MAKE COINS MORE PROFITABLE FOR YOU THAN FOR THE DEALER!

Do you know why a 1909-S V.D.B. Lincoln cent is worth more than the much rarer 1876 nickel three-cent piece? How to guarantee that a coin's condition is what the seller says it is? What to pay for a 1913 Buffalo nickel? What today's value is for a 1963 proof set that originally cost $2.10? Why "cleaning" is a dirty word for serious collectors?

Top authority Scott A. Travers makes sure you know the bottom line on U.S. coins—their condition, their scarcity, and *the price they bring right now*! You can feel confident when you buy and satisfied when you sell because you have at hand the best coin book in America—

THE INSIDER'S GUIDE TO U.S. COIN VALUES 1996

Also by Scott A. Travers:

The Coin Collector's Survival Manual
The Investor's Guide to Coin Trading
One-Minute Coin Expert
Travers' Rare Coin Investment Strategy

QUANTITY SALES

Most Dell books are available at special quantity discounts when purchased in bulk by corporations, organizations, or groups. Special imprints, messages, and excerpts can be produced to meet your needs. For more information, write to: Dell Publishing, 1540 Broadway, New York, NY 10036. Attention: Special Markets.

INDIVIDUAL SALES

Are there any Dell books you want but cannot find in your local stores? If so, you can order them directly from us. You can get any Dell book currently in print. For a complete up-to-date listing of our books and information on how to order, write to: Dell Readers Service, Box DR, 1540 Broadway, New York, NY 10036.

The
INSIDER'S GUIDE
to
U.S. COIN VALUES
1996

SCOTT A. TRAVERS

A Dell Book

Published by
Dell Publishing
a division of
Bantam Doubleday Dell Publishing Group, Inc.
1540 Broadway
New York, New York 10036

Not all coin photos are reproduced to scale.

ON THE COVER: PhotoProof digital image of 1900 Indian Head cent, MS-66 Red.

ISBN: 0-440-22151-X

Printed in the United States of America

Published simultaneously in Canada

January 1996
10 9 8 7 6 5 4 3 2 1
OPM

Table of Contents

Eisenhower Dollars
Anthony Dollars
Gold Dollars
$2.50 Gold Pieces
$3 Gold Pieces
$4 Gold Pieces
$5 Gold Pieces
$10 Gold Pieces
$20 Gold Pieces
Commemoratives
American Eagle Bullion Coins

ACKNOWLEDGMENTS

I especially appreciate the support, advice, and in some instances, the pricing data and information provided to me by a number of persons. The following list is, I believe, all-encompassing; however, I apologize if I have omitted anyone.

John Albanese, David T. Alexander, Michael Alster, Charles Anastasio, Richard A. Bagg, Dennis Baker, Andrew Barnet, Steve Blum, Q. David Bowers, Jeanne Cavelos, William L. Corsa Sr., Silvano Di Genova, Cathy Dumont, William Fivaz, Harry Forman, Leo Frese, Michael Fuljenz, Klaus W. Geipel, Larry Gentile Sr., Salvatore Germano, David Hall, James L. Halperin, David C. Harper, John Highfill, Charles Hoskins, Steve Ivy, Robert W. Julian, Chester L. Krause, Ronald E. Lasky, Julian Leidman, Robert J. Leuver, Kevin J. Lipton, Dwight Manley, Steve Mayer, Bruce McNall, Raymond N. Merena, Bob Merrill, James L. Miller, Lee S. Minshull, John Pasciuti Sr., Martin Paul, Ed Reiter, Maurice Rosen, Michael Keith Ruben, John Sack, Mark Salzberg, Florence Schook, Hugh Sconyers, Michael W. Sherman, John Slack, Harvey G. Stack, Rick Sundman, Anthony J. Swiatek, Armen Vartian, Mark Yaffe, and Keith M. Zaner.

Bowers and Merena Galleries provided invaluable assistance by supplying excellent photographs for every single coin pictured in this book. The company's talented photographer, Cathy Dumont, spent countless days poring through its files to compile the clear, crisp photos. They greatly enhance this book, and I'm grateful both to her and to the firm.

Heritage Capital Corporation, and especially Michael W. Sherman, also contributed greatly to the success of this project by furnishing the price chart at the end of the book. We look forward to incorporating updated versions of these charts as a regular yearly feature.

John Albanese, founder of the Numismatic Guaranty Corporation of America (NGC), provided invaluable assistance in the compilation of values for Barber dimes, quarters and half dollars. Albanese is a preeminent authority on this segment of the coin market. He selflessly devoted many hours to this project, drawing upon both his in-depth book knowledge of these series and his many years of practical experience as a trader.

Jack Beymer, a longtime coin dealer from Santa Rosa, California, graciously agreed to assist me in compiling the prices for U.S. copper coins. This is an area in which Beymer is a leading authority and one of the nation's most important dealers. His guidance on the prices was invaluable, and I'm pleased and proud to have had such an expert's services available to me in this project.

Michael R. Fuljenz of Universal Coin & Bullion in Beaumont, Texas, updated the values for gold eagles through double eagles. He is one of the nation's highest-profile and most esteemed gold coin authorities. His contributions, like the metal itself, glitter.

John W. Highfill, a highly esteemed coin dealer and author from Broken Arrow, Oklahoma, was a pillar of strength in the compilation of prices for silver dollars. Highfill is an expert without peer in this segment of the coin market. Among his many accomplishments, he is the founder of the National Silver Dollar Roundtable and the author of "The Comprehensive U.S. Silver Dollar Encyclopedia," a massive and magnificent book on this popular subject.

Norman W. Pullen of Portland, Maine, a coin dealer whose knowledge is deep as well as broad, furnished particular expertise on the pricing of small cents. His guidance, based on decades as an authoritative market-maker in this area, was immensely helpful and reinforces my confidence in the accuracy of the prices.

The late Bob Rose of Renrob Coins in New Brunswick, New Jersey, compiled prices for Standing Liberty quarters. Rose's firm was one of the most respected and influential coin dealerships in the nation, and he himself was extremely knowledgeable not only in numismatics but also in economics and mathematics. This unusual combination of talents made him an indispensable contributor.

Maurice Rosen of Plainview, New York, is not only a major dealer in his own right but also a peerless coin market analyst. His award-winning newsletter, "The Rosen Numismatic Advisory," has an uncanny knack not only for spotting trends but also for predicting them. Rosen's brilliance shines through in this book in the sections on early silver coins, where he provided tremendous assistance.

Michael Keith Ruben of Silver Spring, Maryland, is one of the busiest and savviest coin traders in the business. Ruben probably handles more "super-grade" coins—coins in extremely high levels of preservation—than any other dealer in the world. He generously shared his vast knowledge by helping me prepare and refine the prices for Seated Liberty coinage.

Anthony J. Swiatek of Manhasset, New York, is known throughout the coin hobby as "Mister Commemorative," and the title fits him perfectly. Swiatek is the world's greatest authority on U.S. commemorative coins, as well as co-author of the landmark "Encyclopedia of United States Silver and Gold Commemorative Coins." He personally oversaw the compilation of prices not only for commemorative coins but also for Walking Liberty half dollars, another series on which he is a renowned authority.

The United States Mint Public Information Office assisted me in compiling mintage figures.

PREFACE

If you're like most people, you've probably found a penny lying in the street. Maybe you've even come across a nickel or a dime—or really hit the big time and picked up a stray half dollar.

Did it ever occur to you that coins like these might be worth a lot of money? The odds are against it, of course; most of the "lucky pennies" that turn up at our feet are as common as three-leaf clovers, and so are most of the coins we get in our pocket change. But every now and then, Lady Luck flashes an extra-special smile and directs our attention to a truly exceptional coin—one that's worth a premium of hundreds or thousands of dollars to collectors. And it happens a lot more often than you might think.

That coin may not appear on the sidewalk or the street; instead, you may discover it in a long-forgotten cigar box or tucked away in the drawer of an old, unused dresser in your attic. When it does turn up, however, you'll need a reliable way to determine how much it's worth. *The Insider's Guide to U.S. Coin Values* gives you that information in simple and accurate form, making it far more likely you'll receive a fair price for that special coin when you go to sell it.

Sometimes, the stakes can be staggering. I know of one coin dealer who had a rare coin worth $25,000 in his pocket while riding in a New York City taxicab, but when he got out of the cab the coin was missing. He offered a reward of many thousands of dollars for its return. If you had been fortunate enough to find it, you could have earned yourself a small fortune. And once you've read this book, you'll have a big advantage in knowing what to look for and what the coins you find are really worth.

People who buy or sell coins have traditionally faced three primary risks. The first of these has been an acquisition risk—the risk that they might buy something for $1,000 and then learn it was worth only $100. The second has been a marketplace risk—the risk that they might buy something for $1,000 that was really worth $1,000, but that it might go down in value later because of market conditions. The third has been a sale risk—the risk that if they went to sell a coin worth $1,000, a dealer might take advantage of their ignorance and give them a great deal less.

The Insider's Guide to U.S. Coin Values will be especially helpful to you in minimizing the sale risk. The information contained in these pages will give you the knowledge you need to keep from being the victim of a rip-off.

Recently, someone I know found a coin worth $200 in his pocket change. He took it to a coin shop near his home and the dealer offered him $10. Someone else I know had some valuable old 25-cent pieces that had been in her family for many years. These coins were valued at $2,000 each—but when she took them to a local dealer, he offered her $10 each. There are many honest dealers, but a few bad apples can spoil things for everyone, and you should be prepared to recognize and avoid them.

Armed with the facts and figures in *The Insider's Guide to U.S. Coin Values*, you'll never fall prey to unscrupulous buyers such as these. Knowledge is power, and this book will enable you to always deal from strength when buying or selling coins.

Read on. And happy hunting!

—Scott A. Travers
Scott Travers Rare Coin Galleries Inc.
Box 1711, F.D.R. Station
New York, N.Y. 10150
1-212-535-9135
January 1996

Chapter One

THE LURE OF COINS

Coins have kindled people's imagination and aroused their collecting instincts ever since the first crude examples were struck in Asia Minor more than five hundred years before the birth of Christ.

Coins are hand-held works of art . . . miniature milestones along the march of time. Many times, they're stores of precious metal. Rare coins are worth far more than face value (the value stamped on their surface)—and far more than just their metal content—as collectibles. They can even be an exceptional investment. And, best of all, collecting them can be tremendous fun.

In a sense, collecting coins is like digging up buried treasure. The treasure isn't hidden underground, and finding it doesn't require a secret map, but still there's a sense of adventure, an air of excitement—and ultimately a thrill of discovery—in locating needed coins to complete a set (a group of similar coins containing one example from every different date and every different mint that struck the coins). For those who buy wisely and well, there's also an ultimate payoff, for collecting rare coins, like tracking buried treasure, has the potential to be a richly rewarding pursuit.

No longer the private preserve of wealthy princes, coin collecting today is among the most popular spare-time diversions in the world. Millions of Americans collect coins on a regular basis, and many others dabble in the field.

Most confine their collecting to U.S. coinage, but many use a broader frame of reference in terms of both history and geography, collecting coins from earlier ages—all the way back to ancient times—and from hundreds of other countries around the globe.

In recent years, the far-flung base of traditional collectors has been broadened substantially by newcomers who think of themselves not as pure hobbyists but rather as collector/investors. For them, the profit motive is important —and rare coins' profit performance has been excellent when they are held over time.

Frequently, people who enter the rare coin market as investors find the field's lure irresistible and cross over the line to become pure collectors. This gives them an opportunity to enjoy the best of both worlds—the fun of a fascinating hobby and the profit of a fine investment, too.

Although the instinct to save and savor coins is as old as coinage itself, coin collecting didn't reach the masses until the twentieth century. Prior to that, it was largely an indulgence of the nobility and scholars—people with time and money to devote to such a pursuit. As recently as the early 1900s, major U.S. coin shows seldom attracted more than a few hundred participants, and the major activity wasn't the buying and selling of coins, but rather the exhibiting of collections.

The democratization of coin collecting got under way in earnest in the 1920s and '30s. During that period, Americans were starting to find themselves with more leisure time (some of it enforced, during the 1930s, by the Great

THE LURE OF COINS

Depression). What's more, the United States Mint was turning out dozens of commemorative coins, which piqued people's interest and drew many thousands into the hobby.

Special holders for storing and displaying coins started to appear around that time, along with guidebooks listing the coins' value—and those set up a framework that made collecting easier for the many new devotees.

During the next few decades, rare coins evolved from a drawing-room diversion into a field with true mass appeal and a massive collector base.

The coin market's growth was hastened by developments at the Mint. In the 1950s, for instance, many new collectors became involved with coins by buying annual proof sets—sets of specimen coins—from Uncle Sam. The Mint resumed production of these in 1950, following an eight-year lapse, and by the end of the decade, sales had mushroomed from fewer than 52,000 sets in 1950 to more than 1.1 million in 1959.

In 1960, the growth became a full-fledged boom, largely on the strength of a single new "mint-error" coin. The coin in question was the so-called "small-date" cent. In the spring of 1960, sharp-eyed collectors noticed that there were two major varieties of current-year Lincoln cents, one of which had a perceptibly smaller date. It soon became apparent that the "small-date" variety was scarce—especially the version struck at the nation's main mint in Philadelphia. A nationwide scavenger hunt ensued, and coins became the object of widespread coverage in the media. That, in turn, drew many new participants to the hunt and to coin collecting, as well.

Just four years later, in 1964, the Mint introduced a new half dollar honoring President John F. Kennedy following his assassination—and that, too, stirred widespread interest. In 1965, the rising cost of silver forced the Mint to issue a new kind of dime and quarter: "sandwich-type" coinage made from copper and nickel, with no precious metal at all. The half dollar kept a reduced amount of silver until 1971, when it, too, became fiat money—money whose acceptance is based on public trust in the government, not on its own intrinsic worth. The dawn of clad coinage wasn't a happy time for collectors, but it did focus new attention on the rare coin field—and that, in turn, attracted more recruits.

The 1970s witnessed continued growth, and also a new direction in the marketing of coins. For the first time, many dealers were reaching beyond traditional collectors to lure noncollectors, especially wealthy professionals, into purchasing rare coins as an investment. Instead of building collections, buyers were now assembling portfolios.

Again, the federal government played a pivotal role in stimulating interest in coins. First came the sale of surplus silver dollars by the General Services Administration. Most of these dollars were low-mintage coins from the Carson City Mint, and their release to the market in a series of ballyhooed sales did much to raise public consciousness of rare coins in general and Morgan silver dollars in particular.

In 1974, the government gave coins another big, though indirect, boost by lifting the long-standing ban on U.S. citizens' right to buy, sell, and own gold bullion. That sparked new interest in bullion-type coins such as South Africa's Krugerrand, and the interest carried over into numismatic coinage, or collectible coins, as well.

Coin prices rose throughout the 1970s—steadily at first, then dramatically. In 1972, for the very first time, a single coin changed hands for $100,000. The sale was a private transaction and the coin was an 1804 silver dollar.

By 1979, that seemed puny. As the decade neared a close, in November '79, a Brasher doubloon—a gold piece minted privately in 1787 by New York City jeweler Ephraim Brasher—was gaveled down for a stratospheric $725,000 at an auction of rare coins from the famous Garrett Collection.

For nearly a decade, that remained the highest price ever paid for any single coin at a public auction. The record was finally broken in July 1989, when an 1804 silver dollar brought $990,000, missing the million-dollar mark by just a single bid.

In 1990, a rare U.S. gold coin was sold in a private transaction for more than $1.5 million. The coin was a 1907 double eagle, or $20 gold piece, designed by famed sculptor Augustus Saint-Gaudens. While all Saint-Gaudens double eagles are considered to be magnificent works of coinage art, this one was distinguished by both its exquisite sharpness of detail (it's said to have "extremely high relief") and its virtually flawless condition.

Low mintage and high condition are the two main ingredients buyers seek in a coin, and these combine with supply and demand to determine its market value. While rarity is important, the stress in recent years has been on quality. Investors covet nothing but the best, and are willing to pay for it. Consequently, coins command far higher premiums in pristine mint condition than in grades only slightly lower. There are even degrees of pristineness: the Mint-State range has 11 different grades, with premiums rising steeply as a coin ascends the scale.

Coins are now graded on a scale of 1 to 70, with 1 representing a coin that is barely identifiable as to its type and 70 signifying a coin that is absolutely perfect. The use of numbers to designate grades is a practice of relatively recent origin. In the past, collectors used words instead, describing coins as "uncirculated," "fine," and "good," for example. These were less precise, but were adequate for the needs of a less sophisticated marketplace. The numbers now in use do correspond to descriptive words. For instance, coins graded 60 to 70 are said to be Mint State.

To assure that buyers and sellers get coins that have been accurately graded, independent third-party grading services have come into being. These companies, operated and staffed by knowledgeable, reputable experts, have effectively removed the risk that coins may be overgraded and therefore overpriced on the basis of grade.

The "grading revolution" began in 1986 with the establishment of the Professional Coin Grading Service (PCGS). The following year, a second major grading service—the Numismatic Guaranty Corporation of America (NGC)—opened its doors.

These companies provide unbiased opinions regarding the grade, or state of preservation, of coins that are submitted for their review. They then encapsulate each coin in a sonically sealed, tamper-resistant hard plastic holder (or "slab"), along with a paper insert indicating its date, type, and grade.

In 1990, the nonprofit American Numismatic Association sold ANACS, its certification service, to Amos Press, Inc., of Sidney, Ohio. When the new ANACS began operations, the coins it certified were not traded as fluidly as those certified by NGC and PCGS. Over time, ANACS's standards became about on par with standards of NGC and PCGS.

Together, PCGS and NGC have certified millions of coins. They also have made a valuable contribution to the marketplace by issuing regular "population" or "census" reports telling how many coins of each type and date they have certified in each different grade. These have become valuable reference tools in determining rarity and value.

Fun and profit can and do overlap in the rare coin field. Consider the case of New York City lawyer Harold Bareford, a man who approached rare coins as a pure collector but whose acquisitions proved to be a marvelous investment.

Bareford began acquiring coins just before World War II and remained an active buyer for several decades. He seldom paid more than a few hundred dollars, but he bought with great care, insisting on the ultimate in quality.

In all, he spent about $40,000 assembling sets of U.S. coins struck from gold and silver. Shortly after his death in 1978, the coins were sold at auction and brought a combined total of $3.1 million. One coin—a specimen-quality 1827 dime—had cost Bareford $20 in 1947. Not much more than three decades later, it brought his estate an eye-popping $29,000.

Bareford's insistence on quality was the key: he always demanded the best at a time when other collectors were content to settle for less. And during the years when he was buying coins, prices were laughably low by current standards.

Can similar huge profits still be achieved by people buying rare coins today? Only time will tell, but Harold Bareford's story has a rather intriguing footnote: Bareford stopped buying U.S. coins in 1955, years before the market began to really boom.

He thought they were getting too expensive.

Chapter Two

FIGURING OUT WHAT IT'S WORTH

What's it worth?

That's the first question most people ask when they see an old or unusual-looking coin. They take it for granted that something so intriguing must be worth a lot of money.

Many times, they're right—but not necessarily for the reason they believe. Coins don't gain added value simply because they're old; you can buy Roman coins from the time of Julius Caesar for just a few dollars apiece. Nor does odd appearance always command a premium; a great many coins with dramatic minting mistakes, although they may be terrific conversation pieces, bring very little as collectibles.

THREE KEYS TO VALUE

Three basic factors determine just how much a coin is worth—or, on the other hand, how much it isn't worth. The first of these is the grade of the coin—its level of preservation. The second is the coin's collector base—the number of collectors who covet it enough to pay a bonus price for it. The third is the coin's availability—the number of examples that exist.

The grade of a coin is the most important factor, and because it is so crucial I'll be dealing with this subject in much greater detail in the next chapter. I do want to give you some basic guidelines now, though, on how a coin's grade and value are intertwined.

When asked to describe their coins, the uninitiated often like to say they're in "good condition." They're using that expression in a general sense, of course, but to knowledgeable collectors the term "good condition" has a very specific meaning—and that meaning is just the opposite of what most laypersons think. Among the established grade levels, Good is one of the lowest, not the highest: it signifies a coin that has passed through a great many hands and undergone heavy wear but still possesses all the basic elements needed to identify its design.

As I explained in Chapter One, experts grade U.S. coins on a scale of 1 to 70, with 1 representing a coin that can barely be identified and 70 denoting a coin that is sheer perfection. The coins that enjoy the greatest demand and bring the biggest premiums are those that have never passed from hand to hand; these are said to be in "uncirculated" condition and identified by grades within an eleven-number Mint State range. This range is at the top of the 1-through-70 spectrum, covering the numbers from 60 to 70.

Perfection is highly prized by many coin collectors and investors. They will pay a great deal more for a Mint State coin than they will for a similar coin that is worn ever so slightly—even when that wear is all but undetectable without the use of powerful magnification. What's more, they will frequently pay several times as much for one Mint State coin than they will for a second Mint State coin just one or two numbers lower on the grading scale.

Prices rise sharply in grades above Mint State-65 (MS-65, for short). As coins approach the perfection denoted by the grade of 70, their prices very often approach the stratosphere. You may find, for example, that a coin with a value of $500 in MS-65 condition is worth ten times as much in MS-67—and one hundred times as much in MS-69. This difference reflects the fact that hardly any exist in the highest grades. People who collect these coins are willing to pay top dollar for top quality not only because the coins are breathtakingly beautiful in these very high levels of preservation, but also because they're flat-out rare.

PROOF COINS

"Proof" coins are graded similarly to regular coins but separately. A proof is a specimen coin—one that has been struck two or more times to give it greater sharpness of detail. The same numerical scale is used in grading proofs, but instead of being labeled, say, Mint State-65, a proof would be given a grade of Proof-65.

The process of minting proof coins is really quite simple. Think of what would happen if you pressed a rubber stamp onto a piece of paper, then pressed it down again in the very same spot. After you did this the second time, the impression on the paper would be sharper, deeper, and darker. Likewise, the multiple striking brings out every nuance of a proof coin's design in razor-sharp detail.

Proof coins won't appear in your everyday pocket change. But you might very well encounter such a coin—or a whole set of proof coins—among your family's keepsakes in the drawer or cigar box that I mentioned in this book's Preface. Every year the United States Mint puts together proof sets containing proof examples of all five current U.S. coins: the Lincoln cent, Jefferson nickel, Roosevelt dime, Washington quarter, and Kennedy half dollar. It sells these sets to collectors for a premium—currently $12.50 per set. For further information on how to order such sets, write to: The United States Mint, P.O. Box 13576, Philadelphia, PA 19162-0011.

SUPPLY AND DEMAND

Some coins are more popular than others. Lincoln cents, for instance, have always held great appeal to a broad cross section of collectors. Obscure and obsolete coins have far fewer followers; the Lincoln Cent Fan Club is enormous, for example, compared to the number of hobbyists actively pursuing three-cent pieces and twenty-cent pieces, two coin series the United States abandoned in the late 1800s.

Popularity, or unpopularity, has enormous implications for the value of a coin. What it boils down to is the age-old law of supply and demand: the greater the demand for a given supply of coins, the higher the price will be—and popularity is, of course, just another name for demand.

Consider the case of the 1909-S V.D.B. Lincoln cent. This is a famous coin minted in San Francisco in 1909, the year Lincoln cents first appeared, and bearing the initials of Victor David Brenner, the artist who designed the coin. The San Francisco Mint produced 484,000 examples of this coin, so it hardly qualifies as a great rarity. Yet, there are literally millions of collectors who would love to own one. As a result, this coin is worth several hundred dollars even in well-worn condition.

Now consider the case of the 1876 nickel three-cent piece (a coin with the same metallic composition as our present-day Jefferson nickel but a face value, or denomination, of only three cents). The Mint produced only 162,000 examples of this coin—barely a third as many as the number of 1909-S V.D.B. Lincoln cents. Furthermore, this coin is older by thirty-three years. Yet, it's only worth 10 to 20 dollars in worn condition. The explanation is simple: The number of collectors pursuing this coin is significantly smaller than the number of pieces available.

The third and final determinant of the value of a coin is the flip side of demand: the coin's supply.

In general, you can gauge the number of coins available by checking the number minted in the first place. The United States Mint has a long-standing policy of disclosing mintage figures, and *The Insider's Guide to U.S. Coin Values* furnishes those figures for each and every date that each and every U.S. coin was made. You'll find them conveniently located right beside the listings of year-by-year market values.

There are instances, however, where unusual circumstances led to the loss or destruction of large numbers of coins after the Mint produced them. Many silver dollars from the turn-of-the-century era were melted, for example, when the government needed silver for other uses. So were many gold coins left in federal vaults, or surrendered by the public, when the nation suspended gold coinage in 1933. More recently, untold millions of modern silver coins wound up in the melting pot when silver rose in value to $50 an ounce at the start of the 1980s. In that case, the coins were melted because they had more value as metal than as money.

In recent years, buyers and sellers have gained a major new tool in their effort to assess the available supply of certain coins. Companies known as "grading services," which evaluate rare coins, have issued periodic reports detailing the number of coins their personnel have graded— type by type, date by date, and grade by grade. These "population" and "census" reports provide important guidance to what is known as "condition rarity"—a circumstance where coins, however high their mintages and however available they may be in lower grades, are scarce and even rare in very high grades.

MINT MARKS

Supply and demand—and consequently value—can be influenced greatly by the presence or absence of one or more tiny letters on a coin. These letters are known as "mint marks," and they designate the mint where the coin was produced.

In 1792, when the United States Mint came into being, there was just one mint facility, a modest mint building in Philadelphia. As the nation and its coinage needs grew, Congress began to authorize branch mints in other locations around the country, chosen for their advantageous geographic locations or sometimes their proximity to sources of the precious metal needed in making coins. The San Francisco Mint was opened, for example, following the California Gold Rush.

During much of U.S. history, the branch mints' coinage output has been substantially smaller than that of the mother mint in Philadelphia. Thus, if a mint mark appears on a coin, the chances are good that the mintage (or number made) may be relatively low, enhancing that coin's value to collectors.

Until recent years, the Philadelphia Mint didn't place a mint mark on its coins. Coins from that mint could be recognized instead by the absence of any such mark. Since 1980, the Philadelphia Mint has stamped the letter "P" on all the coins it makes except the cent.

At present, there are three U.S. branch mints. Their locations, and the mint marks of their coins, are as follows: Denver (D); San Francisco (S); and West Point, New York (W). In earlier years, there also were branch mints in Charlotte, North Carolina (C); Carson City, Nevada (CC); Dahlonega, Georgia (D); and New Orleans (O). Although the mint mark "D" appears on coins produced in both Dahlonega and Denver, no confusion exists because those mints were active in different eras. The Dahlonega Mint was closed in 1861, and the Denver Mint didn't begin operations until 1906.

For a detailed list of where mint marks appear on various coins, see Appendix C.

COMMEMORATIVE COINS

In addition to making regular-issue coins for use in the nation's commerce, the United States Mint also has produced a wide variety of commemorative coins. These are special coins authorized by Congress to recognize important people, places, and events. Centennials of statehood, anniversaries of battles, and the staging of Olympic Games have been among the subjects honored on these coins. Normally, they are minted in just a single year and in limited quantities; however, in some cases, production has continued for as long as thirteen years. Rather than being placed in circulation, these coins are offered for sale at a premium.

U.S. commemorative coins are divided into two general groups: those from the "traditional" period, from 1892 to 1954, and those from the "modern" era, which got under way in 1982. Issuance of commemoratives was suspended from 1954 to 1982 because of opposition by the Treasury Department.

As with regular-issue coinage, the value of commemoratives depends upon the coins' level of preservation and the workings of supply and demand. A number of the traditional commemoratives command impressive premiums, especially in very high grades. However, the modern issues haven't yet shown great market strength. Most have been sold by the Mint at relatively high initial prices, and then had difficulty sustaining those price levels. Abundant supply has held prices down in the resale market: mintages of the modern commemoratives have been consistently higher than those of their traditional counterparts.

Typically, U.S. commemoratives not only pay tribute to the subjects they portray but also raise funds for some related cause. The 1986 Statue of Liberty coins, for instance, marked the centennial of that national shrine and also helped generate money to finance its repair and restoration. Since 1982, legislation authorizing commemoratives has spelled out how much of a "surcharge" should be added to benefit the designated cause.

BULLION COINS

In 1986 the Mint began producing a series of special coins called American Eagles. These are what is known as "bullion coins"—precious-metal coins whose price goes up or down, depending on fluctuations in the value of the metal they contain. They are made not to be spent, but rather to be sold as stores of precious metal.

American Eagles come in gold and silver. There are four different gold coins in the series: a one-ounce piece plus fractional coins with gold contents of $1/2$, $1/4$, and $1/10$ of an ounce, respectively. There is just one silver coin, and it weighs an ounce. All these coins carry denominations well below the bullion value of their gold or silver. The one-ounce gold American Eagle, for instance, has a face value of $50—less than one-sixth what an ounce of gold is worth at this writing. The silver American Eagle has a face value of $1, but its metal value would be four times that much.

To make the American Eagles more appealing to collectors, the Mint chose designs based partially on classics of the past. The "heads" side of each of the four gold coins carries the portrait of Miss Liberty designed by famous sculptor Augustus Saint-Gaudens for the U.S. double eagle, or $20 gold piece, minted from 1907 to 1933. The heads side of the silver American Eagle duplicates the Walking Liberty design that graced the half dollar from 1916 to 1947. New designs appear on the bullion coins' reverses.

In addition to the regular American Eagles, the Mint also makes proof versions every year for sale at an added premium as collectibles.

GETTING THE BEST OFFER

Clearly, the bottom line when you go to sell a coin is to get the highest price you possibly can. To do this, you need to be aware of the factors that affect overall values in the coin market and the steps that you can take to minimize your risk and maximize your return.

Keep in mind that coins, like any other commodities, can vary in value greatly as time goes by and market conditions change. Inflation, for example, tends to push coin values up; much like precious metals, coins are excellent hedges against a shrinking dollar, and many people turn to them for shelter in inflationary times. Recessions, on the other hand, tend to cause coin prices to decline. When times are tough and people can barely afford life's necessities, they're far less likely to spend their limited funds on "extras" such as coins.

Coin market cycles, and the interrelationship of coins and the economy, are examined in greater detail in two of my earlier books, *One-Minute Coin Expert* and *The Coin Collector's Survival Manual.* Those who would like to learn more about these fascinating subjects will find both of these books well worth reading.

The price you get for a coin can also depend, to a very great extent, on the circumstances surrounding the sales transaction itself. You're likely to receive a substantially higher offer if, for example, the dealer you approach perceives you as a knowledgeable collector, or at least an informed amateur, rather than a hapless babe in the woods.

Typically, coin dealers' offers fall into a number of readily identifiable categories. To show you what I mean, here are three examples:

The low-ball offer. A low-ball offer isn't the same as a rip-off; the offer is low, but the dealer isn't trying to get the coin for just a tiny fraction of its value. Let's say you have a coin that the dealer would sell for $1,000 to a knowledgeable consumer. He could pay you $700 or even $800 and still turn a normal profit, but instead he makes you an offer of $300. If you were knowledgeable, you could probably get him to upgrade the offer by holding out for more—especially if he had a potential buyer in mind. The lesson here is clear: Knowledge is power—the kind of power measured in cold, hard cash.

The fair-market wholesale offer. This is the kind of offer a dealer would make to another dealer, or possibly to a collector who was reasonably familiar with the value of the coin. If you were in no hurry to sell your coin, you also could receive a fair-market wholesale price by consigning it to a reputable coin auction firm for sale at a public auction.

Fair market value. When a dealer offers you "fair market value" for a coin, what he's really offering is a price somewhere between fair-market wholesale value and fair-market retail value. He'll still make a decent profit when he resells it, but not quite as much as he would have made if he had paid you a strictly wholesale price. Fair market value is the price that is arrived at when both the buyer and seller are ready and willing to consummate a deal, both of them are knowledgeable regarding the coin's market value, and neither of them is under special pressure to make the deal.

The price listings used in this book are based upon fair market value.

Chapter Three

MAKING THE GRADE IN COINS

Coins are made to be spent. But collectors prefer coins that have never been spent at all—coins that are still as shiny and sharp as the day they left the mint—and they're willing to pay big premiums to obtain them.

"Quality" is a very important word in coin collecting today, and a very important word for you, as well, if you have any plans to buy or sell coins in today's marketplace. Buying the best will cost you more money, but you'll get more money back when you go to sell, and chances are, those high-quality coins will hold their value better in the meantime. Conversely, if you're thinking of selling any coins you already own, you'll find potential buyers placing heavy stress on the coins' condition.

The condition or "grade" of a coin—its level of preservation—has become a primary key in determining how much that coin is worth. A brand-new coin, one in what is called Mint State or "uncirculated" condition, is often worth many times as much as another coin of the same type and date that has passed from hand to hand. What's more, there are nuances of "newness." Coins aren't looked upon as simply "new" or "used": experts now recognize no fewer than eleven different grade levels within the Mint State range, and a shift of just one or two levels can mean a difference of many thousands of dollars in the value of a coin.

RECOGNIZED GRADING STANDARDS

The coin market's preoccupation with quality has led to the establishment of industrywide standards for grading coins. These standards were promulgated in 1977 by the American Numismatic Association (ANA), the world's largest organization of coin collectors, and have come to be accepted and observed throughout the marketplace.

The system set up by the ANA rates coins on a scale of 1 to 70, with the numbers ascending as the level of quality rises. A coin graded 1 can barely be identified; if it were a Lincoln cent, for instance, you could tell that's what it was, but little more. A coin graded 70 would be positively perfect in every respect: a coin with no nicks, no flaws, no scratches, and no imperfections of any kind. It also wouldn't have the slightest bit of friction on its highest points from having been touched or passed from hand to hand.

"Uncirculated" becomes "circulated" if just two tiny letters are removed. It's similarly easy to transform a Mint State coin into something a little less than that—and a lot less valuable. Suppose you had a coin worth $5,000 to collectors because of its virtual perfection—a coin that looked as new as the day it left the mint because it had never been spent and its owners had never mishandled it even once. If you were to take a sweat-soaked finger and wipe it lightly over that coin, it wouldn't be considered Mint State anymore; experts would downgrade it all the way to About Uncirculated, a grade that corresponds to the number 58—perhaps 10 points lower on the scale. The real damage would show up on your ledger sheet, for the value of that coin might now be just a few hundred dollars—and possibly even less.

Even the slightest mishandling can damage a coin irreparably. And once a coin passes from hand to hand, the most exposed parts of the metal begin to wear down, causing the loss of detail—detail that can never be replaced.

The grade assigned to each coin includes not only a number but also a word description. That perfect coin, for instance, would be designated Mint State-70. If it were a proof, or specimen coin, its grade would be Proof-70. Proofs are graded separately from regular coins (also known as "business strikes"), but the same 1-to-70 scale is used.

The ANA may have standardized grading with its 1-to-70 scale, but it didn't invent the concept of using specific terms to describe a coin's condition. Long before the present system evolved, dealers and collectors were utilizing such adjectives as "good," "fine," "choice," and "gem" to characterize their coins. These adjectives provided a convenient kind of shorthand for long-distance buyers and sellers, mail-order coin dealers, for example. They could carry out transactions by telephone or mail with reasonable confidence because there was general agreement on the meaning of the basic grading terms. This type of confidence is important in the rare coin business, for coins by their nature lend themselves well to long-distance sales. Coins are small, extremely portable, and often quite valuable, so deals involving very high values can be carried out easily through the mail, using registered mail to protect against possible loss.

THE ELEMENTS OF GRADING

A number of different elements help to determine the grade of a coin. It's beyond the scope of this book to examine these elements in detail, but a brief discussion will give you a general idea of what's involved. For a much fuller treatment, I recommend that you read my companion book *One-Minute Coin Expert*, which also is a Dell paperback.

When a professional numismatist—usually a coin dealer —looks at a coin, he focuses on several different factors, and all of these have a bearing on how he grades the coin. He checks, of course, to see if there is wear—and, if so, how much. He also looks for obvious imperfections such as cuts, scratches, or nicks: Smooth *surfaces* enhance a coin's appearance and its grade. With a Mint State coin, in particular, the expert puts great emphasis on the *strike*— the sharpness of detail imparted to the coin when it was made. He also takes into account the *luster* of the coin— the way it reflects light. Finally, he considers everything all together by gauging the coin's *eye appeal.* Sometimes a coin may seem to have much to recommend it in each of the individual categories but somehow comes up short when viewed as a whole.

THE MOST IMPORTANT GRADES

There may be 70 numbers on the ANA grading scale, but not all those numbers are created equal. The 11 grades at the top of the scale, those between 60 and 70, constitute the Mint State range, and this is where the action is in today's coin market. This is where we see the overwhelming majority of important coin transactions—those involving substantial amounts of money. This is also the area where accurate grading is most crucial and where the greatest potential exists for disputes and costly mistakes.

Mint State coins cannot have any wear; by definition, a coin cannot be uncirculated if it has entered circulation—that is to say, been passed from hand to hand—and suffered even the slightest loss of detail. Mint State coins can have flaws, but any such imperfections must have occurre at the mint. For example, they can have "bag marks" from coming into contact with other coins at the mint. They still would be considered Mint State coins, but the marks would reduce their grade.

In practice, few coins qualify for designation as Mint State-70. This is really more of a theoretical grade, a utopian goal that is constantly pursued but seldom attained. MS-69 and MS-68 are attainable, but only with great difficulty. To qualify for one of these grades, a coin must be free of all but the tiniest flaws.

Here are some of the most important grades in the current marketplace:

· **MS-67.** A coin in this grade can have one or two small defects that are visible under 5-power magnification. However, these would not be apparent to the naked eye and the coin would seem practically perfect upon first being viewed.

· **MS-65.** While clearly not perfect, a coin in this grade is still highly desirable. In fact, coins graded MS-65 fall just short of what is called "super-grade" status. They possess great appeal but are held back by a single minor blemish.

· **MS-63.** A coin in this grade is still desirable, but even the naked eye can detect some flaws. There may be an obvious bag mark, for example, or spots on the surface of the coin.

· **MS-60.** A coin graded MS-60 is uncirculated—but just barely. It hasn't been passed from hand to hand, so technically it doesn't have any wear. But it does have very obvious mint-made imperfections. These may include scratches, nicks, and even large gashes in prominent locations.

· **About Uncirculated.** This is the grading level just below the Mint State range. It has three main components: AU-58, AU-55, and AU-50. Coins graded AU-58 may have considerable eye appeal; in fact, they may be more attractive at first glance than many Mint State coins. However, closer scrutiny will reveal slight wear on the highest points. These coins have passed through people's hands—but only through a few.

· **Extremely Fine.** Next in line, as we move down the scale, are coins graded EF-45 and EF-40. These coins have light wear on their highest points, but overall they're still detailed and attractive.

· **Very Fine.** Coins graded VF-30 and VF-20 are moderately worn, but all their major features remain sharp.

· **Fine.** A coin graded Fine-12 has passed through many hands and emerged with moderate to heavy wear. However, the wear is even and all the major features are still clearly discernible.

· **Very Good.** When we reach the grade of VG-8, we're obviously approaching the bottom of the scale. A coin in this grade is well worn. Its design remains clear, but it's flat and lacks details.

· **Good.** It soon becomes evident that this is not what the uninitiated have in mind when they say that their coins are "in good condition." Far from being desirable, G-4 coins are heavily worn. The design and inscriptions are still discernible; however, they're faint here and there.

· **About Good.** For all practical purposes, AG-3 is the lowest collectible grade—and most collectors shun it except in the case of scarce-date coins. On an AG-3 coin, the design remains visible only in outline and parts of the date and inscriptions are worn smooth.

For in-depth information on coin grading, I recommend that you read the *Official A.N.A. Grading Standards for United States Coins,* compiled, arranged, and edited by Ken Bressett and A. Kosoff. This book sets forth the grading standards of the national coin collector organization in great detail and provides illustrations for all the major types of U.S. coins. The first edition was published in 1977 and the latest, fourth edition in 1991 by Western Publishing Company Inc. of Racine, Wisconsin.

CLEANING COINS

Uninformed individuals mistakenly believe that dark, dull, or damaged coins can be magically restored to something approaching their original brilliance through the application of baking soda and elbow grease. This is a disastrous misconception.

Never clean a coin. Far from enhancing the value of a coin, cleaning almost always diminishes—or destroys—whatever appeal that coin might have held for collectors. A coin that has been cleaned may look bright and shiny to the untrained eye, but under a magnifying glass its surfaces will reveal unsightly scratches. The friction involved in cleaning a coin wears down the metal on its surface. This actually lowers the grade of the coin. What's more, many collectors find cleaned coins repugnant and flatly refuse to put them in their collections.

There are ways of cleaning coins that minimize the damage; museums, for example, have experts who are skilled in removing foreign substances from coins. For everyone else, however, the message is clear: When it comes to your coins, "cleaning" is a very dirty word.

GRADING SERVICES

The so-called "good old days" may stir our sense of nostalgia, but the old days weren't always all that good. Consider what used to happen when people had valuable coins to sell.

There wasn't any system in place in those days to offer people guidance on how much their coins were worth. Experienced collectors knew where to turn; besides being knowledgeable themselves about coins, they also knew which coin dealers could be counted upon to render honest appraisals. But those unschooled in the ways of the coin world had no such protection. They ended up taking their coins to local coin shops and putting themselves, quite literally, at the dealers' mercy. And all too often, those dealers weren't merciful: they offered ridiculously low sums for coins that were actually rare and valuable, then, after buying the coins, turned around and sold them for huge profits.

Today, there is a safety net for consumers—meaning you! Companies known as grading services provide impartial opinions on the grades of rare coins that are sent in to them for review. They don't come right out and say what your coins are worth, but since a coin's value is determined by its grade, it's a very simple matter to figure out

MAKING THE GRADE IN COINS

the value once you know the grade. Those of you who dabble in the stock market are undoubtedly familiar with Moody's Investor Services, a company that offers independent ratings of stocks. The grading services play a similar role today in the coin market: they offer independent third-party opinions on the grades of the coins they examine, based upon the 1-to-70 scale.

Three top grading services are the Numismatic Guaranty Corporation of America (NGC), the Professional Coin Grading Service (PCGS), and ANACS. For a fee of approximately $25 per coin, these companies will examine your coins, assign appropriate grades, then encapsulate each coin in a hard plastic holder along with an insert stating the grade. Coins in these holders are said to be "certified coins." They enjoy wide acceptance in the marketplace, and this will facilitate sale of your coins for fair market prices.

When you think of it, $25 is a small price to pay for the peace of mind and protection you receive. As you can see from reading through this book, it's not at all impossible that you may have a coin worth many thousands of dollars. If you walk into a coin shop without first having that coin certified, you're likely to receive a low-ball offer—and possibly even a rip-off offer. Once you get it certified, you'll know what it's worth and you can then deal from a position of strength in seeking a buyer. Furthermore, its status as a certified coin will make it much easier to sell.

NGC and PCGS do not accept direct submissions of coins from the public. Both maintain networks of authorized submission centers. ANA members may submit coins directly to PCGS. The centers will advise you on how to submit your coins. For information and lists of authorized centers, write to NGC and PCGS as follows:

Numismatic Guaranty Corporation of America Inc.
P.O. Box 1776
Parsippany, NJ 07054

Professional Coin Grading Service
P.O. Box 9458
Newport Beach, CA 92658

Wherever possible, the prices quoted in Chapter Four of this book represent fair market values for certified coins of the dates and mints listed—coins graded by NGC, PCGS, or ANACS. These are far and away the most accurate statements of real market value—the prices at which coins actually change hands in the current marketplace.

In cases where insufficient numbers of certain coins have been certified to establish firm price levels, the prices represent fair market values for uncertified coins. These are the prices at which those coins would change hands in a transaction between two people who are reasonably knowledgeable of the facts, are willing participants, and are under no special compulsion to consummate the transaction.

Mintage figures—the quantities produced by the mint—are shown alongside the listing of each coin's date, grade, and value. To further assist you, I have included a number of high-quality photographs to illustrate the major coin types and varieties. These will help you identify each of your coins. All of these photographs were obtained on a courtesy basis from Bowers and Merena Galleries Inc., Box 1224, Wolfeboro, NH 03894-1224.

I'm confident that this book will enable you to determine how much your coins are worth. I'm sure it will also help you obtain a fair price if you choose to sell them. More than this, however, I firmly believe that after reading this book, you will be richer not only in dollars and cents but also in knowledge. And that's the best kind of wealth that money can buy.

PRICE PERFORMANCE STATISTICS

Statistics can be highly useful. They also can be abused. For that reason, you always should be wary when confronted with statistics touting rare coins' investment performance and potential.

There isn't any question that over the long term, truly rare coins that are free from imperfections and wear have appreciated in value handsomely—even spectacularly. Over shorter terms, however, coins encounter ups and downs just like any other investment you might make. Thus, it would be misleading to take a fairly short time span—a year or two, for instance—and argue that just because coins did very well (or very poorly) during that period, they were likely to perform similarly in the future.

Consider what happened in 1990 and 1991. The coin market, like many other parts of the U.S. economy, experienced widespread setbacks during that two-year period. Some rare coins lost more than half their value. But things began to turn around during the early part of 1992, and prices rebounded dramatically. If someone drew up a chart showing coins' performance from 1989 through 1991, the downward-pointing arrows would alarm the most cock-eyed optimist. Yet in the long-term scheme of things, that was just a narrow—and not at all typical—band in the market's performance. And it certainly didn't serve as an accurate barometer of what lay ahead, even in the very near term.

It would be extremely difficult to fashion an accurate chart of coin price performance over, say, a period of fifty years. The reason is that over the long haul, major changes have taken place in how rare coins are graded—how buyers and sellers assess those coins' level of preservation.

It would certainly be possible to go back fifty years and come up with statistics on how much certain coins were selling for at that time, then compare those figures with the prices of similar coins forty years ago, thirty years ago, and so on. But all those figures wouldn't be very meaningful unless the grade was constant for each and every coin being charted. In other words, the "uncirculated" coin from fifty years ago would have to correspond exactly to the Mint State coin of today. In practice, grading standards have changed significantly even within the last fifteen years, much less the last fifty.

The truest test of coins' price performance is to see how well (or how poorly) coin buyers have done after holding their acquisitions for many years. Those who purchased desirable material years ago at market-related prices—prices that were fair at the time of the transaction—have fared quite well indeed. I know of numerous cases where people assembled collections for just a few thousand dollars several decades ago and sold them in recent years for enormous profits. Some of these people ended up close to being millionaires. On the other hand, people who purchased coins that weren't as desirable may have very little to show for those acquisitions, even after holding them many years.

U.S. COIN VALUES

(NOTE: All photographs in this chapter were provided by Bowers and Merena Galleries Inc., with special assistance furnished by company photographer Cathy Dumont.)

IMPORTANT NOTE: Values for Mint State and Proof copper coins are for specimens which exhibit both *red* and *brown* color, except where indicated.

Following are fair market values for U.S. coins issued from 1792 to the present. The coins are arranged from the smallest-value denomination (the half cent) through the highest (the $20 gold piece), with commemoratives and American Eagle bullion coins listed separately.

The values are provided in several different grades, or levels of preservation; the better the condition of a coin, the higher its value will be. In some cases, you will find only two or three grades listed for certain coins. It may be that these coins are normally encountered only in those grades; other times, they may have no special value except in the very highest grades.

You will find a number of listings for "overdates." These are coins on which one or more of the numbers in the date are engraved over other numbers. This was a common occurrence in the U.S. Mint's early years, when dies from prior years were reused—and the new dates were cut over the old ones—in order to save money. Dies are the pieces of metal used to stamp coins; you might think of them as being like the cookie cutters used to press designs into cookies.

The italicized numbers after the dates of certain coins denote the number of proofs—or specimen coins—that were struck in that year at that mint. Proof mintage figures for 1994 are tentative.

HALF CENTS (1793–1857)

Liberty Cap Portrait (1793–1797)

Portrait Facing Left (1793)

	Mintage	Good-4	Fine-12	EF-40
1793	35,334	$1,600	$3,400	$8,750

Portrait Facing Right (1794–1797)

	Mintage	Good-4	Fine-12	EF-40
1794	81,600	$240	$700	$2,300
1795	139,690	220	525	1,750
1796 combined total.	1,390			
1796 with pole		5,500	11,000	26,500
1796 without pole		13,500	27,000	—
1797 combined total.	127,840			
1797 plain edge.		240	575	1,950
1797 lettered edge.		550	2,000	8,500

Draped Bust Portrait (1800–1808)

	Mintage	Good-4	Fine-12	EF-40
1800	202,908	$25.00	$60.00	$300
1802 combined total.	20,266			
1802/0 overdate with same reverse as 1800		7,500	22,500	—
1802/0 with new reverse		275	1,100	7,000
1803	92,000	30.00	60.00	350
1804 combined total.	1,055,312			
1804 with "spiked" chin		25.00	50.00	300
1804, all others		22.50	45.00	225
1805 combined total.	814,464			
1805 with small 5 and stems		275	1,100	—

	Mintage	Good-4	Fine-12	EF-40
1805, all others		27.50	55.00	220
1806 combined total.	356,000			
1806 with small 6 and stems		110	375	1,900
1806, all others		27.50	55.00	220
1807	476,000	30.00	60.00	240
1808 combined total.	400,000			
1808 regular date		30.00	65.00	275
1808/7 overdate		80.00	240	1,500

Classic Head Portrait (1809–1836)

	Mintage	Good-4	Fine-12	EF-40	Proof-63
1809 combined total	1,154,572				
1809 regular date		$22.50	$37.50	$100	
1809/6 overdate.		24.00	40.00	110	
1810.	215,000	25.00	52.50	250	
1811.	63,140	100	325	2,100	
1825.	63,000	24.00	40.00	100	
1826.	234,000	20.00	35.00	95.00	
1828 combined total	606,000				
1828 with 13 stars.		20.00	32.50	85.00	
1828 with 12 stars.		22.50	37.50	100	
1829.	487,000	20.00	32.50	85.00	
1831 original	2,200	—	—	6,000	
1831 restrike with large berries (proof only) . . . . *unknown*		—	—	—	7,000
1831 restrike with small berries (proof only) . . . . *unknown*		—	—	—	11,000
1832.	154,000	25.00	32.50	75.00	
1833.	120,000	25.00	32.50	75.00	
1834.	141,000	25.00	32.50	75.00	
1835.	398,000	24.00	31.00	72.50	

	Mintage	Good-4	Fine-12	EF-40	Proof-63
1836 original (proof only) ..... *unknown*	—	—	—	5,000
1836 restrike (proof only) ..... *unknown*	—	—	—	6,000

Coronet Portrait (1840–1857)

	Mintage	Good-4	Fine-12	EF-40	Proof-63
1840–1848 original (proof only) ..... *unknown*	—	—	—	$4,850
1840–1848 restrike (proof only) ..... *unknown*	—	—	—	3,700
1849 large date	39,364	$30.00	$52.50	$100	
1849 small date original (proof only) ..... *unknown*	—	—	—	3,800
1849 small date restrike (proof only) ..... *unknown*	—	—	—	3,900
1850	39,812	32.50	55.00	110	
1851	147,672	27.50	50.00	90.00	
1852 restrike (proof only)	*unknown*	—	—	—	3,900
1853	129,694	27.50	50.00	90.00	
1854	55,358	30.00	52.50	100	
1855	56,500	30.00	52.50	100	
1856	40,430	32.50	55.00	110	
1857	35,180	35.00	57.50	120	

LARGE CENTS (1793–1857)

Flowing Hair Portrait (1793)

Chain on Reverse (1793)

	Mintage	Good-4	Fine-12	EF-40
1793 combined total.	36,103			
1793 with AMERICA spelled out		$2,400	$5,250	$18,000
1793 with AMERICA abbreviated AMERI.		2,750	5,500	19,000

Wreath on Reverse (1793)

	Mintage	Good-4	Fine-12	EF-40
1793 combined total.	63,353			
1793 with vine and bars on edge.		$900	$2,250	$7,000
1793 lettered edge.		950	2,400	7,000
1793 with strawberry leaves above the date	4 known	—		(unknown in higher grades)

Liberty Cap Portrait (1793–1796)

	Mintage	Good-4	Fine-12	EF-40
1793	11,056	$1,600	$3,750	$23,000
1794 combined total.	918,521			
1794 with same head as 1793		275	1,750	11,500
1794 with new head.		150	450	2,250
1794 with stars on the reverse		6,500	19,500	—
1795 lettered edge.	37,000	150	450	2,250
1795 plain edge.	501,500	125	375	1,750
1795 Jefferson head		3,000	10,000	—
1796	109,825	150	450	2,250

Draped Bust Portrait (1796–1807)

	Mintage	Good-4	Fine-12	EF-40
1796 combined total.	363,375			
1796 with same reverse as 1794		$125	$375	$1,750
1796 with regular 1796 reverse		120	360	1,700
1796 with same reverse as 1797		115	345	1,650
1796 with LIBERTY spelled LIHERTY		135	425	4,000
1797 combined total.	897,510			
1797 with gripped edge		60.00	275	1,650

LARGE CENTS (1793–1857)

	Mintage	Good-4	Fine-12	EF-40
1797 plain edge		65.00	290	1,750
1797 with new reverse and stems on wreath		55.00	220	1,350
1797 with new reverse and no stems		85.00	255	3,000
1798 combined total.	1,841,745			
1798 with old hair style		32.50	150	1,200
1798 with new hair style		32.50	150	1,000
1798 with same reverse as 1796		65.00	300	2,900
1798/7 overdate		75.00	325	2,800
1799 regular date	42,540	1,000	4,000	—
1799/8 overdate (mintage included with 1798)		1,100	4,250	—
1800 combined total.	2,822,175			
1800 regular date		30.00	120	750
1800/1798 overdate with old hair style	—	32.50	130	1,800
1800, 80/79 overdate with new hair style		30.00	120	875
1801 combined total.	1,362,837			
1801 with regular reverse. . . .		32.50	130	875
1801 with fraction 1/000		32.50	130	950
1801 with fraction 1/100 over 1/000		35.00	150	1,350
1801 with 3 errors (1/000, only one stem and IINITED instead of UNITED).		60.00	240	2,000
1802 combined total.	3,435,100			
1802 with regular reverse. . . .		32.50	120	750
1802 with no stems on wreath		32.50	120	800
1802 with fraction 1/000		35.00	140	825
1803 combined total.	3,131,691			
1803 small date		32.50	120	750
1803 large date with small fraction		2,400	7,250	—
1803 large date with large fraction		60.00	240	1,900
1803 with no stems on wreath		32.50	120	850
1803 with fraction 1/100 over 1/000		32.50	120	850
1804	96,500	350	1,400	6,000
1805	941,116	32.50	120	850

	Mintage	Good-4	Fine-12	EF-40
1806	348,000	35.00	140	1,000
1807 combined total.	829,221			
1807 with small fraction		32.50	130	925
1807 with large fraction		30.00	120	800
1807/6 overdate with small 7		1,750	6,000	24,500
1807/6 overdate with large 7		32.50	120	825

Classic Head Portrait (1808–1814)

	Mintage	Good-4	Fine-12	EF-40
1808	1,007,000	$37.50	$140	$900
1809	222,867	75.00	300	1,825
1810 combined total.	1,458,500			
1810 regular date		32.50	120	800
1810/09 overdate		32.50	120	800
1811 combined total.	218,025			
1811 regular date		60.00	240	1,750
1811/0 overdate		65.00	250	2,100
1812	1,075,500	32.50	120	800
1813	418,000	45.00	160	1,100
1814	357,830	32.50	120	975

Coronet Portrait (1816–1857)

	Mintage	Good-4	Fine-12	EF-40	AU-55	MS-63
1816.	2,820,982	$9.50	$22.00	$100	$225	$400
1817 combined total	3,948,400					
1817 with 13 stars.		9.50	22.00	100	200	400
1817 with 15 stars.		12.50	27.50	150	300	800
1818.	3,167,000	9.50	22.00	100	200	375
1819 combined total	2,671,000					
1819 regular date		9.50	22.00	100	200	375
1819/8 overdate.		11.00	24.00	110	250	400
1820 combined total	4,407,550					
1820 regular date		9.50	20.00	110	240	375
1820/19 overdate		11.00	24.00	120	275	400
1821.	389,000	17.50	47.50	375	1,750	—
1822.	2,072,339	9.50	22.00	125	325	550
1823 combined total	68,061					
1823 regular date		27.50	110	1,000	1,750	—
1823/2 overdate.		25.00	100	850	1,500	—
1824 combined total	1,193,939					
1824 regular date		9.50	22.00	250	1,250	2,350
1824/2 overdate.		15.00	45.00	500	1,750	—
1825.	1,461,100	9.50	22.00	125	375	800
1826 combined total	1,517,425					
1826 regular date		9.50	22.00	110	350	700
1826/5 overdate.		15.00	45.00	225	900	1,800
1827.	2,357,732	9.50	22.00	100	200	350
1828 combined total	2,260,624					
1828 small date		10.00	22.50	47.50	375	800
1828 large date		9.50	22.00	45.00	350	775
1829 combined total	1,414,500					
1829 with medium letters		11.00	24.00	150	750	—
1829 with large letters		9.50	22.00	100	200	350
1830 combined total	1,711,500					
1830 with medium letters		17.50	52.50	275	1,000	—

LARGE CENTS (1793–1857)

	Mintage	Good-4	Fine-12	EF-40	AU-55	MS-63
1830 with large letters		9.50	22.00	100	200	350
1831.	3,359,260	9.50	22.00	100	200	350
1832.	2,362,000	9.50	22.00	100	200	350
1833.	2,739,000	9.50	22.00	100	200	350
1834 combined total	1,855,100					
1834 with small 8, large stars and medium letters		9.50	22.00	100	200	350
1834 with large 8, small stars and medium letters		9.50	22.00	100	200	350
1834 with large 8, large stars and medium letters		22.50	52.50	225	900	—
1834 with large 8, large stars and large letters		10.00	25.00	110	220	375
1835 combined total	3,878,400					
1835 with same head as 1834		10.00	22.50	120	240	400
1835 with same head as 1836		9.50	22.00	110	220	425
1836.	2,111,000	9.50	22.00	100	200	375
1837.	5,558,300	9.00	20.00	100	200	350
1838.	6,370,200	9.00	20.00	100	200	350
1839 combined total . . .	3,128,661					
1839 with regular head . . .		9.50	22.00	100	200	375
1839 with "silly" head		11.00	24.00	120	400	1,100
1839 with "booby" head. . .		9.50	22.50	100	300	850
1839/6 overdate.		120	480	2,750	—	—
1840 combined total	2,462,700					
1840 regular date		9.00	12.00	65.00	125	325
1840 with small 18 over large 18.		9.50	15.00	90.00	200	375
1841.	1,597,367	9.00	12.00	65.00	130	350
1842.	2,383,390	9.00	12.00	65.00	125	300
1843 combined total	2,425,342					
1843 with small head and small letters		9.00	12.00	65.00	125	300
1843 with small head and large letters.		11.00	27.50	120	400	800
1843 with large head and large letters.		9.00	17.50	75.00	130	350
1844 combined total	2,398,752					
1844 regular date		8.50	11.00	65.00	125	300
1844/81 error		11.00	27.50	150	450	—
1845.	3,894,804	8.50	11.00	65.00	125	300
1846 combined total	4,120,800					

	Mintage	Good-4	Fine-12	EF-40	AU-55	MS-63
1846 regular date		8.50	11.00	60.00	120	285
1846 small date.		8.00	10.50	57.50	110	280
1847 combined total	6,183,669					
1847 regular date		8.00	10.50	57.50	110	280
1847 with 7 over small 7 . . .		11.00	22.50	90.00	150	—
1848.	6,415,799	7.50	10.00	75.00	125	300
1849.	4,178,500	7.50	10.00	75.00	125	300
1850.	4,426,844	7.50	10.00	57.50	110	300
1851 combined total	9,889,707					
1851 regular date		7.50	10.00	52.50	110	300
1851/81 error		11.00	20.00	90.00	180	375
1852.	5,063,094	7.50	10.00	52.50	100	275
1853.	6,641,131	7.50	10.00	52.50	100	275
1854.	4,236,156	7.50	10.00	52.50	100	275
1855 combined total . . .	1,574,829					
1855 with slanting 5 and						
knob on ear		8.50	15.00	60.00	110	285
1855, all other		7.50	10.00	52.50	100	275
1856.	2,690,463	7.50	10.00	52.50	100	275
1857 combined total	333,456					
1857 small date.		22.50	45.00	65.00	125	300
1857 large date		20.00	40.00	60.00	120	325

FLYING EAGLE CENTS (1856–1858)

	Mintage	Good-4	Fine-12	EF-40	AU-55	MS-63	MS-65	Proof-65
1856 pattern	1,000	$2,400	$3,250	$4,000	$5,000	$6,750	$15,000	$12,000
1857 . . *485*	17,450,000	12.50	17.50	67.50	135	350	2,700	11,000
1858 combined total	24,600,000							
1858 with small								
letters . . *200*.		12.50	17.50	67.50	135	350	2,700	11,000
1858 with large								
letters . . *80*		12.50	17.50	67.50	135	350	2,700	11,000
1858/7 overdate.		50.00	125	400	800	1,350	—	—

INDIAN HEAD CENTS (1859–1909)

Copper-Nickel Composition (1859–1864)

Wreath on Reverse Without Shield (1859)

	Mintage	Good-4	Fine-12	EF-40	AU-55	MS-63	MS-65	Proof-65
1859 . . *800*	36,400,000	$7.50	$10.00	$75.00	$150	$285	$1,500	$3,000

INDIAN HEAD CENTS (1859–1909)

Wreath and Shield on Reverse (1860–1909)

	Mintage	Good-4	Fine-12	EF-40	AU-55	MS-63	MS-65	Proof-65
1860 . . *1,000*	20,566,000	$6.00	$9.00	$27.50	$55.00	$150	$750	$1,700
1861 . . *1,000*	10,100,000	12.50	22.50	65.00	100	170	850	1,700
1862 . . *550*	28,075,000	5.00	7.50	25.00	52.50	150	750	1,700
1863 . . *460*	49,840,000	4.00	6.00	22.50	45.00	150	750	1,700
1864 . . *370*	13,740,000	11.00	21.00	32.50	65.00	165	800	1,700

Bronze Composition (1864–1909)

	Mintage	Good-4	Fine-12	EF-40	AU-55	MS-63	MS-65	Proof-65
1864 combined total	39,233,714							
1864 with no L . . *150*. . .		$6.00	$9.00	$25.00	$37.50	$120	$300	$650
1864 with L on								
headdress . . *20*		30.00	57.50	120	180	350	750	6,000
1865 . . *500*	35,429,286	5.00	7.50	27.50	37.50	110	225	500
1866 . . *725*	9,826,500	27.50	37.50	90.00	120	200	400	500
1867 . . *625*	9,821,000	27.50	37.50	90.00	120	200	400	600
1868 . . *600*	10,266,500	27.50	37.50	90.00	120	200	400	600
1869 combined total	6,420,000							
1869 regular date . . *600*		32.50	110	240	300	400	725	675
1869/9 overdate.		100	200	400	600	1,000	2,500	
1870 . . *1,000*	5,275,000	27.50	120	240	300	400	725	575
1871 . . *960*	3,929,500	30.00	125	250	300	400	725	600
1872 . . *950*	4,042,000	50.00	150	300	350	475	1,200	650
1873 combined total	11,676,500							
1873 with closed								
3 . . *1,100*		12.00	27.50	75.00	100	300	500	500

INDIAN HEAD CENTS (1859–1909)

	Mintage	Good-4	Fine-12	EF-40	AU-55	MS-63	MS-65	Proof-65
1873 with open 3		12.00	25.00	45.00	60.00	175	300	
1873 with double letters on LIBERTY		75.00	300	750	1,250	2,750	5,500	
1874 . . 700	14,187,500	12.00	20.00	60.00	80.00	150	375	500
1875 . . 700	13,528,000	12.00	20.00	60.00	80.00	150	375	500
1876 . . 1,150	7,944,000	17.50	35.00	80.00	110	225	450	550
1877 . . 900	852,500	250	450	1,000	1,250	2,400	4,500	2,000
1878 . . 2,350	5,799,850	20.00	37.50	90.00	120	240	420	275
1879 . . 3,200	16,231,200	4.00	7.50	25.00	32.50	75.00	225	275
1880 . . 3,955	38,964,955	3.00	4.50	15.00	25.00	65.00	200	275
1881 . . 3,575	39,211,575	3.00	4.50	15.00	25.00	65.00	200	275
1882 . . 3,100	38,581,100	3.00	4.50	15.00	25.00	65.00	200	275
1883 . . 6,609	45,598,109	3.00	4.50	15.00	25.00	65.00	200	275
1884 . . 3,942	23,261,742	3.25	5.00	17.50	27.50	70.00	210	275
1885 . . 3,790	11,765,384	3.75	10.00	30.00	40.00	90.00	225	275
1886 . . 4,290	17,654,290	3.50	8.00	35.00	47.50	95.00	225	275
1887 . . 2,960	45,226,483	1.50	3.00	12.50	20.00	65.00	160	275
1888 combined total	37,494,414							
1888 regular date . . 4,582		1.50	3.00	12.50	20.00	65.00	160	275
1888/7 overdate		250	650	1,250	1,500	12,500	—	
1889 . . 3,336	48,869,361	1.50	2.50	11.00	20.00	65.00	160	275
1890 . . 2,740	57,182,854	1.50	2.50	11.00	17.50	65.00	160	275
1891 . . 2,350	47,072,350	1.50	2.50	11.00	17.50	65.00	160	275
1892 . . 2,745	37,649,832	1.50	2.50	11.00	17.50	65.00	160	275
1893 . . 2,195	46,642,195	1.50	2.50	11.00	17.50	65.00	160	275
1894 . . 2,632 . . . . , . .	16,752,132	2.25	4.50	17.50	27.50	100	300	275
1895 . . 2,062	38,343,636	1.00	2.00	10.00	17.50	60.00	150	275
1896 . . 1,862	39,057,293	1.00	2.00	10.00	16.00	60.00	150	275
1897 . . 1,938	50,466,330	1.00	2.00	10.00	16.00	60.00	150	275
1898 . . 1,795	49,823,079	1.00	2.00	10.00	16.00	60.00	150	275
1899 . . 2,031	53,600,031	1.00	2.00	10.00	16.00	60.00	150	275
1900 . . 2,262	66,833,764	.85	1.75	7.50	15.00	55.00	140	275
1901 . . 1,985	79,611,143	.85	1.75	7.50	15.00	55.00	140	275
1902 . . 2,018	87,376,722	.75	1.50	6.00	12.50	55.00	140	275
1903 . . 1,790	85,094,493	.75	1.50	6.00	12.50	55.00	140	275
1904 . . 1,817	61,328,015	.75	1.50	6.00	12.50	55.00	140	275
1905 . . 2,152	80,719,163	.75	1.50	6.00	12.50	55.00	140	275
1906 . . 1,725	96,022,255	.75	1.50	6.00	12.50	55.00	140	275
1907 . . 1,475	108,138,618	.75	1.50	6.00	12.50	55.00	140	275
1908 . . 1,620	32,327,987	.80	1.60	6.75	13.50	57.50	145	275
1908-S	1,115,000	22.50	30.00	70.00	100	225	400	
1909 . . 2,175	14,370,645	1.00	2.00	10.00	20.00	60.00	150	275
1909-S	309,000	140	165	250	300	450	750	

LINCOLN CENTS (1909–PRESENT)

Wheat-Ears Reverse (1909–1958)

Bronze Composition (1909–1942)

	Mintage	Good-4	Fine-12	EF-40	AU-55	MS-63	MS-65	Proof-65
1909 with initials								
V.D.B. on back . . *420*	27,994,580	$2.00	$2.50	$3.75	$5.25	$15.00	$40.00	$1,650
1909-S V.D.B.	484,000	300	350	400	450	550	1,250	
1909 without								
initials . . *2,198*. . . .	72,700,420	.60	.80	2.00	4.50	22.50	48.00	300
1909-S	1,825,000	42.50	50.00	90.00	125	195	250	
1910 . . *2,405*	146,798,813	.15	.30	1.80	3.50	22.50	80.00	300
1910-S	6,045,000	7.50	9.00	22.50	40.00	120	190	
1911 . . *1,733*	101,176,054	.20	.50	4.00	6.00	32.50	150	300
1911-D	12,672,000	3.75	5.75	27.50	42.50	95.00	300	
1911-S	4,026,000	17.50	20.00	35.00	50.00	220	800	
1912 . . *2,145*	68,150,915	.30	1.50	9.00	15.00	35.00	140	300
1912-D	10,411,000	4.25	6.75	37.50	47.50	150	750	
1912-S	4,431,000	11.00	14.00	37.50	47.50	150	950	
1913 . . *2,848*	76,529,504	.25	.90	7.50	10.00	37.50	150	300
1913-D	15,804,000	2.25	3.75	20.00	37.50	150	750	
1913-S	6,101,000	6.50	8.50	22.50	45.00	210	975	
1914 . . *1,365*	75,237,067	.25	1.20	8.00	12.50	75.00	200	300
1914-D	1,193,000	80.00	120	360	575	1,250	3,750	
1914-S	4,137,000	9.50	12.50	35.00	57.50	360	3,000	
1915 . . *1,150*	29,090,970	1.00	3.50	35.00	50.00	120	325	300
1915-D	22,050,000	.85	1.75	9.00	17.50	110	375	
1915-S	4,833,000	7.00	8.50	27.50	40.00	195	975	
1916 . . *1,050*	131,832,627	.15	.40	2.00	3.50	27.50	120	300
1916-D	35,956,000	.20	.90	7.50	22.50	100	650	
1916-S	22,510,000	.85	1.65	8.00	25.00	120	975	
1917	196,429,785	.15	.30	2.00	4.00	27.50	65.00	
1917-D	55,120,000	.30	.85	7.00	20.00	120	525	

LINCOLN CENTS (1909–PRESENT)

	Mintage	Good-4	Fine-12	EF-40	AU-55	MS-63	MS-65	Proof-65
1917-S	32,620,000	.30	.90	7.25	25.00	130	1,250	
1918	288,104,634	.15	.30	2.00	4.50	27.50	120	
1918-D	47,830,000	.25	.75	6.00	12.50	110	675	
1918-S	34,680,000	.35	.80	6.50	14.00	130	1,450	
1919	392,021,000	.15	.30	1.75	3.25	22.50	90.00	
1919-D	57,154,000	.25	.50	5.00	8.50	85.00	450	
1919-S	139,760,000	.20	.40	2.25	3.50	75.00	650	
1920	310,165,000	.10	.25	1.75	3.25	20.00	100	
1920-D	49,280,000	.20	.65	6.00	11.00	90.00	475	
1920-S	46,220,000	.20	.45	3.50	12.00	110	900	
1921	39,157,000	.25	.65	4.50	10.00	75.00	225	
1921-S	15,274,000	.75	1.50	12.50	42.50	250	2,000	
1922-D combined total.	7,160,000							
1922-D		5.25	7.50	17.50	40.00	120	375	
1922 Plain (without D)		150	275	1,500	2,500	7,500	14,000	
1923	74,723,000	.20	.40	3.00	6.00	22.50	100	
1923-S	8,700,000	1.60	3.25	20.00	65.00	375	2,100	
1924	75,178,000	.15	.35	4.00	6.50	45.00	110	
1924-D	2,520,000	10.00	12.50	47.50	95.00	375	1,900	
1924-S	11,696,000	.80	1.60	15.00	30.00	190	2,150	
1925	139,949,000	.10	.25	2.00	3.50	20.00	80.00	
1925-D	22,580,000	.30	.60	6.50	10.00	90.00	700	
1925-S	26,380,000	.25	.40	6.00	9.00	130	2,250	
1926	157,088,000	.10	.25	2.00	3.25	17.50	47.50	
1926-D	28,020,000	.30	.55	5.00	8.50	80.00	900	
1926-S	4,550,000	3.25	4.25	12.50	45.00	190	2,400	
1927	144,440,000	.10	.25	1.75	3.00	17.50	75.00	
1927-D	27,170,000	.25	.45	3.00	8.00	70.00	825	
1927-S	14,276,000	.50	1.25	7.50	15.00	130	1,050	
1928	134,116,000	.10	.25	1.75	3.00	17.50	70.00	
1928-D	31,170,000	.25	.40	2.50	5.00	52.50	300	
1928-S	17,266,000	.35	.65	3.75	7.50	110	925	
1929	185,262,000	.10	.25	1.75	3.25	14.00	65.00	
1929-D	41,730,000	.15	.30	1.75	3.50	30.00	130	
1929-S	50,148,000	.15	.30	1.75	3.25	17.50	120	
1930	157,415,000	.10	.25	1.20	2.00	10.00	32.50	
1930-D	40,100,000	.15	.30	1.50	3.50	27.50	85.00	
1930-S	24,286,000	.20	.35	1.50	3.00	12.50	65.00	
1931	19,396,000	.40	.60	2.00	4.00	37.50	110	
1931-D	4,480,000	2.50	3.25	7.25	22.50	90.00	250	
1931-S	866,000	32.50	37.50	42.50	50.00	90.00	150	
1932	9,062,000	1.50	2.25	3.00	7.50	30.00	52.50	

LINCOLN CENTS (1909–PRESENT)

	Mintage	Good-4	Fine-12	EF-40	AU-55	MS-63	MS-65	Proof-65
1932-D	10,500,000	.75	1.25	3.00	7.50	32.50	57.50	
1933	14,360,000	.90	1.35	3.25	7.50	30.00	57.50	
1933-D	6,200,000	1.80	2.25	4.50	9.00	35.00	65.00	

Note: Mint State and Proof values are for Lincoln cents 1934 to present exhibiting full red *color.*

	Mintage	Fine-12	EF-40	AU-55	MS-60	MS-63	MS-65	Proof-65
1934	219,080,000	$.15	$.50	$1.00	$2.50	$5.00	$12.50	
1934-D	28,446,000	.25	1.00	7.50	17.50	27.50	55.00	
1935	245,388,000	.15	.50	.85	1.50	2.50	6.50	
1935-D	47,000,000	.15	.50	1.25	2.50	5.00	12.50	
1935-S	38,702,000	.25	1.00	5.00	7.50	12.50	52.50	
1936 . . 5,569	309,632,000	.10	.50	.85	1.50	3.00	6.00	800
1936-D	40,620,000	.15	.50	1.00	1.75	3.25	7.50	
1936-S	29,130,000	.20	.60	1.25	2.00	3.50	9.00	
1937 . . 9,320	309,170,000	.10	.40	.75	1.25	2.25	5.00	125.
1937-D	50,430,000	.15	.45	.85	2.00	3.00	6.50	
1937-S	34,500,000	.15	.45	.85	1.75	3.25	9.50	
1938 . . 14,734	156,682,000	.10	.30	.75	1.50	2.50	6.25	85.00
1938-D	20,010,000	.20	.50	1.00	2.25	3.50	8.50	
1938-S	15,180,000	.30	.60	1.10	2.40	3.75	10.00	
1939 . . 13,520	316,466,000	.10	.25	.50	.75	1.25	3.50	70.00
1939-D	15,160,000	.45	.75	1.50	2.50	3.50	11.00	
1939-S	52,070,000	.15	.35	.75	1.25	1.75	9.00	
1940 . . 15,872	586,810,000	.10	.20	.35	.70	1.10	3.50	65.00
1940-D	81,390,000	.10	.20	.40	.75	1.25	4.50	
1940-S	112,940,000	.10	.20	.50	.80	1.35	6.00	
1941 . . 21,100	887,018,000	—	.15	.25	.65	1.00	3.50	65.00
1941-D	128,700,000	—	.15	.75	2.00	2.75	7.50	
1941-S	92,360,000	—	.15	.90	2.25	3.00	8.50	
1942 . . 32,600	657,796,000	—	.10	.20	.50	.75	2.50	70.00
1942-D	206,698,000	—	.10	.25	.60	.90	3.50	
1942-S	85,590,000	—	.15	.90	3.50	5.25	22.50	

Zinc-Coated Steel Composition (1943)

	Mintage	Fine-12	EF-40	AU-55	MS-60	MS-63	MS-65	Proof-65
1943	684,628,670	$.10	$.25	$.50	$.75	$1.00	$3.50	

	Mintage	Fine-12	EF-40	AU-55	MS-60	MS-63	MS-65	Proof-65
1943-D	217,660,000	.10	.25	.50	.85	1.50	5.25	
1943-S	191,550,000	.15	.45	.75	1.25	2.25	9.00	

Bronze Composition (1944–1958)

	Mintage	Fine-12	EF-40	AU-55	MS-60	MS-63	MS-65	Proof-65
1944	1,435,400,000	—	$.10	$.15	$.35	$.60	$1.25	
1944-D combined total	430,578,000							
1944-D regular mint mark		—	.10	.15	.40	.90	1.50	
1944-D/S Variety 1 (more obvious)		75.00	150	225	300	450	900	
1944-D/S Variety 2		60.00	120	180	240	360	720	
1944-S	282,760,000	—	.10	.15	.40	.80	1.50	
1945	1,040,515,000	—	.10	.15	.40	.80	1.50	
1945-D	266,268,000	—	.10	.15	.40	.80	1.50	
1945-S	181,770,000	—	.10	.15	.40	.80	1.50	
1946	991,655,000	—	.10	.15	.40	.80	1.50	
1946-D	315,690,000	—	.10	.15	.40	.80	1.50	
1946-S	198,100,000	—	.10	.15	.40	.80	1.50	
1947	190,555,000	—	.10	.15	.40	.80	1.50	
1947-D	194,750,000	—	.10	.15	.40	.80	1.50	
1947-S	99,000,000	—	.10	.15	.40	.85	1.60	
1948	317,570,000	—	.10	.15	.40	.80	1.50	
1948-D	172,637,500	—	.10	.15	.40	.80	1.50	
1948-S	81,735,000	—	.10	.15	.40	.85	1.75	
1949	217,775,000	—	.10	.15	.40	.75	1.50	
1949-D	153,132,500	—	.10	.15	.40	.75	1.75	
1949-S	64,290,000	—	.15	.20	.75	1.25	4.00	
1950 . . 51,386	272,635,000	—	.10	.15	.40	.85	1.25	30.00
1950-D	334,950,000	—	.10	.15	.40	.75	1.10	
1950-S	118,505,000	—	.10	.15	.40	.80	1.20	
1951 . . 57,500	284,576,000	—	.10	.15	.40	.90	1.50	20.00
1951-D	625,355,000	—	.10	.15	.25	.60	.90	
1951-S	136,010,000	—	.10	.15	.35	.75	1.75	
1952 . . 81,980	186,775,080	—	.10	.15	.25	.60	.90	19.00
1952-D	746,130,000	—	.10	.15	.25	.60	.75	
1952-S	137,800,004	—	.10	.15	.35	1.00	2.25	
1953 . . 128,800	256,755,000	—	.10	.15	.25	.60	.70	15.00
1953-D	700,515,000	—	.10	.15	.25	.60	.70	
1953-S	181,835,000	—	.10	.15	.25	.75	1.00	
1954 . . 233,300	71,640,050	—	.15	.25	.35	.65	1.25	8.00
1954-D	251,552,500	—	.10	.15	.20	.30	.40	

	Mintage	Fine-12	EF-40	AU-55	MS-60	MS-63	MS-65	Proof-65
1954-S	96,190,000	—	.15	.20	.25	.50	.75	
1955 combined total	330,580,000							
1955 regular								
date . . 378,200.		—	.10	.15	.20	.25	.35	7.50
1955 with doubled-die								
obverse		300	450	525	750	1,250	4,000	
1955-D	563,257,500	—	.10	.15	.20	.25	.35	
1955-S	44,610,000	—	.20	.40	.60	.75	1.00	
1956 . . 669,384	420,745,000	—	—	—	.15	.20	.30	2.50
1956-D	1,098,201,100	—	—	—	.15	.20	.30	
1957 . . 1,247,952.	282,540,000	—	—	—	.15	.20	.30	2.00
1957-D	1,051,342,000	—	—	—	.15	.20	.30	
1958 . . 875,652	252,525,000	—	—	—	.15	.20	.30	2.25
1958-D	800,953,300	—	—	—	.15	.20	.30	

Lincoln Memorial Reverse (1959–Present)

Bronze Composition (1959–1962)

	Mintage	Fine-12	EF-40	AU-55	MS-60	MS-63	MS-65	Proof-65
1959 . . 1,149,291.	609,715,000	—	—	—	—	$.10	$.20	$1.50
1959-D	1,279,760,000	—	—	—	—	.10	.20	
1960 combined								
total . . 1,691,602	586,405,000							
1960 with large date.		—	—	—	—	.10	.20	1.25
1960 with small date		$.50	$.75	$.90	$1.50	2.00	3.00	12.50
1960-D combined total. . . .	1,580,884,000							
1960-D with large date		—	—	—	—	.10	.20	
1960-D with small date. . . .		.10	.15	.20	.30	.40	.50	
1961 . . 3,028,244.	753,345,000	—	—	—	—	.10	.15	1.00
1961-D	1,753,266,700	—	—	—	—	.10	.15	
1962 . . 3,218,019.	606,045,000	—	—	—	—	.10	.15	1.00
1962-D	1,793,148,400	—	—	—	—	.10	.15	

LINCOLN CENTS (1909–PRESENT)

Brass Composition (1963–1982)

	Mintage	Fine-12	EF-40	AU-55	MS-60	MS-63	MS-65	Proof-65
1963 . . 3,075,645.	754,110,000	—	—	—	—	—	$.10	$1.00
1963-D	1,774,020,400						.10	
1964 . . 3,950,762.	2,648,575,000	—	—	—	—	—	.10	1.00
1964-D	3,799,071,500	—	—	—	—	—	.10	
1965	1,497,224,900	—	—	—	—	—	.15	
1966	2,188,147,783	—	—	—	—	—	.15	
1967	3,048,667,100	—	—	—	—	—	.15	
1968	1,707,880,970	—	—	—	—	—	.20	
1968-D	2,886,269,600	—	—	—	—	—	.10	
1968-S . . 3,041,506	258,270,001	—	—	—	—	—	.15	1.00
1969	1,136,910,000	—	—	—	—	—	.30	
1969-D	4,002,832,200	—	—	—	—	—	.10	
1969-S . . 2,934,631	544,375,000	—	—	—	—	—	.15	1.00
1970	1,898,315,000	—	—	—	—	—	.20	
1970-D	2,891,438,900	—	—	—	—	—	.10	
1970-S combined								
total . . 2,632,810	690,560,004							
1970-S with small date		12.50	17.50	22.50	32.50	37.50	42.50	75.00
1970-S with large date		—	—	—	—	—	.15	1.00
1971	1,919,490,000	—	—	—	—	—	.20	
1971-D	2,911,045,600	—	—	—	—	—	.20	
1971-S . . 3,220,733	525,133,459	—	—	—	—	—	.15	1.00
1972 combined total	2,933,255,000							
1972 regular date		—	—	—	—	—	.10	
1972 with doubled-die								
obverse		100	120	140	175	200	225	
1972-D	2,665,071,400	—	—	—	—	—	.10	
1972-S . . 3,260,996	376,939,108	—	—	—	—	—	.15	1.00
1973	3,728,245,000	—	—	—	—	—	.10	
1973-D	3,549,576,588	—	—	—	—	—	.10	
1973-S . . 2,760,339	317,177,295	—	—	—	—	—	.15	1.00
1974	4,232,140,523	—	—	—	—	—	.10	
1974-D	4,235,098,000	—	—	—	—	—	.10	
1974-S . . 2,612,568	409,426,660	—	—	—	—	—	.15	1.00
1975	5,451,476,142	—	—	—	—	—	.10	
1975-D	4,505,275,300	—	—	—	—	—	.10	
1975-S (proof only)	2,845,450	—	—	—	—	—	—	3.00
1976	4,674,292,426	—	—	—	—	—	.10	
1976-D	4,221,592,455	—	—	—	—	—	.10	
1976-S (proof only)	4,149,730	—	—	—	—	—	—	1.50

LINCOLN CENTS (1909–PRESENT)

	Mintage	Fine-12	EF-40	AU-55	MS-60	MS-63	MS-65	Proof-65
1977	4,469,930,000	—	—	—	—	—	.10	
1977-D	4,194,062,300	—	—	—	—	—	.10	
1977-S (proof only)	3,251,152	—	—	—	—	—	—	1.50
1978	5,558,605,000	—	—	—	—	—	.10	
1978-D	4,280,233,400	—	—	—	—	—	.10	
1978-S (proof only)	3,127,781	—	—	—	—	—	—	2.00
1979	6,018,515,000	—	—	—	—	—	.10	
1979-D	4,139,357,254	—	—	—	—	—	.10	
1979-S combined total (proof only)	3,677,175							
1979-S with clogged S		—	—	—	—	—	—	2.00
1979-S with clear S		—	—	—	—	—	—	6.00
1980	7,414,705,000	—	—	—	—	—	.10	
1980-D	5,140,098,660	—	—	—	—	—	.10	
1980-S (proof only)	3,554,806	—	—	—	—	—	—	1.25
1981	7,491,750,000	—	—	—	—	—	.10	
1981-D	5,373,235,677	—	—	—	—	—	.10	
1981-S (proof only)	4,063,083	—	—	—	—	—	—	1.25
1982 combined total	10,712,525,000							
1982 with small date		—	—	—	—	—	.15	
1982 with large date		—	—	—	—	—	.10	
1982-D with large date		—	—	—	—	—	.10	
1982-S (proof only)	3,857,479	—	—	—	—	—	—	1.50

Copper-Plated Zinc Composition
(1982–Present)

	Mintage	Fine-12	EF-40	AU-55	MS-60	MS-63	MS-65	Proof-65
1982 mintage included in combined total								
1982 with small date		—	—	—	—	—	$.60	
1982 with large date		—	—	—	—	—	.40	
1983 combined total	7,752,355,000							
1983 with regular reverse		—	—	—	—	—	.10	
1983 with doubled-die reverse		$90.00	$105	$125	$150	$180	225	
1983-D	6,467,199,428	—	—	—	—	—	.10	
1983-S (proof only)	3,279,126	—	—	—	—	—	—	$3.00
1984 combined total	8,151,079,000							
1984 with regular obverse		—	—	—	—	—	.10	
1984 with doubled-die obverse		40.00	50.00	60.00	75.00	105	140	
1984-D	5,569,238,906	—	—	—	—	—	.10	

LINCOLN CENTS (1909–PRESENT)

	Mintage	Fine-12	EF-40	AU-55	MS-60	MS-63	MS-65	Proof-65
1984-S (proof only)	3,065,110	—	—	—	—	—	—	4.00
1985.	5,648,489,887	—	—	—	—	—	.10	
1985-D	5,287,399,926	—	—	—	—	—	.10	
1985-S (proof only)	3,362,821	—	—	—	—	—	—	2.75
1986.	4,491,395,493	—	—	—	—	—	.10	
1986-D	4,442,866,698	—	—	—	—	—	.10	
1986-S (proof only)	3,010,497	—	—	—	—	—	—	7.00
1987.	4,682,466,931	—	—	—	—	—	.10	
1987-D	4,879,389,514	—	—	—	—	—	.10	
1987-S (proof only)	3,792,233	—	—	—	—	—	—	2.75
1988.	6,092,810,000	—	—	—	—	—	.10	
1988-D	5,253,740,443	—	—	—	—	—	.10	
1988-S (proof only)	3,262,948	—	—	—	—	—	—	4.00
1989.	7,261,535,000	—	—	—	—	—	.10	
1989-D	5,345,467,111	—	—	—	—	—	.10	
1989-S (proof only)	3,215,728	—	—	—	—	—	—	4.00
1990.	6,851,765,000	—	—	—	—	—	.10	
1990-D	4,922,894,533	—	—	—	—	—	.10	
1990-S without S mint mark	3,555	—	—	—	—	—	—	2,600
1990-S with S	3,296,004	—	—	—	—	—	—	6.00
1991.	5,165,940,000	—	—	—	—	—	.10	
1991-D	4,158,442,076	—	—	—	—	—	.10	
1991-S (proof only)	2,867,787	—	—	—	—	—	—	6.75
1992.	4,648,905,000	—	—	—	—	—	.10	
1992-D	4,448,673,300	—	—	—	—	—	.10	
1992-S (proof only)	4,176,544	—	—	—	—	—	—	5.00
1993.	5,684,705,000	—	—	—	—	—	—	
1993-D	6,426,650,571	—	—	—	—	—	—	
1993-S (proof only)	3,360,876	—	—	—	—	—	—	5.00
1994.	6,502,060,896	—	—	—	—	—	.10	
1994-D	7,132,975,896	—	—	—	—	—	.10	
1994-S (proof only)	3,212,792	—	—	—	—	—	—	5.75
1995.		—	—	—	—	—	.10	
1995 with doubled-die obverse		—	—	10.00	15.00	25.00	40.00	
1995-D		—	—	—	—	—	.10	
1995-S (proof only)		—	—	—	—	—	—	5.75

TWO-CENT PIECES (1864–1873)

	Mintage	Fine-12	EF-40	AU-55	MS-60	MS-63	MS-65	Proof-65
1864 combined total	19,847,400							
1864 with small motto		$52.50	$90.00	$240	$300	$750	$2,300	—
1864 with large motto . . *100*		6.00	10.00	32.50	65.00	140	225	$800
1865 . . *500*	13,639,500	6.00	10.00	32.50	65.00	140	225	800
1866 . . *725*	3,176,275	6.00	10.00	32.50	65.00	140	225	800
1867 . . *625*	2,938,125	6.00	10.00	32.50	65.00	140	225	800
1868 . . *600*	2,803,150	6.50	11.00	35.00	70.00	175	300	900
1869 combined total	1,545,900							
1869 regular date . . *600*		7.50	12.50	37.50	75.00	225	400	900
1869/8 overdate		175	250	400	—	—	—	—
1870 . . *1,000*	860,250	9.00	17.50	60.00	90.00	325	500	1,000
1871 . . *960*	720,290	10.00	20.00	75.00	105	350	600	1,000
1872 . . *950*	64,050	70.00	140	350	475	1,050	2,300	1,200
1873 closed 3 (proof only)	*600*	—	—	—	—	—	—	1,000
1873 open 3 (restrike, proof only)	*500*	—	—	—	—	—	—	2,000

SILVER THREE-CENT PIECES (1851–1873)

	Mintage	Good-4	Fine-12	EF-40	AU-55	MS-63	MS-65	Proof-65
1851	5,447,400	$11.00	$17.50	$60.00	$110	$225	$1,350	
1851-O	720,000	17.50	32.50	120	200	450	3,250	

SILVER THREE-CENT PIECES (1851–1873)

	Mintage	Good-4	Fine-12	EF-40	AU-55	MS-63	MS-65	Proof-65
1852	18,663,500	11.00	17.50	57.50	115	225	1,350	
1853	11,400,000	11.00	17.50	52.50	115	225	1,350	
1854	671,000	12.50	25.00	100	200	540	5,000	—
1855	139,000	17.50	42.50	160	240	1,050	15,500	6,000
1856	1,458,000	11.00	20.00	85.00	175	540	5,000	6,000
1857	1,042,000	11.00	20.00	80.00	190	540	5,000	6,000
1858	1,604,000	11.00	22.50	90.00	180	540	5,000	6,000
1859 . . 800	364,200	11.00	20.00	52.50	110	300	1,050	1,400
1860 . . 1,000	286,000	11.00	20.00	52.50	110	300	1,050	1,400
1861 . . 1,000	497,000	11.00	20.00	52.50	110	300	1,050	1,400
1862 combined total	343,000							
1862 regular								
date . . 550		11.00	20.00	52.50	110	300	1,050	1,400
1862/1 overdate		14.00	22.50	70.00	150	350	1,150	
1863 combined								
total . . 460	21,000							
1863 regular date		175	250	325	375	750	1,800	1,600
1863/2 overdate		200	275	350	400	800	1,900	1,800
1864 . . 470	12,000	225	300	375	425	850	1,900	1,600
1865 . . 500	8,000	235	325	375	425	900	2,000	1,600
1866 . . 725	22,000	200	275	325	375	900	1,800	1,600
1867 . . 625	4,000	250	325	375	450	875	2,600	1,600
1868 . . 600	3,500	250	325	375	450	1,200	2,800	1,600
1869 combined								
total . . 600	4,500							
1869 regular date		250	325	400	475	1,050	2,800	1,600
1869/8 overdate		350	425	500	575	1,300	2,900	1,650
1870 . . 1,000	3,000	250	325	375	450	900	2,000	1,600
1871 . . 960	3,400	250	325	400	475	825	1,800	1,600
1872 . . 950	1,000	275	400	550	650	1,250	2,800	1,600
1873 closed-3								
(proof only) 600		—	—	—	—	—	—	2,500

NICKEL THREE-CENT PIECES (1865–1889)

	Mintage	Good-4	Fine-12	EF-40	AU-55	MS-63	MS-65	Proof-65
1865 . . 500	11,381,500	$5.50	$7.50	$15.00	$35.00	$150	$700	$550
1866 . . 725	4,800,275	5.50	7.50	15.00	35.00	150	700	550
1867 . . 625	3,914,375	5.50	7.50	15.00	35.00	150	700	550
1868 . . 600	3,251,400	5.50	7.50	15.00	35.00	150	700	550
1869 . . 600	1,603,400	5.50	7.50	15.00	37.50	150	700	550
1870 . . 1,000	1,334,000	6.00	8.25	17.50	40.00	150	700	550
1871 . . 960	603,040	6.00	8.25	17.50	40.00	200	900	550
1872 . . 950	861,050	6.00	8.25	17.50	40.00	175	900	550
1873 closed								
3 . . . 1,100	388,900	6.00	8.00	17.50	40.00	180	950	550
1873 open 3	783,000	6.00	8.00	17.50	40.00	180	950	550
1874 . . 700	789,300	6.00	8.00	17.50	40.00	190	950	550
1875 . . 700	227,300	7.50	10.00	22.50	60.00	200	950	550
1876 . . 1,150	160,850	10.00	15.00	32.50	90.00	300	950	550
1877 (proof only)	510	—	—	—	—	—	—	2,200
1878 (proof only)	2,350	—	—	—	—	—	—	800
1879 . . 3,200	38,000	42.50	57.50	90.00	125	375	900	600
1880 . . 3,955	21,000	57.50	75.00	120	160	425	900	600
1881 . . 3,575	1,077,000	5.50	7.50	15.00	35.00	150	700	550
1882 . . 3,100	22,200	57.50	75.00	110	150	450	900	600
1883 . . 6,609	4,000	120	160	240	275	650	1,400	750
1884 . . 3,942	1,700	275	350	400	450	700	1,700	750
1885 . . 3,790	1,000	325	400	475	550	750	1,600	750
1886 (proof only)	4,290	—	—	—	—	—	—	675
1887 combined								
total . . 2,960.	5,001							
1887 regular date		250	325	400	450	750	900	675
1887/6 overdate (proof only)		—	—	—	—	—	—	775
1888 . . 4,582	36,501	40.00	50.00	75.00	120	400	900	675
1889 . . 3,436	18,125	60.00	75.00	110	140	350	700	675

HALF DISMES (1792)

1792.	1,500	$3,000	$5,000	$10,000

HALF DIMES (1794–1873)

Flowing Hair Portrait (1794–1795)

	Mintage	Good-4	Fine-12	EF-40
1794.	7,756	$700	$1,200	$2,500
1795.	78,660	525	900	1,800

Draped Bust Portrait with Small Eagle on Reverse (1796–1797)

	Mintage	Good-4	Fine-12	EF-40
1796 combined total.	10,230			
1796 regular date		$675	$1,200	2,500
1796/5 overdate		725	1,325	2,800
1796 with LIBERTY spelled LIKERTY		675	1,250	3,000
1797 combined total.	44,527			
1797 with 15 stars		650	1,200	2,500
1797 with 16 stars		675	1,250	2,600
1797 with 13 stars		750	1,500	3,500

Draped Bust Portrait with Heraldic Eagle on Reverse (1800–1805)

	Mintage	Good-4	Fine-12	EF-40
1800 LIBERTY	24,000	$450	$675	$2,000
1800 LIBEKTY	16,000	460	685	2,100
1801	27,760	525	750	2,500
1802	3,060	7,500	17,500	52,500
1803	37,850	500	700	2,300
1805	15,600	625	900	3,000

Capped Bust Portrait (1829–1837)

	Mintage	Good-4	Fine-12	EF-40	AU-55	MS-63
1829	1,230,000	$13.00	$23.00	$95.00	$250	$650
1830	1,240,000	13.00	23.00	95.00	250	650
1831	1,242,700	13.00	23.00	95.00	250	650
1832	965,000	13.00	23.00	100	275	675
1833	1,370,000	13.00	23.00	95.00	250	650
1834	1,480,000	13.00	23.00	95.00	250	650
1835	2,760,000	13.00	23.00	95.00	250	650
1836	1,900,000	13.00	23.00	95.00	250	650
1837 combined total	871,000					
1837 with small 5c		24.00	40.00	200	575	2,250
1837 with large 5c		14.00	24.00	100	275	700

Seated Liberty Portrait (1837–1873)

Without Stars on Obverse (1837–1838)

	Mintage	Good-4	Fine-12	EF-40	AU-55	MS-63	MS-65
1837 combined total	1,405,000						
1837 with small date		$20.00	$40.00	$175	$350	$1,250	$3,700
1837 with large date. . . .		20.00	40.00	175	350	1,000	3,500
1838-O.	70,000	60.00	140	400	750	4,000	12,000

With Stars on Obverse (1838–1859)

	Mintage	Good-4	Fine-12	EF-40	AU-55	MS-63	MS-65
1838 combined total	2,225,000						
1838 with regular stars. . . .		$5.00	$10.00	$50.00	$100	$700	$2,000
1838 with small stars		15.00	40.00	150	350	1,000	—
1839.	1,069,150	5.00	10.00	50.00	100	700	2,000
1839-O.	1,034,039	6.00	10.00	60.00	130	1,000	—
1840 without drapery from elbow	1,034,000	5.00	10.00	50.00	100	700	2,000
1840 with drapery from elbow	310,085	15.00	40.00	130	350	800	2,000
1840-O without drapery from elbow	695,000	6.00	14.00	60.00	175	1,300	—
1840-O with drapery from elbow	240,000	20.00	90.00	300	750	4,000	—
1841.	1,150,000	5.00	9.00	50.00	90.00	480	1,900
1841-O.	815,000	9.00	20.00	90.00	300	1,500	4,000
1842.	815,000	5.00	9.00	50.00	90.00	500	1,400
1842-O.	350,000	20.00	45.00	225	500	1,100	12,000
1843.	1,165,000	5.00	9.00	50.00	80.00	400	1,250
1844.	430,000	5.00	9.00	50.00	80.00	400	1,250
1844-O.	220,000	50.00	130	800	1,800	—	—
1845.	1,564,000	5.00	9.00	50.00	80.00	400	1,250
1846.	27,000	150	300	900	2,000	6,000	—
1847.	1,274,000	5.00	9.00	50.00	80.00	400	1,250
1848 combined total	668,000						
1848 regular date		5.00	9.00	50.00	80.00	400	1,250
1848 with large date.		9.00	22.00	75.00	200	1,300	—
1848-O.	600,000	9.00	20.00	75.00	150	525	1,400
1849 combined total	1,309,000						
1849 with regular date. . . .		5.00	9.00	50.00	80.00	400	1,250
1849/6 overdate.		7.00	15.00	90.00	150	700	—
1849/8 overdate.		9.00	20.00	90.00	170	900	—

	Mintage	Good-4	Fine-12	EF-40	AU-55	MS-63	MS-65
1850	955,000	5.00	9.00	50.00	80.00	400	1,250
1850-O	690,000	8.00	15.00	70.00	220	1,800	1,900
1851	781,000	5.00	9.00	50.00	80.00	400	1,250
1851-O	860,000	7.00	17.00	62.50	180	750	3,000
1852	1,000,500	5.00	9.00	50.00	80.00	400	1,250
1852-O	260,000	20.00	50.00	200	300	1,300	—
1853 without arrows	135,000	140	250	900	2,200	9,000	18,500
1853-O without arrows	160,000	125	240	900	2,000	9,000	18,500

With Arrows Beside the Date (1853–1855)

	Mintage	Good-4	Fine-12	EF-40	AU-55	MS-63	MS-65	Proof-65
1853	13,210,020	$6.00	$9.00	$50.00	$90.00	$500	$1,900	
1853-O	2,200,000	8.00	9.00	60.00	90.00	600	2,500	
1854	5,740,000	8.00	9.00	60.00	90.00	600	2,400	
1854-O	1,560,000	6.00	12.00	60.00	100	700	2,500	
1855	1,750,000	6.00	8.00	50.00	90.00	500	1,800	20,000
1855-O	600,000	12.00	30.00	125	190	1,100	—	

Without Arrows Beside the Date (1856–1859)

	Mintage	Good-4	Fine-12	EF-40	AU-55	MS-63	MS-65	Proof-65
1856	4,880,000	$5.00	$9.00	$50.00	$80.00	$200	$1,500	—
1856-O	1,100,000	9.00	18.00	80.00	250	1,000	2,000	
1857	7,280,000	5.00	9.00	50.00	80.00	200	1,500	4,000
1857-O	1,380,000	9.00	15.00	60.00	200	300	1,400	
1858 combined total	3,500,000							
1858 regular date		5.00	9.00	50.00	80.00	200	1,500	4,000
1858 with inverted date underneath		20.00	40.00	150	225	400	1,800	
1858-O	1,660,000	6.00	10.00	60.00	140	400	2,200	
1859 combined total	340,000							
1859 with regular date		7.00	20.00	60.00	110	275	1,900	4,000
1859-O	560,000	8.00	20.00	90.00	200	400	1,900	

With Motto on Obverse (1860–1873)

	Mintage	Good-4	Fine-12	EF-40	AU-55	MS-63	MS-65	Proof-65
1860 . . *1,000*	798,000	$5.00	$7.00	$20.00	$50.00	$300	$1,600	$2,000
1860-O	1,060,000	5.00	8.00	30.00	70.00	400	1,600	
1861 combined total	3,360,000							
1861 regular date . . *1,000*		5.00	8.00	20.00	60.00	300	1,400	2,000
1861/0 overdate		20.00	50.00	250	350	—	—	
1862 . . *550*	1,492,000	5.00	8.00	26.00	57.50	320	1,600	1,700
1863 . . *460*	18,460	135	180	375	485	1,150	1,800	1,800
1863-S	100,000	15.00	27.50	80.00	200	1,500	2,900	
1864 . . *470*	48,000	210	350	700	900	1,600	2,600	1,700
1864-S	90,000	40.00	80.00	300	400	900	3,500	
1865 . . *500*	13,000	225	325	640	725	1,500	3,500	1,900
1865-S	120,000	15.00	25.00	125	325	1,825	—	
1866 . . *725*	10,000	225	325	640	725	1,600	3,500	1,900
1866-S	120,000	12.00	30.00	110	300	1,300	5,000	
1867 . . *625*	8,000	325	450	650	800	1,400	—	1,800
1867-S	120,000	15.00	30.00	100	300	1,000	—	
1868 . . *600*	88,600	40.00	60.00	300	400	900	2,900	1,800
1868-S	280,000	6.00	15.00	30.00	90.00	900	—	
1869 . . *600*	208,000	6.00	15.00	30.00	90.00	900	2,100	1,600
1869-S	230,000	7.00	9.00	30.00	90.00	500	—	
1870 . . *1,000*	535,000	6.00	9.00	20.00	50.00	300	1,400	1,800
1870-S	1 known	(graded MS-60)					—	
1871 . . *960*	1,873,000	6.00	9.00	20.00	50.00	300	1,400	1,700
1871-S	161,000	7.00	35.00	65.00	150	500	3,000	
1872 . . *950*	2,947,000	5.00	10.00	25.00	50.00	300	1,800	1,700
1872-S combined total	837,000							
1872-S with S inside the wreath		5.00	9.00	25.00	60.00	300	1,400	
1872-S with S below the wreath		5.00	9.00	25.00	60.00	300	1,400	
1873 . . *600*	712,000	5.00	9.00	25.00	60.00	300	1,875	1,500
1873-S	324,000	5.00	9.00	25.00	60.00	300	1,400	

NICKELS (1866–Present)

Shield Portrait (1866–1883)

	Mintage	Good-4	Fine-12	EF-40	AU-55	MS-63	MS-65	Proof-65
1866 with rays between the stars . . . *125*	14,742,375	$16.00	$21.00	$90.00	$125	$275	$2,300	$3,800
1867 with rays . . . *25.*	2,018,975	16.00	25.00	115	225	275	2,300	3,800
1867 without rays . . *600*	28,880,900	7.50	11.00	22.50	45.00	150	675	675
1868 . . *600*	28,816,400	7.50	11.00	20.00	42.50	150	675	675
1869 . . *600*	16,394,400	7.50	11.00	25.00	47.50	150	675	675
1870 . . *1,000*	4,805,000	8.25	12.50	27.50	52.50	150	675	675
1871 . . *960*	560,040	27.50	42.50	90.00	150	225	825	800
1872 . . *950*	6,035,050	8.25	12.50	27.50	65.00	150	675	675
1873 with closed 3 . . *1,100*	434,950	10.00	25.00	75.00	105	225	825	800
1873 with open 3	4,113,950	8.25	12.50	30.00	60.00	150	675	
1874 . . *700*	3,537,300	8.50	13.00	32.50	65.00	150	675	675
1875 . . *700*	2,086,300	8.50	15.00	37.50	75.00	175	1,100	675
1876 . . *1,150*	2,528,900	8.50	15.00	35.00	70.00	185	725	675
1877 (proof only)	*510*	—	—	—	—	—	—	1,250
1878 (proof only)	*2,350*	—	—	—	—	—	—	800
1879 . . *3,200*	25,900	235	340	450	525	650	1,000	675
1880 . . *3,955*	16,000	260	325	475	550	725	1,750	675
1881 . . *3,575*	68,800	160	240	360	410	550	1,000	675
1882 . . *3,100*	11,472,900	9.00	12.00	27.50	45.00	185	675	675
1883 combined total	1,456,919							
1883 regular date . . *5,419*		9.00	12.00	27.50	47.50	180	675	675
1883/2 overdate		20.00	70.00	140	180	475	1,425	

Liberty Head Portrait (1883–1912)

	Mintage	Good-4	Fine-12	EF-40	AU-55	MS-63	MS-65	Proof-65
1883 without CENTS on reverse . . 5,219	5,474,300	$2.40	$3.75	$7.50	$12.50	$40.00	$325	$600
1883 with CENTS . . 6,783	16,026,200	7.50	12.50	37.50	62.50	80.00	575	500
1884 . . 3,942	11,270,000	8.00	15.00	40.00	65.00	150	825	500
1885 . . 3,790	1,472,700	175	325	575	650	700	1,500	600
1886 . . 4,290	3,326,000	47.50	120	235	350	500	1,600	600
1887 . . 2,960	15,260,692	5.50	12.50	30.00	57.50	175	575	500
1888 . . 4,582	10,715,901	8.00	15.00	40.00	75.00	150	800	500
1889 . . 3,336	15,878,025	4.50	11.00	30.00	57.50	120	575	500
1890 . . 2,740	16,256,532	4.50	11.00	30.00	60.00	135	900	500
1891 . . 2,350	16,832,000	4.00	11.00	30.00	57.50	100	800	500
1892 . . 2,745	11,696,897	4.00	11.00	30.00	60.00	100	800	500
1893 . . 2,195	13,368,000	4.00	11.00	30.00	60.00	100	800	500
1894 . . 2,632	5,410,500	6.00	22.50	65.00	110	170	1,100	500
1895 . . 2,062	9,977,822	3.00	10.00	30.00	57.50	100	975	500
1896 . . 1,862	8,841,058	4.50	11.00	32.50	65.00	110	975	500
1897 . . 1,938	20,426,797	2.50	5.00	17.50	47.50	90.00	975	500
1898 . . 1,795	12,530,292	2.00	5.00	17.50	50.00	90.00	575	500
1899 . . 2,031	26,027,000	1.25	4.50	17.50	42.50	80.00	575	500
1900 . . 2,262	27,253,733	.75	3.50	15.00	37.50	80.00	575	500
1901 . . 1,985	26,478,228	.75	3.50	14.00	35.00	80.00	575	500
1902 . . 2,018	31,487,561	.75	3.50	14.00	35.00	80.00	575	500
1903 . . 1,790	28,004,935	.75	3.50	14.00	35.00	80.00	575	500
1904 . . 1,817	21,403,167	.75	3.50	14.00	35.00	80.00	575	500
1905 . . 2,152	29,825,124	.75	3.50	14.00	35.00	80.00	575	500
1906 . . 1,725	38,612,000	.75	3.50	14.00	35.00	80.00	575	500
1907 . . 1,475	39,213,325	.75	3.50	14.00	35.00	80.00	575	500
1908 . . 1,620	22,684,557	.75	3.50	14.00	35.00	80.00	575	500
1909 . . 4,763	11,585,763	.90	4.00	16.00	40.00	100.00	600	500
1910 . . 2,405	30,166,948	.75	3.50	14.00	35.00	80.00	575	500
1911 . . 1,733	39,557,639	.75	3.50	14.00	35.00	80.00	575	500

	Mintage	Good-4	Fine-12	EF-40	AU-55	MS-63	MS-65	Proof-65
1912 . . *2,145*	26,234,569	.75	3.50	14.00	35.00	85.00	585	595
1912-D	8,474,000	1.25	4.50	37.50	75.00	170	600	
1912-S	238,000	37.50	60.00	350	475	590	2,000	
1913 (not an authorized Mint issue) . . . . . *5 known*	—	—	—	—	—	—	963,500	

"Buffalo" Portrait (1913–1938)

Bison Standing on Mound (1913)

	Mintage	Good-4	Fine-12	EF-40	AU-55	MS-63	MS-65	Proof-65
1913 . . *1,520*	30,992,000	$4.50	$6.00	$12.50	$20.00	$45.00	$85.00	$2,000
1913-D	5,337,000	7.50	10.00	20.00	32.50	55.00	190	
1913-S	2,105,000	12.50	17.50	35.00	45.00	65.00	700	

Bison Standing on Plain Line (1913–1938)

	Mintage	Good-4	Fine-12	EF-40	AU-55	MS-63	MS-65	Proof-65
1913 . . *1,514*	29,857,186	$4.50	$6.50	$13.00	$20.00	$40.00	$300	$1,000
1913-D	4,156,000	32.50	47.50	75.00	110	175	800	
1913-S	1,209,000	75.00	130	190	225	300	2,000	
1914 . . *1,275*	20,665,463	4.50	6.50	16.00	25.00	50.00	300	1,000
1914-D	3,912,000	27.50	47.50	90.00	125	205	1,000	
1914-S	3,470,000	5.50	12.50	37.50	52.50	200	2,500	
1915 . . *1,050*	20,986,220	2.25	4.50	12.00	20.00	50.00	210	1,000
1915-D	7,569,000	2.25	17.50	52.50	77.50	210	2,000	
1915-S	1,505,000	12.50	22.50	120	200	400	2,000	
1916 combined total	63,497,466							
1916 regular date . . *600*		.85	1.75	6.00	12.50	55.00	250	1,000

NICKELS (1866–Present)

	Mintage	Good-4	Fine-12	EF-40	AU-55	MS-63	MS-65	Proof-65
1916 with doubled obverse		1,300	3,900	7,800	9,000	13,000	52,500	
1916-D	13,333,000	5.25	9.50	47.50	75.00	190	2,100	
1916-S	11,860,000	3.25	7.00	42.50	70.00	225	1,950	
1917	51,424,019	.85	2.00	9.50	22.50	60.00	365	
1917-D	9,910,000	5.25	14.00	80.00	125	330	2,200	
1917-S	4,193,000	4.50	14.00	95.00	185	450	2,400	
1918	32,086,314	1.00	2.25	16.00	32.50	70.00	1,200	
1918-D combined total.	8,362,000							
1918-D regular date		5.25	17.50	150	225	350	2,500	
1918/7-D overdate		375	750	3,750	5,750	21,000	85,000	
1918-S	4,882,000	4.50	12.50	140	200	840	7,000	
1919	60,868,000	.85	1.25	7.50	20.00	85.00	320	
1919-D	8,006,000	5.25	15.00	160	240	690	2,600	
1919-S	7,521,000	3.25	9.00	150	225	710	4,500	
1920	63,093,000	.75	1.25	8.50	22.50	45	500	
1920-D	9,418,000	3.75	12.50	200	275	560	3,500	
1920-S	9,689,000	2.00	7.00	135	180	725	9,000	
1921	10,663,000	1.25	2.50	20.00	37.50	80.00	400	
1921-S	1,557,000	14.00	42.50	550	700	960	4,000	
1923	35,715,000	.75	1.25	7.50	15.00	48.00	350	
1923-S	6,142,000	2.25	5.25	160	225	440	5,000	
1924	21,620,000	.75	1.25	8.50	22.50	70.00	425	
1924-D	5,258,000	2.75	7.50	135	200	325	2,000	
1924-S	1,437,000	5.00	22.50	825	1,000	1,850	3,200	
1925	35,565,100	.75	1.50	7.50	20.00	48.00	180	
1925-D	4,450,000	4.50	16.00	120	180	395	2,800	
1925-S	6,256,000	2.00	7.50	135	200	750	13,500	
1926	44,693,000	.50	.85	4.50	13.50	33.00	125	
1926-D	5,638,000	2.50	12.50	125	170	285	1,750	
1926-S	970,000	6.00	15.00	750	1,000	2,000	16,000	
1927	37,981,000	.50	.75	4.50	15.00	37.00	180	
1927-D	5,730,000	1.50	4.00	37.50	70.00	142	1,950	
1927-S	3,430,000	.85	2.50	60.00	100	875	9,250	
1928	23,411,000	.50	.85	5.25	15.00	42.00	250	
1928-D	6,436,000	1.00	3.50	15.00	22.50	45.00	595	
1928-S	6,936,000	.80	1.75	12.50	25.00	325	3,500	
1929	36,446,000	.50	.75	5.00	12.50	40.00	165	
1929-D	8,370,000	1.00	1.75	14.00	22.50	55.00	825	
1929-S	7,754,000	.60	1.10	8.50	25.00	50.00	220	
1930	22,849,000	.50	.85	5.25	13.00	30.00	100	
1930-S	5,435,000	.60	.90	7.50	22.50	65.00	375	
1931-S	1,200,000	3.00	5.00	10.50	25.00	55.00	175	

	Mintage	Good-4	Fine-12	EF-40	AU-55	MS-63	MS-65	Proof-65
1934	20,213,003	.40	.65	3.75	12.50	25.00	225	
1934-D	7,480,000	.45	.75	6.50	15.00	45.00	900	
1935	58,264,000	.30	.50	3.00	7.50	22.50	80.00	
1935-D	12,092,000	.35	.60	3.75	15.00	50.00	370	
1935-S	10,300,000	.35	.60	3.25	8.50	25.00	175	
1936 . . . *4,420*	118,997,000	.30	.50	3.00	7.50	22.50	47.50	800
1936-D	24,814,000	.35	.60	3.25	9.00	25.00	60.00	
1936-S	14,930,000	.35	.60	3.25	11.00	25.00	75.00	
1937 . . . *5,769*	79,480,000	.35	.50	3.00	6.50	20.00	30.00	800
1937-D combined total	17,826,000							
1937-D with normal reverse		.35	.60	3.25	8.00	22.50	30.00	
1937-D with 3-legged bison		90.00	155	275	525	2,275	8,500	
1937-S	5,635,000	.35	.60	3.25	8.00	20.00	40.00	
1938-D combined total	7,020,000							
1938-D with normal mint mark		.35	.50	2.50	7.50	17.50	30.00	
1938-D/D		.90	2.75	4.50	9.00	22.50	85.00	
1938-D/S		4.50	7.00	10.50	15.00	30.00	120	

Jefferson Portrait (1938–Present)

	Mintage	Good-4	Fine-12	EF-40	AU-55	MS-63	MS-65	Proof-65
1938 . . . *19,365*	19,496,000	$.10	$.20	$.50	$.75	$1.50	$3.50	$35.00
1938-D	5,376,000	.50	.75	1.25	1.60	3.00	5.00	
1938-S	4,105,000	1.00	1.50	2.00	2.50	5.00	7.50	
1939 combined total	120,615,000							
1939 with regular reverse . . *12,535*		—	.10	.20	.25	.50	1.00	30.00
1939 with double image on MONTICELLO and FIVE CENTS		5.00	9.00	35.00	50.00	—	—	
1939-D	3,514,000	2.00	3.00	3.75	7.50	25.00	50.00	

NICKELS (1866–Present)

	Mintage	Good-4	Fine-12	EF-40	AU-55	MS-63	MS-65	Proof-65
1939-S	6,630,000	.25	.50	1.75	3.50	10.00	20.00	
1940 . . *14,158*	176,485,000	—	—	.10	.15	.75	1.25	30.00
1940-D	43,540,000	—	—	.20	.30	1.25	2.50	
1940-S	39,690,000	—	—	.15	.20	1.00	2.00	
1941 . . *18,720*	203,265,000	—	—	.10	.15	.60	1.20	25.00
1941-D	53,432,000	—	—	.10	.20	1.00	2.00	
1941-S	43,445,000	—	—	.10	.20	1.10	2.25	
1942 . . *29,600*	49,789,000	—	—	.10	.15	.60	1.20	20.00
1942-D	13,938,000	—	—	1.00	2.00	4.00	10.00	

Wartime Composition,
Mint Mark Above Monticello (1942–1945)

	Mintage	Good-4	Fine-12	EF-40	AU-55	MS-63	MS-65	Proof-65
1942-P . . *27,600*	57,873,000	—	—	$.50	$.60	$3.00	$7.50	$90
1942-S	32,900,000	—	—	.50	.60	2.50	5.00	
1943-P combined total	271,165,000							
1943-P regular date		—	—	.50	.60	2.00	4.00	
1943/2 overdate.		—	—	90.00	150	250	500	
1943-D	15,294,000	—	—	.50	.60	2.50	4.50	
1943-S	104,060,000	—	—	.50	.60	2.00	4.00	
1944-P	119,150,000			.50	.60	2.00	4.00	
1944-D	32,309,000			.50	.60	2.00	4.00	
1944-S	21,640,000	—	—	.50	.60	2.50	4.50	
1945-P	119,150,000	—	—	.50	.60	2.00	4.00	
1945-D	37,158,000	—	—	.50	.60	2.00	4.00	
1945-S	58,939,000	—	—	.50	.60	2.00	4.00	

Regular Composition Returns (1946–Present)

	Mintage	Fine-12	EF-40	AU-55	MS-63	MS-65	Proof-65
1946.	161,116,000	—	$.10	$.15	$.25	$.50	
1946-D	45,292,200	—	.15	.20	.35	.65	
1946-S	13,560,000	—	.20	.25	.40	.70	
1947.	95,000,000	—	.10	.15	.25	.50	
1947-D	37,822,000	—	.15	.20	.35	.65	
1947-S	24,720,000	—	.15	.20	.35	.65	
1948.	89,348,000	—	.10	.15	.25	.50	
1948-D	44,734,000	—	.15	.20	.35	1.00	
1948-S	11,300,000	—	.15	.20	.35	1.00	
1949.	60,652,000	—	.10	.15	.25	.90	

NICKELS (1866–Present)

	Mintage	Fine-12	EF-40	AU-55	MS-63	MS-65	Proof-65
1949-D combined total. . . .	36,498,000						
1949-D with regular mint mark		—	.15	.20	.30	.80	
1949-D/S		17.50	60.00	75.00	200	350	
1949-S	9,716,000	.10	.20	.25	.45	1.00	
1950 . . 51,386	9,796,000	.10	.20	.25	.45	1.00	40.00
1950-D	2,630,030	5.00	5.50	6.00	7.50	9.00	
1951 . . 57,500	28,552,000	—	.10	.15	.25	.90	20.00
1951-D	20,460,000	—	.10	.15	.25	.90	
1951-S	7,776,000	.10	.15	.20	.35	1.25	
1952 . . 81,980	63,988,000	—	.10	.15	.25	.50	19.00
1952-D	30,638,000	—	.15	.20	.35	1.00	
1952-S	20,572,000	—	.10	.15	.25	.60	
1953 . . 128,800	46,644,000	—	.10	.15	.25	.50	18.00
1953-D	59,878,600	—	.10	.15	.25	.50	
1953-S	19,210,900	—	.10	.15	.25	.60	
1954 . . 233,300	47,684,050	—	.10	.15	.25	.50	10.00
1954-D	117,183,060	—	.10	.15	.25	.50	
1954-S combined total	29,384,000						
1954-S with regular mint mark		—	.10	.15	.25	.50	
1954-S/D		4.00	7.50	9.00	22.50	37.50	
1955 . . 378,200	7,888,000	.10	.15	.20	.35	1.00	10.00
1955-D combined total. . . .	74,464,100						
1955-D with regular mint mark		—	.10	.15	.25	.50	
1955-D/S		5.00	10.00	15.00	35.00	60.00	
1956 . . 669,384	35,216,000	—	—	.10	.20	.30	6.00
1956-D	67,222,940	—	—	.10	.20	.30	
1957 . . 1,247,952.	38,408,000	—	—	.10	.20	.30	4.00
1957-D	136,828,900	—	—	.10	.20	.30	
1958 . . 875,652	17,088,000	—	—	.15	.30	.40	5.00
1958-D	168,249,120	—	—	.10	.20	.30	
1959 . . 1,149,291.	27,248,000	—	—	.10	.25	.35	4.00
1959-D	160,738,240	—	—	.10	.20	.30	
1960 . . 1,691,602.	55,416,000	—	—	—	.10	.15	3.00
1960-D	192,582,180	—	—	—	.10	.15	
1961 . . 3,028,144.	73,640,100	—	—	—	.10	.15	2.50
1961-D	229,342,760	—	—	—	.10	.15	
1962 . . 3,218,019.	97,384,000	—	—	—	.10	.15	2.50
1962-D	280,195,720	—	—	—	.10	.15	
1963 . . 3,075,645.	175,776,000	—	—	—	.10	.15	2.50
1963-D	276,829,460	—	—	—	.10	.15	
1964 . . 3,950,762.	1,024,672,000	—	—	—	.10	.15	2.25

NICKELS (1866–Present)

	Mintage	Fine-12	EF-40	AU-55	MS-63	MS-65	Proof-65
1964-D	1,787,297,160	—	—	—	.10	.15	
1965	136,131,380	—	—	—	.10	.15	
1966	156,208,283	—	—	—	.10	.15	
1967	107,325,800	—	—	—	.10	.15	
1968-D	91,227,880	—	—	—	.10	.15	
1968-S . . 3,041,506	100,396,004	—	—	—	.10	.15	1.00
1969-D	202,807,500	—	—	—	.10	.15	
1969-S . . 2,934,631	120,075,000	—	—	—	.10	.15	1.00
1970-D	515,485,380	—	—	—	.10	.15	
1970-S . . 2,632,810	238,832,004	—	—	—	.10	.15	1.60
1971	106,884,000	—	—	—	.25	.50	
1971-D	316,144,800	—	—	—	.10	.15	
1971-S combined total (proof only)	3,220,733						
1971-S with S		—	—	—	—	—	1.00
1971-S proof with no mint mark		—	—	—	—	—	700
1972	202,036,000	—	—	—	.10	.15	
1972-D	351,694,600	—	—	—	.10	.15	
1972-S (proof only)	3,260,996	—	—	—	—	—	1.10
1973	384,396,000	—	—	—	.10	.15	
1973-D	261,405,000	—	—	—	.10	.15	
1973-S (proof only)	2,760,339	—	—	—	—	—	1.20
1974	601,752,000	—	—	—	.10	.15	
1974-D	277,373,000	—	—	—	.15	.20	
1974-S (proof only)	2,612,568	—	—	—	—	—	1.35
1975	181,772,000	—	—	—	—	.10	
1975-D	401,875,300	—	—	—	—	.10	
1975-S (proof only)	2,845,450	—	—	—	—	—	1.60
1976	367,124,000	—	—	—	—	.10	
1976-D	563,964,147	—	—	—	—	.10	
1976-S (proof only)	4,149,730	—	—	—	—	—	1.40
1977	585,376,000	—	—	—	—	.10	
1977-D	297,313,422	—	—	—	—	.15	
1977-S (proof only)	3,251,152	—	—	—	—	—	1.50
1978	391,308,000	—	—	—	—	.10	
1978-D	313,092,780	—	—	—	—	.10	
1978-S (proof only)	3,127,781	—	—	—	—	—	1.60
1979	463,188,000	—	—	—	—	.10	
1979-D	325,867,672	—	—	—	—	.10	
1979-S combined total (proof only)	3,677,175						
1979-S with clear S		—	—	—	—	—	12.00

NICKELS (1866–Present)

	Mintage	Fine-12	EF-40	AU-55	MS-63	MS-65	Proof-65
1979-S with clogged S		—	—	—	—	—	1.50
1980-P	593,004,000	—	—	—	—	.10	
1980-D	502,323,448	—	—	—	—	.10	
1980-S (proof only)	3,554,806	—	—	—	—	—	1.60
1981-P	657,504,000	—	—	—	—	.10	
1981-D	364,801,843	—	—	—	—	.10	
1981-S (proof only)	4,063,083	—	—	—	—	—	1.40
1982-P	292,355,000	—	—	—	—	.10	
1982-D	373,726,544	—	—	—	—	.10	
1982-S (proof only)	3,857,479	—	—	—	—	—	1.50
1983-P	561,615,000	—	—	—	—	.10	
1983-D	536,726,276	—	—	—	—	.10	
1983-S (proof only)	3,279,126	—	—	—	—	—	1.60
1984-P	746,769,000	—	—	—	—	.10	
1984-D	517,675,146	—	—	—	—	.10	
1984-S (proof only)	3,065,110	—	—	—	—	—	2.50
1985-P	647,114,962	—	—	—	—	.10	
1985-D	459,747,446	—	—	—	—	.10	
1985-S (proof only)	3,362,821	—	—	—	—	—	1.60
1986-P	536,883,483	—	—	—	—	.10	
1986-D	361,819,140	—	—	—	—	.10	
1986-S (proof only)	3,010,497	—	—	—	—	—	4.50
1987-P	371,499,481	—	—	—	—	.10	
1987-D	410,590,604	—	—	—	—	.10	
1987-S (proof only)	3,792,233	—	—	—	—	—	1.50
1988-P	771,360,000	—	—	—	—	.10	
1988-D	663,771,652	—	—	—	—	.10	
1988-S (proof only)	3,262,948	—	—	—	—	—	2.50
1989-P	898,812,000	—	—	—	—	.10	
1989-D	570,842,474	—	—	—	—	.10	
1989-S (proof only)	3,215,728	—	—	—	—	—	2.00
1990-P	661,636,000	—	—	—	—	.10	
1990-D	663,938,503	—	—	—	—	.10	
1990-S (proof only)	3,299,559	—	—	—	—	—	3.50
1991-P	614,104,000	—	—	—	—	.10	
1991-D	436,496,678	—	—	—	—	.10	
1991-S (proof only)	2,867,787	—	—	—	—	—	2.50
1992-P	399,552,000	—	—	—	—	.10	
1992-D	450,565,113	—	—	—	—	.10	
1992-S (proof only)	4,176,544	—	—	—	—	—	2.00
1993-P	412,076,000	—	—	—	—	.10	
1993-D	406,084,135	—	—	—	—	.10	
1993-S (proof only)	3,360,876	—	—	—	—	—	2.00

	Mintage	Fine-12	EF-40	AU-55	MS-63	MS-65	Proof-65
1994-P	723,370,896	—	—	—	—	.10	
1994-D	716,973,006	—	—	—	—	.10	
1994-S (proof only)	*3,212,792*	—	—	—	—	—	2.00
1995-P		—	—	—	—	.10	
1995-D		—	—	—	—	.10	
1995-S (proof only)		—	—	—	—	2.00	

DIMES (1796–PRESENT)

Draped Bust Portrait with Small Eagle on Reverse (1796–1797)

	Mintage	Good-4	Fine-12	EF-40
1796	22,135	$825	$1,775	$4,000
1797 combined total	25,261			
1797 with 16 stars		850	1,800	4,500
1797 with 13 stars		850	1,800	4,400

Draped Bust Portrait with Heraldic Eagle on Reverse (1798–1805)

	Mintage	Good-4	Fine-12	EF-40
1798 combined total	27,550			
1798 regular date		$400	$700	$2,000

	Mintage	Good-4	Fine-12	EF-40
1798/7 overdate with 16 stars on reverse		440	800	2,400
1798/7 overdate with 13 stars on reverse		1,500	3,750	7,500
1798 with small 8		500	900	2,700
1800	21,760	410	710	2,100
1801	34,640	410	800	2,800
1802	10,975	600	1,300	5,000
1803	33,040	385	750	2,300
1804	8,265	900	2,100	7,000
1805	120,780	370	675	1,900
1807	165,000	370	675	1,900

Capped Bust Portrait (1809–1837)

	Mintage	Good-4	Fine-12	EF-40	AU-55	MS-63
1809	51,065	$85.00	$325	$900	$2,100	$5,000
1811/09 overdate	65,180	41.00	120	725	1,750	5,000
1814 combined total	421,500					
1814 small date		30.00	90.00	475	1,100	3,500
1814 large date		16.00	40.00	300	675	2,250
1814 STATESOFAMERICA		16.00	40.00	330	725	2,300
1820 combined total	942,587					
1820 small 0		13.00	34.00	280	650	2,200
1820 large 0		13.00	32.00	270	650	2,200
1820 STATESOFAMERICA		16.00	40.00	350	875	2,500
1821 combined total	1,186,512					
1821 small date		18.00	46.00	300	700	2,600
1821 large date		13.00	32.00	275	675	2,200
1822	100,000	300	725	2,000	4,250	14,000
1823/2 overdate	440,000	13.00	30.00	260	700	2,400
1824/2 overdate	100,000	17.00	45.00	450	950	2,800
1825	410,000	12.00	30.00	260	625	2,000
1827	1,215,000	12.00	30.00	260	625	2,000

	Mintage	Good-4	Fine-12	EF-40	AU-55	MS-63
1828 combined total	125,000					
1828 large date		24.00	60.00	400	1,100	—
1828 small date		24.00	70.00	300	800	2,100
1829 combined total	770,000					
1829 with curl-base 2		3,500	8,000	—	—	—
1829 small 10c		14.00	28.00	180	500	1,800
1829 large 10c		30.00	80.00	350	750	2,400
1830 combined total	510,000					
1830 regular date		11.00	19.00	150	410	1,350
1830/29 overdate		35.00	90.00	350	750	3,000
1831	771,350	11.00	19.00	150	400	1,350
1832	522,500	11.00	19.00	150	400	1,350
1833	485,000	11.00	19.00	150	400	1,350
1834	635,000	11.00	19.00	150	400	1,350
1835	1,410,000	11.00	19.00	150	400	1,350
1836	1,190,000	11.00	19.00	150	400	1,350
1837	359,500	11.00	19.00	150	400	1,400

Seated Liberty Portrait (1837–1891)

Without Stars on Obverse (1837–1838)

	Mintage	Good-4	Fine-12	EF-40	AU-55	MS-63	MS-65
1837	682,500	$24.00	$52.50	$425	$675	$2,000	$5,500
1838-O	406,034	90.00	175	950	1,500	6,000	14,500

With Stars on Obverse (1838–1859)

	Mintage	Good-4	Fine-12	EF-40	AU-55	MS-63	MS-65
1838 combined total	1,992,500						
1838 with regular stars		$6.00	$10.00	$65.00	$130	$925	$3,250
1838 with small stars		18.00	42.50	150	225	2,500	6,000

	Mintage	Good-4	Fine-12	EF-40	AU-55	MS-63	MS-65
1838 with partial drapery from elbow.		27.50	65.00	190	385	3,850	5,800
1839.	1,053,115	6.00	10.00	65.00	130	925	2,200
1839-O.	1,323,000	7.50	15.00	75.00	300	1,500	4,500
1840.	981,500	8.00	12.50	72.50	150	1,000	2,000
1840-O.	1,175,000	12.50	25.00	100	350	3,750	5,500

Drapery Added from Liberty's Elbow
(1840–1891)

	Mintage	Good-4	Fine-12	EF-40	AU-55	MS-63	MS-65
1840.	377,500	$30.00	$75.00	$350	$1,100	—	—
1841.	1,622,500	5.00	10.00	37.50	150	675	2,800
1841-O.	2,007,500	9.00	17.50	42.50	175	975	4,000
1842.	1,887,500	5.00	10.00	37.50	150	675	2,500
1842-O.	2,020,000	9.00	17.50	42.50	250	—	—
1843.	1,370,000	5.00	10.00	37.50	150	675	2,800
1843-O.	150,000	50.00	150	750	1,250	—	—
1844.	72,500	50.00	125	450	1,100	—	—
1845.	1,755,000	5.00	10.00	37.50	150	675	2,800
1845-O.	230,000	25.00	75.00	750	1,250	—	—
1846.	31,300	80.00	175	900	1,500	—	—
1847.	245,000	11.00	27.50	110	275	1,500	5,000
1848.	451,500	9.00	17.50	52.50	175	1,000	7,000
1849.	839,000	9.00	14.00	37.50	95.00	900	3,000
1849-O.	300,000	17.50	27.50	275	1,100	4,000	—
1850.	1,931,500	5.00	10.00	42.50	150	675	2,800
1850-O.	510,000	12.50	25.00	110	175	1,500	5,000
1851.	1,026,500	6.00	11.00	32.50	100	700	2,850
1851-O.	400,000	15.00	25.00	120	200	2,250	—
1852.	1,535,500	5.00	10.00	32.50	90.00	675	2,850
1852-O.	430,000	17.50	32.50	200	325	2,000	—
1853 without arrows.	95,000	45.00	100	275	375	900	4,000

With Arrows Beside the Date (1853–1855)

	Mintage	Good-4	Fine-12	EF-40	AU-55	MS-63	MS-65	Proof-65
1853.	12,078,010	$5.00	$7.50	$36.00	$110	$600	$2,500	
1853-O.	1,100,000	8.00	12.00	92.50	350	1,650	7,500	
1854.	4,470,000	5.00	7.50	36.00	110	600	2,500	36,000

	Mintage	Good-4	Fine-12	EF-40	AU-55	MS-63	MS-65	Proof-65
1854-O	1,770,000	6.00	9.00	38.00	120	800	3,000	
1855	2,075,000	5.00	7.50	36.00	110	775	3,500	35,000

Arrows Removed (1856)

	Mintage	Good-4	Fine-12	EF-40	AU-55	MS-63	MS-65	Proof-65
1856	5,780,000	$5.00	$10.00	$27.50	$75.00	$675	$2,000	$10,000
1856-O	1,100,000	7.50	12.50	30.00	85.00	700	2,000	
1856-S	70,000	65.00	200	350	600	5,000	—	
1857	5,580,000	4.00	8.00	24.00	70.00	475	2,850	5,600
1857-O	1,540,000	6.00	11.00	28.00	80.00	500	3,150	
1858	1,540,000	4.00	8.00	24.00	70.00	500	2,850	4,000
1858-O	290,000	15.00	35.00	75.00	250	800	4,500	
1858-S	60,000	80.00	200	300	500	—	—	
1859 . . 800	429,200	6.00	11.00	28.00	80.00	500	2,000	4,000
1859-O	480,000	7.50	12.50	30.00	85.00	500	2,800	

With Motto on Obverse (1860–1873)

	Mintage	Good-4	Fine-12	EF-40	AU-55	MS-63	MS-65	Proof-65
1860 . . 1,000	608,000	$4.00	$6.00	$25.00	$80.00	$200	$1,400	$1,200
1860-O	40,000	400	900	2,500	4,500	—	—	
1861 . . 1,000	1,883,000	4.00	6.00	25.00	80.00	200	1,400	1,200
1861-S	172,500	25.00	40.00	200	400	5,000	14,000	
1862 . . 550	847,000	4.00	6.00	25.00	80.00	200	1,400	1,200
1862-S	180,750	25.00	45.00	135	900	2,500	9,500	
1863 . . 460	14,000	75.00	240	375	650	900	4,250	1,200
1863-S	157,500	25.00	75.00	185	900	2,500	9,000	
1864 . . 470	11,000	75.00	240	375	650	900	3,000	1,200
1864-S	230,000	25.00	75.00	185	900	2,000	8,000	
1865 . . 500	10,000	75.00	240	375	650	900	3,800	1,200
1865-S	175,000	22.50	65.00	160	800	2,500	7,800	
1866 . . 725	8,000	140	425	675	1,000	3,200	9,000	1,200
1866-S	135,000	20.00	70.00	175	600	2,100	5,000	
1867 . . 625	6,000	140	425	675	2,000	3,800	9,000	1,200
1867-S	140,000	15.00	65.00	150	600	1,500	4,000	
1868 . . 600	464,000	12.00	24.00	40.00	90.00	500	2,500	1,200
1868-S	260,000	12.00	70.00	150	250	1,200	3,500	
1869 . . 600	256,000	11.00	24.00	60.00	150	500	3,000	1,200
1869-S	450,000	9.00	42.50	95.00	210	610	3,800	
1870 . . 1,000	470,500	5.00	8.00	38.00	110	300	1,800	1,200
1870-S	50,000	150	220	450	1,200	3,000	7,000	

	Mintage	Good-4	Fine-12	EF-40	AU-55	MS-63	MS-65	Proof-65
1871 . . *960*	906,750	6.00	8.00	27.50	110	375	1,800	1,200
1871-CC	20,100	450	1,500	3,000	—	—	—	
1871-S	320,000	14.00	30.00	130	350	1,600	6,250	
1872 . . *950*	2,395,500	5.00	9.00	30.00	150	800	4,250	1,200
1872-CC	35,480	250	900	1,800	—	—	—	
1872-S	190,000	30.00	90.00	240	650	2,000	4,000	
1873 closed 3 . . *1,100* . .	1,506,900	4.00	6.00	45.00	90.00	300	1,400	1,200
1873 open 3	60,000	25.00	50.00	185	650	1,500	3,800	
1873-CC	(unique)	—	—	—	—	—	—	

With Arrows Beside the Date (1873–1874)

	Mintage	Good-4	Fine-12	EF-40	AU-55	MS-63	MS-65	Proof-65
1873 . . *800*	2,377,700	$6.00	$14.00	$110	$250	$1,000	$4,000	$5,000
1873-CC	18,791	500	1,450	3,000	9,000	—	—	
1873-S	455,000	20.00	75.00	150	350	1,300	5,000	
1874 . . *700*	2,940,000	6.00	14.00	110	250	1,000	4,000	5,000
1874-CC	10,817	850	1,400	2,450	11,000	—	—	
1874-S	240,000	20.00	95.00	250	450	1,500	6,850	

Arrows Removed (1875)

	Mintage	Good-4	Fine-12	EF-40	AU-55	MS-63	MS-65	Proof-65
1875 . . *700*	10,350,000	$4.00	$6.00	$15.00	$40.00	$175	$900	$1,200
1875-CC combined total . . .	4,645,000							
1875-CC with CC below wreath		5.00	8.00	30.00	60.00	175	975	
1875-CC with CC inside wreath		4.00	6.00	20.00	110	175	975	
1875-S combined total	9,070,000							
1875-S with S below wreath		4.00	6.00	15.00	40.00	175	900	
1875-S with S inside wreath		4.00	6.00	17.50	100	175	900	
1876 . . *1,150*	11,460,000	4.00	6.00	15.00	40.00	175	900	1,200
1876-CC	8,270,000	5.00	6.50	20.00	42.50	175	900	

DIMES (1796–PRESENT)

	Mintage	Good-4	Fine-12	EF-40	AU-55	MS-63	MS-65	Proof-65
1876-S	10,420,000	4.00	6.00	15.00	40.00	175	900	
1877 . . *510*	7,310,000	4.00	6.00	15.00	40.00	175	900	1,200
1877-CC	7,700,000	5.00	6.50	20.00	42.50	175	975	
1877-S	2,340,000	4.00	6.00	15.00	40.00	175	900	
1878 . . *800*	1,678,000	6.00	8.00	18.00	55.00	250	2,000	1,200
1878-CC	200,000	40.00	130	250	400	1,100	2,500	
1879 . . *1,100*	14,000	140	325	475	800	1,250	2,000	
1880 . . *1,355*	36,000	75.00	140	340	650	1,000	1,800	1,200
1881 . . *975*	24,000	90.00	275	425	800	1,100	2,000	1,200
1882 . . *1,100*	3,910,000	4.00	6.00	15.00	40.00	300	900	1,200
1883 . . *1,039*	7,674,673	4.00	6.00	15.00	40.00	300	900	1,200
1884 . . *875*	3,365,505	4.00	6.00	15.00	40.00	300	900	1,200
1884-S	564,969	12.50	25.00	70.00	110	475	1,800	
1885 . . *930*	2,532,497	4.00	6.00	15.00	40.00	300	900	1,200
1885-S	43,690	150	350	600	1,250	2,250	2,800	
1886 . . *886*	6,376,684	4.00	6.00	15.00	40.00	300	900	1,200
1886-S	206,524	15.00	45.00	92.50	110	550	1,600	
1887 . . *710*	11,283,229	4.00	6.00	15.00	40.00	300	900	1,200
1887-S	4,454,450	4.00	6.00	15.00	40.00	300	900	
1888 . . *832*	5,495,655	4.00	6.00	15.00	40.00	300	900	1,200
1888-S	1,720,000	4.00	6.00	15.00	40.00	300	900	
1889 . . *711*	7,380,000	4.00	6.00	15.00	40.00	300	900	1,200
1889-S	972,678	9.00	20.00	92.50	110	475	1,000	
1890 . . *590*	9,910,951	4.00	6.00	15.00	40.00	300	900	1,200
1890-S	1,423,076	7.50	15.00	50.00	100	475	1,250	
1891 . . *600*	15,310,000	4.00	6.00	15.00	40.00	300	900	1,200
1891-O	4,540,000	4.00	6.00	18.00	60.00	350	975	
1891-S	3,196,116	4.00	6.00	16.00	45.00	310	925	

Barber or Liberty Head Portrait (1892–1916)

	Mintage	Good-4	Fine-12	EF-40	AU-55	MS-63	MS-65	Proof-65
1892 . . *1,245*	12,120,000	$2.00	$6.00	$20.00	$50.00	$205	$650	$1,200
1892-O	3,841,700	4.00	10.00	25.00	65.00	300	1,500	

	Mintage	Good-4	Fine-12	EF-40	AU-55	MS-63	MS-65	Proof-65
1892-S	990,710	30.00	65.00	95.00	180	700	3,500	
1893 combined total	3,340,000							
1893 regular date . . 792		5.00	10.00	25.00	55.00	210	725	1,200
1893/2 overdate.	—	—	125	210	850	2,500		
1893-O	1,760,000	13.00	50.00	85.00	110	375	3,250	
1893-S	2,491,401	6.00	18.00	50.00	95.00	425	2,500	
1894 . . 972	1,330,000	6.00	45.00	85.00	110	395	900	1,200
1894-S (proof; not								
officially authorized) . . .	24	50,000	—	—	—	—	—	250,000
1895 . . 880	690,000	60.00	185	300	350	795	1,500	1,200
1895-O.	440,000	150	400	750	1,850	2,850	8,000	
1895-S	1,120,000	20.00	45.00	80.00	175	990	4,000	
1896 . . 762	2,000,000	5.00	15.00	45.00	95.00	250	1,500	1,200
1896-O.	610,000	50.00	150	300	475	900	4,000	
1896-S	575,056	50.00	80.00	200	425	990	4,000	
1897 . . 731	10,868,533	2.00	3.00	20.00	50.00	205	650	1,200
1897-O.	666,000	35.00	110	250	495	900	5,000	
1897-S	1,342,844	8.00	30.00	75.00	175	675	5,000	
1898 . . 735	16,320,000	2.00	4.00	20.00	50.00	205	650	1,200
1898-O.	2,130,000	4.00	45.00	110	150	750	2,000	
1898-S	1,702,507	4.00	14.00	35.00	90.00	550	3,500	
1899 . . 846	19,580,000	2.00	4.00	20.00	50.00	205	650	1,200
1899-O.	2,650,000	4.00	35.00	100	195	750	2,500	
1899-S	1,867,493	4.00	11.00	30.00	80.00	495	2,850	
1900 . . 912	17,600,000	2.00	4.00	20.00	50.00	205	650	1,200
1900-O.	2,010,000	5.00	50.00	135	240	850	2,500	
1900-S	5,168,270	3.00	7.00	25.00	65.00	325	1,500	
1901 . . 813	18,859,665	2.00	4.00	20.00	50.00	205	650	1,200
1901-O.	5,620,000	3.00	8.00	40.00	110	495	2,000	
1901-S	593,022	35.00	175	350	525	900	3,000	
1902 . . 777	21,380,000	2.00	4.00	20.00	50.00	205	650	1,200
1902-O.	4,500,000	3.00	8.00	40.00	95.00	550	1,950	
1902-S	2,070,000	4.00	22.00	70.00	125	550	1,950	
1903 . . 755	19,500,000	2.00	4.00	20.00	50.00	205	650	1,200
1903-O.	8,180,000	3.00	6.00	25.00	85.00	475	4,000	
1903-S	613,300	25.00	165	650	750	875	3,700	
1904 . . 670	14,600,357	2.00	4.00	20.00	50.00	205	650	1,200
1904-S	800,000	19.00	75.00	225	350	875	3,600	
1905 . . 727	14,551,623	2.00	4.00	20.00	50.00	205	600	1,200
1905-O.	3,400,000	3.00	12.00	35.00	95.00	390	3,800	
1905-S	6,855,199	3.00	7.00	25.00	70.00	365	1,000	
1906 . . 675	19,957,731	2.00	4.00	20.00	50.00	205	650	1,200

DIMES (1796–PRESENT)

	Mintage	Good-4	Fine-12	EF-40	AU-55	MS-63	MS-65	Proof-65
1906-D	4,060,000	3.00	6.00	25.00	70.00	325	1,000	
1906-O	2,610,000	3.00	25.00	40.00	110	325	900	
1906-S	3,136,640	2.00	10.00	30.00	85.00	325	975	
1907 . . 575	22,220,000	2.00	4.00	20.00	50.00	205	650	1,200
1907-D	4,080,000	2.00	7.00	30.00	80.00	225	2,000	
1907-O	5,058,000	2.00	13.00	25.00	70.00	375	1,300	
1907-S	3,178,470	3.00	9.00	40.00	95.00	425	2,900	
1908 . . 545	10,600,000	2.00	4.00	20.00	50.00	205	650	1,200
1908-D	7,490,000	2.00	6.00	25.00	55.00	205	700	
1908-O	1,789,000	3.00	27.00	55.00	110	495	1,000	
1908-S	3,220,000	2.00	8.00	27.50	85.00	495	1,250	
1908 . . 650	10,240,000	2.00	4.00	20.00	50.00	205	650	1,200
1909-D	954,000	3.00	25.00	80.00	140	550	2,000	
1909-O	2,287,000	2.00	8.00	27.50	85.00	325	1,000	
1909-S	1,000,000	3.00	39.00	125	250	475	2,500	
1910 . . 551	11,520,000	2.00	4.00	20.00	50.00	205	650	1,200
1910-D	3,490,000	2.00	8.00	30.00	80.00	300	1,000	
1910-S	1,240,000	2.00	25.00	52.50	135	300	1,000	
1911 . . 543	18,870,000	2.00	4.00	20.00	50.00	205	650	1,200
1911-D	11,209,000	2.00	4.00	20.00	50.00	205	650	
1911-S	3,520,000	2.00	8.00	25.00	80.00	325	700	
1912 . . 700	19,350,000	2.00	4.00	20.00	50.00	205	650	1,200
1912-D	11,760,000	2.00	5.00	20.00	50.00	205	650	
1912-S	3,420,000	2.00	6.00	25.00	70.00	280	1,000	
1913 . . 622	19,760,000	2.00	4.00	20.00	50.00	205	650	1,200
1913-S	510,000	8.00	50.00	155	275	375	1,000	
1914 . . 425	17,360,230	2.00	4.00	20.00	50.00	205	650	1,500
1914-D	11,908,000	2.00	4.00	20.00	50.00	205	650	
1914-S	2,100,000	3.00	6.00	25.00	60.00	225	1,000	
1915 . . 450	5,620,000	2.00	3.00	20.00	50.00	205	650	1,400
1915-S	960,000	2.00	8.00	40.00	110	400	1,000	
1916	18,490,000	2.00	3.00	20.00	55.00	205	650	
1916-S	5,820,000	2.00	3.00	20.00	55.00	205	650	

Winged Liberty Head or "Mercury" Portrait (1916–1945)

	Mintage	Good-4	Fine-12	EF-40	AU-55	MS-63	MS-65	Proof-65
1916.	22,180,080	$3.00	$3.75	$10.00	$25.00	$50.00	$100	
1916-D	264,000	300	1,000	3,000	3,500	4,000	10,000	
1916-S	10,450,000	3.00	6.00	20.00	25.00	80.00	200	
1917.	55,230,000	2.00	3.00	9.00	12.00	70.00	200	
1917-D	9,402,000	3.00	6.00	40.00	65.00	300	1,500	
1917-S	27,330,000	1.75	3.00	16.00	25.00	200	1,000	
1918.	26,680,000	1.75	4.00	25.00	35.00	190	500	
1918-D	22,674,800	1.85	3.00	25.00	36.00	275	1,200	
1918-S	19,300,000	1.85	3.00	15.00	30.00	200	1,000	
1919.	35,740,000	1.25	3.00	12.00	25.00	150	450	
1919-D	9,939,000	2.25	5.00	35.00	65.00	400	2,000	
1919-S	8,850,000	2.00	4.75	30.00	65.00	500	1,600	
1920.	59,030,000	1.50	2.75	8.00	15.00	90.00	300	
1920-D	19,171,000	2.00	3.50	13.00	35.00	400	1,200	
1920-S	13,820,000	2.00	3.50	12.00	38.00	325	1,200	
1921.	1,230,000	20.00	75.00	500	750	1,500	3,000	
1921-D	1,080,000	30.00	100	550	775	1,800	3,000	
1923.	50,130,000	2.00	3.00	5.00	20.00	75.00	100	
1923-S	6,440,000	2.20	4.00	45.00	75.00	300	1,200	
1924.	24,010,000	2.00	3.00	10.00	25.00	100	250	
1924-D	6,810,000	2.00	4.00	40.00	90.00	350	1,200	
1924-S	7,120,000	2.00	3.75	40.00	90.00	575	2,500	
1925.	25,610,000	2.00	2.75	8.00	20.00	90.00	300	
1925-D	5,117,000	3.00	9.00	90.00	200	600	1,600	
1925-S	5,850,000	2.00	3.50	40.00	100	450	2,000	
1926.	32,160,000	2.00	2.75	8.00	20.00	75.00	300	
1926-D	6,828,000	2.00	4.00	15.00	35.00	250	600	
1926-S	1,520,000	4.00	15.00	200	400	1,500	3,000	
1927.	28,080,000	2.00	3.00	6.00	12.00	75.00	200	
1927-D	4,812,000	2.00	4.00	40.00	80.00	450	1,000	
1927-S	4,770,000	2.00	3.00	20.00	35.00	350	900	
1928.	19,480,000	2.00	2.00	6.00	15.00	75.00	150	

DIMES (1796–PRESENT)

	Mintage	Good-4	Fine-12	EF-40	AU-55	MS-63	MS-65	Proof-65
1928-D	4,161,000	3.00	5.00	40.00	80.00	250	1,000	
1928-S	7,400,000	2.00	4.00	9.00	30.00	150	400	
1929	25,970,000	2.00	3.00	5.00	10.00	35.00	75.00	
1929-D	5,034,000	2.50	4.00	12.00	20.00	40.00	70.00	
1929-S	4,730,000	2.00	2.50	5.00	15.00	42.00	100	
1930	6,770,000	2.00	2.25	6.00	12.00	45.00	140	
1930-S	1,843,000	2.50	4.00	10.00	40.00	100	135	
1931	3,150,000	2.25	3.00	8.00	20.00	75.00	175	
1931-D	1,260,000	5.00	10.00	30.00	42.00	100	200	
1931-S	1,800,000	2.50	4.00	10.00	35.00	75.00	200	
1934	24,080,000	1.00	1.10	1.20	2.50	20.00	45.00	
1934-D	6,772,000	1.25	1.50	3.50	7.50	35.00	65.00	
1935	58,830,000	.50	.60	.90	1.35	20.00	28.00	
1935-D	10,477,000	.50	.60	.90	1.35	35.00	65.00	
1935-S	15,840,000	.50	.60	.90	1.35	30.00	60.00	
1936 . . 4,130 . . . . . :	87,500,000	.50	.60	.90	1.35	20.00	30.00	800
1936-D	16,132,000	.50	.60	.90	1.35	28.00	40.00	
1936-S	9,210,000	.50	.60	.90	1.35	20.00	30.00	
1937 . . 5,756	56,860,000	.50	.60	.90	1.35	18.00	25.00	225
1937-D	14,146,000	.50	.60	.90	1.35	25.00	45.00	
1937-S	9,740,000	.50	.60	.90	1.35	26.00	35.00	
1938 . . 8,728	22,190,000	.50	.60	.90	1.35	20.00	28.00	180
1938-D	5,537,000	.50	.60	.90	1.35	22.00	30.00	
1938-S	8,090,000	.50	.60	.90	1.35	22.00	35.00	
1939 . . 9,321	67,740,000	.50	.60	.90	1.35	20.00	25.00	200
1939-D	24,394,000	.50	.60	.90	1.35	19.00	25.00	
1939-S	10,540,000	.50	.60	.90	1.35	28.00	40.00	
1940 . . 11,827	65,350,000	.40	.50	.75	1.25	15.00	25.00	125
1940-D	21,198,000	.40	.50	.75	1.25	15.00	25.00	
1940-S	21,560,000	.40	.50	.75	1.25	16.00	25.00	
1941 . . 16,557	175,090,000	.40	.50	.75	1.25	12.00	25.00	120
1941-D	45,634,000	.40	.50	.75	1.25	13.00	30.00	
1941-S	43,090,000	.40	.50	.75	1.25	15.00	25.00	
1942 combined total	205,410,000							
1942 regular date . . 22,329		.40	.50	.75	1.25	12.00	25.00	120
1942/1 overdate		175	225	300	400	2,000	5,700	
1942-D combined total	60,740,000							
1942-D regular date		.40	.50	.75	1.25	15.00	25.00	
1942/1-D overdate		175	225	400	800	2,000	4,000	
1942-S	49,300,000	.40	.50	.75	1.25	16.00	25.00	
1943	191,710,000	.40	.50	.75	1.25	15.00	24.00	
1943-D	71,949,000	.40	.50	.75	1.25	16.00	35.00	

	Mintage	Good-4	Fine-12	EF-40	AU-55	MS-63	MS-65	Proof-65
1943-S	60,400,000	.40	.50	.75	1.25	15.00	25.00	
1944	231,410,000	.40	.50	.75	1.25	15.00	25.00	
1944-D	62,224,000	.40	.50	.75	1.25	15.00	25.00	
1944-S	49,490,000	.40	.50	.75	1.25	15.00	25.00	
1945	159,130,000	.40	.50	.75	1.25	12.00	28.00	
1945-D	40,245,000	.40	.50	.75	1.25	10.00	25.00	
1945 combined total	41,920,000							
1945-S with regular S		.40	.50	.75	1.25	12.00	25.00	
1945-S with microscopic S		.40	.50	.75	1.25	20.00	58.00	

Roosevelt Portrait (1946–Present)

Silver Composition (1946–1964)

	Mintage	Fine-12	EF-40	AU-55	MS-60	MS-63	MS-65	Proof-65
1946	255,250,000	$.50	$.70	$1.10	$1.25	$1.75	$3.50	
1946-D	61,043,500	.60	.80	1.25	1.45	2.25	4.25	
1946-S	27,900,000	.75	.95	1.50	1.75	4.00	12.75	
1947	121,520,000	.60	.80	1.25	1.45	2.25	4.25	
1947-D	46,835,000	.85	1.05	2.00	2.75	5.75	16.50	
1947-S	34,840,000	.75	.95	1.50	1.75	4.00	12.00	
1948	74,950,000	.75	1.05	2.00	2.75	9.00	15.00	
1948-D	52,841,000	.60	1.05	2.50	2.75	8.00	16.50	
1948-S	35,520,000	.50	.70	1.25	2.75	8.00	18.00	
1949	30,940,000	.65	1.40	2.00	6.00	10.00	19.00	
1949-D	26,034,000	.65	1.00	1.25	3.00	5.00	12.00	
1949-S	13,510,000	1.00	1.50	5.00	12.00	15.00	23.00	
1950 . . 51,386	50,130,114	.50	.65	2.00	3.00	3.75	10.00	20.00
1950-D	46,803,000	.50	.65	1.75	2.10	3.00	8.50	
1950-S	20,440,000	.65	1.40	2.00	6.00	10.00	19.00	
1951 . . 57,500	103,880,102	.50	.70	1.10	1.25	1.75	3.50	15.00
1951-D	56,529,000	.50	.70	1.10	1.25	1.75	3.50	
1951-S	31,630,000	.65	1.40	1.75	5.00	8.00	12.00	
1952 . . 81,980	99,040,093	.50	.70	1.10	1.25	1.75	3.50	16.00
1952-D	122,100,000	.50	.70	1.10	1.25	1.75	3.50	

	Mintage	Fine-12	EF-40	AU-55	MS-60	MS-63	MS-65	Proof-65
1952-S	44,419,500	.60	1.05	2.50	2.75	8.00	16.50	
1953 . . . *128,800*	53,490,120	.50	.70	1.10	1.25	1.75	3.50	15.00
1953-D	136,433,000	.50	.70	1.00	1.10	1.25	2.00	
1953-S	39,180,000	.50	.65	.90	1.00	1.20	1.75	
1954 . . . *233,300*	114,010,203	.50	.65	.90	1.00	1.40	1.90	12.00
1954-D	106,397,000	.50	.65	.90	1.00	1.30	1.85	
1954-S	22,860,000	.50	.65	.90	1.10	1.35	1.95	
1955 . . . *378,200*	12,450,181	.65	.75	1.50	1.75	2.25	4.75	9.00
1955-D	13,959,000	.50	.65	.90	1.00	1.50	2.10	
1955-S	18,510,000	.50	.70	1.10	1.25	1.75	2.75	
1956 . . *669,384*	108,640,000	.50	.65	.90	1.00	1.20	1.50	4.00
1956-D	108,015,100	.50	.65	.90	1.00	1.20	1.50	
1957 . . . *1,247,952.* . . .	160,160,000	.50	.70	1.00	1.10	1.35	1.60	3.00
1957-D	113,354,330	.50	.65	.90	1.00	1.50	2.00	
1958 . . . *875,652.* . . .	31,910,000	.50	.65	.90	1.10	1.35	1.90	3.50
1958-D	136,564,600	.50	.65	.90	1.00	1.50	2.00	
1959 . . . *1,149,291.* . . .	85,780,000	.50	.65	.90	1.10	1.35	1.90	2.25
1959-D	164,919,790	.50	.65	.90	1.00	1.50	2.00	
1960 . . . *1,691,602.* . . .	70,390,000	.50	.65	.90	1.00	1.20	1.50	2.00
1960-D	200,160,400	.45	.60	.80	.90	1.00	1.35	
1961 . . . *3,028,244.* . . .	93,730,000	.40	.50	.75	.85	.90	1.25	1.90
1961-D	209,146,550	.40	.50	.75	.85	.90	1.25	
1962 . . . *3,218,019.* . . .	72,450,000	.40	.50	.75	.85	.90	1.25	1.90
1962-D	334,948,380	.40	.50	.75	.85	.90	1.35	
1963 . . . *3,075,645.* . . .	123,650,000	.40	.50	.75	.85	.90	1.35	1.90
1963-D	421,476,530	.40	.50	.75	.85	.90	1.30	
1964 . . . *3,950,762.* . . .	929,360,000	.40	.50	.75	.85	.90	1.30	1.75
1964-D	1,357,517,180	.40	.50	.75	.85	.90	1.30	

Copper-Nickel Clad Composition (1965–Present)

	Mintage	EF-40	MS-65	Proof-65
1965	1,652,140,570	—	.25	
1966	1,382,734,540	—	.25	
1967	2,244,007,320	—	.25	
1968	424,470,400	—	.25	
1968-D	480,748,280	—	.25	
1968-S (proof only)	*3,041,506*	—	—	.50
1969	145,790,000	—	.25	
1969-D	563,323,870	—	.25	
1969-S (proof only)	*2,934,631*	—	—	.50
1970	345,570,000	—	.20	

DIMES (1796–PRESENT)

	Mintage	EF-40	MS-65	Proof-65
1970-D	754,942,100	—	.20	
1970-S combined total (proof only)	2,632,810			
1970-S proof with S		—	—	.50
1970-S proof with no mint mark		—	—	400
1971	162,690,000	—	.25	
1971-D	377,914,240	—	.25	
1971-S (proof only)	3,220,733	—	—	.50
1972	431,540,000	—	.25	
1972-D	330,290,000	—	.25	
1972-S (proof only)	3,260,996	—	—	.75
1973	315,670,000	—	.15	
1973-D	455,032,426	—	.15	
1973-S (proof only)	2,760,339	—	—	.75
1974	470,248,000	—	.15	
1974-D	571,083,000	—		
1974-S (proof only)	2,612,568	—	—	.75
1975	585,673,900	—	.15	
1975-D	313,705,300	—	.15	
1976	568,760,000	—	.15	
1976-D	695,222,774	—	.15	
1976-S (proof only)	4,149,730	—	—	.75
1977	796,930,000	—	.15	
1977-D	376,222,774	—	.15	
1977-S (proof only)	3,251,152	—	—	.75
1978	663,980,000	—	.15	
1978-D	282,847,540	—	.15	
1978-S (proof only)	3,127,781	—	—	.75
1979	315,440,000	—	.15	
1979-D	390,921,184	—	.15	
1979-S combined total (proof only)	3,677,175			
1979-S with clear S		—	—	1.00
1979-S with clogged S		—	—	.75
1980-P	735,170,000	—	.15	
1980-D	719,354,321	—	.15	
1980-S (proof only)	3,554,806	—	—	.65
1981-P	676,650,000	—	.15	
1981-D	712,284,143	—	.15	
1981-S (proof only)	4,063,083	—	—	.60
1982-P combined total	519,475,000			

DIMES (1796–PRESENT)

	Mintage	EF-40	MS-65	Proof-65
1982-P with P		—	.15	
1982-P with no mint mark		—	100	
1982-D	542,713,584	—	.15	
1982-S (proof only)	3,857,479	—	—	.60
1983-P	647,025,000	—	.15	
1983-D	730,129,224	—	.15	
1983-S combined total (proof only)	3,279,126			
1983-S proof with S		—	—	.60
1983-S proof with no mint mark		—	—	310
1984-P	856,669,000	—	.15	
1984-D	704,803,976	—	.15	
1984-S (proof only)	3,065,110	—	—	1.00
1985-P	705,200,962	—	.15	
1985-D	587,979,970	—	.15	
1985-S (proof only)	3,362,821	—	—	.90
1986-P	682,649,693	—	.15	
1986-D	473,326,970	—	.15	
1986-S (proof only)	3,010,497	—	—	1.00
1987-P	762,709,481	—	.15	
1987-D	653,203,402	—	.15	
1987-S (proof only)	3,792,233	—	—	1.00
1988-P	1,030,550,000	—	.15	
1988-D	962,385,489	—	.15	
1988-S (proof only)	3,262,948	—	—	1.00
1989-P	1,298,400,000	—	.15	
1989-D	896,535,597	—	.15	
1989-S (proof only)	3,215,728	—	—	1.00
1990-P	1,034,340,000	—	.15	
1990-D	839,995,824	—	.15	
1990-S (proof only)	3,299,559	—	—	1.00
1991-P	927,220,000	—	.15	
1991-D	601,241,114	—	.15	
1991-S (proof only)	2,867,787	—	—	1.00
1992-P	593,500,000	—	.15	
1992-D	616,273,932	—	.15	
1992-S (proof only) clad . . .	4,176,544*	—	—	1.00
1993-P	766,180,000	—	.15	
1993-D	750,110,166	—	.15	
1993-S (proof only) clad . . .	3,360,876*	—	—	1.00
1994-P	1,190,210,896	—	.15	

	Mintage	EF-40	MS-65	Proof-65
1994-D	1,304,479,006	—	.15	
1994-S (proof only) clad . . .	3,212,792*	—		1.00
1995-P	—	—	.15	
1995-D (proof only) clad. . .	—	—	.15	
1995-S	—	—	.15	1.00

* Includes 90% silver issue

TWENTY-CENT PIECES (1875–1878)

	Mintage	Good-4	Fine-12	EF-40	AU-55	MS-63	MS-65	Proof-65
1875 . . 2,790	36,910	$50.00	$65.00	$150	$400	$1,400	$6,800	$5,100
1875-CC	133,290	50.00	65.00	150	400	1,400	6,800	
1875-S	1,155,000	40.00	60.00	130	300	1,100	6,000	
1876 . . 1,260	14,640	90.00	110	120	260	600	4,000	5,250
1876-CC (fewer than 20 known)	10,000	—	—	40,000	—	—	—	
1877 (proof only)	350	1,100	1,600	2,000	2,500	—	—	6,000
1878 (proof only)	600	800	1,000	1,275	1,500	—	—	5,000

QUARTER DOLLARS (1796–PRESENT)

Draped Bust Portrait with Small Eagle on Reverse (1796)

	Mintage	Good-4	Fine-12	EF-40
1796	6,146	$3,400	$7,250	$15,000

Draped Bust Portrait with Heraldic Eagle on Reverse (1804–1807)

	Mintage	Good-4	Fine-12	EF-40
1804	6,738	$800	$2,200	$7,500
1805	121,394	180	375	2,100
1806 combined total	206,124			
1806 regular date		170	330	2,000
1806/5 overdate		180	375	2,200
1807	220,643	170	330	2,000

Capped Bust Portrait (1815–1838)

Large Size (1815–1828)

	Mintage	Good-4	Fine-12	EF-40	AU-55	MS-63
1815	89,235	$38.00	$100	$610	$1,750	$4,100
1818 combined total	361,174					
1818 regular date		35.00	90.00	560	1,500	3,800
1818/5 overdate		40.00	120	700	1,850	3,900
1819 combined total	144,000					
1819 small 9		35.00	90.00	560	1,500	3,750
1819 large 9		35.00	90.00	560	1,500	3,750
1820 combined total	127,444					
1820 small 0		35.00	95.00	600	1,500	3,750
1820 large 0		35.00	90.00	560	1,500	3,750
1821	216,851	35.00	90.00	560	1,500	3,750
1822 combined total	64,080					
1822 regular 25c		46.00	130	850	2,200	4,200
1822 25/50c		800	1,600	8,000	16,000	—
1823/2 overdate	17,800	5,600	13,750	28,000	—	—
1824/2 overdate	24,000	65.00	180	1,100	3,000	—
1825 combined total	144,000					
1825/2 overdate		75.00	210	1,100	3,000	—
1825/3 overdate		35.00	90.00	560	1,500	3,750
1825/4 overdate		35.00	90.00	560	1,500	3,750
1827 original (curl-base 2 in 25c)	4,000	(only a few proofs known)			—	55,000
1827 restrike (square-base 2 in 25c)		(only a few proofs known)			—	27,500
1828 combined total	125,000					
1828 regular 25c		35.00	90.00	560	1,500	3,750
1828 25/50c		75.00	300	1,300	3,500	—

Reduced Size (1831–1838)

	Mintage	Good-4	Fine-12	EF-40	AU-55	MS-63
1831 combined total	398,000					
1831 with small letters. . . .		$32.00	$46.00	$200	$550	$1,600
1831 with large letters		32.00	46.00	200	550	1,600
1832.	320,000	32.00	46.00	200	550	1,600
1833.	156,000	35.00	50.00	210	600	1,700
1834.	286,000	32.00	46.00	200	550	1,600
1835.	1,952,000	32.00	46.00	200	550	1,600
1836.	472,000	32.00	46.00	200	550	1,600
1837.	252,400	32.00	46.00	200	550	1,600
1838.	366,000	32.00	48.00	210	600	1,700

Seated Liberty Portrait (1838–1891)

	Mintage	Good-4	Fine-12	EF-40	AU-55	MS-63	MS-65
1838.	466,000	$10.00	$23.00	$300	$600	$2,000	$35,000
1839.	491,146	10.00	23.00	300	600	2,000	37,500
1840-O.	382,200	10.00	30.00	350	705	4,000	—

With Drapery Hanging from Elbow (1840–1891)

	Mintage	Good-4	Fine-12	EF-40	AU-55	MS-63	MS-65
1840.	188,127	$15.00	$40.00	$150	$300	$3,000	$9,750
1840-O.	43,000	15.00	50.00	160	475	3,300	—
1841.	120,000	35.00	75.00	140	300	1,600	—
1841-O.	452,000	15.00	35.00	135	310	1,800	7,500
1842 small date		(only a few proofs known)			—	—	—
1842 large date	88,000	55.00	100	350	400	1,800	—
1842-O combined total. . . .	769,000						
1842-O small date		210	605	1,500	3,000	10,500	—
1842-O large date		15.00	28.00	70.00	300	2,800	—
1843.	645,600	10.00	22.00	60.00	200	1,000	—
1843-O.	968,000	15.00	40.00	150	350	2,000	—
1844.	421,200	8.00	20.00	60.00	150	1,100	—
1844-O.	740,000	8.00	22.00	90.00	175	1,800	—
1845.	922,000	8.00	20.00	80.00	110	590	—
1846.	510,300	8.00	23.50	85.00	130	1,000	—
1847.	734,000	8.00	20.00	80.00	110	800	7,000
1847-O.	368,000	20.00	60.00	152.50	260	4,000	—
1848.	146,000	21.00	60.00	130	250	2,250	11,000

	Mintage	Good-4	Fine-12	EF-40	AU-55	MS-63	MS-65
1849	340,000	15.00	40.00	110	200	1,600	8,750
1849-O	16,000	325	640	1,950	3,375	—	—
1850	190,800	22.50	46.00	100	205	1,385	—
1850-O	412,000	18.00	45.00	95.00	215	2,000	—
1851	160,000	30.00	54.00	110	205	1,800	8,000
1851-O	88,000	110	350	1,150	1,850	—	—
1852	177,060	38.00	55.00	150	200	905	—
1852-O	96,000	135	300	865	1,750	6,200	—
1853 without arrows or rays	44,200	140	345	440	825	3,775	—

With Arrows Beside the Date, Rays Around the Eagle (1853)

	Mintage	Good-4	Fine-12	EF-40	AU-55	MS-63	MS-65	Proof-65
1853 combined total	15,210,020							
1853 regular date		$10.00	$25.00	$175	$400	$3,500	$20,000	—
1853/4 overdate		50.00	110	300	900	4,500	—	
1853-O	1,332,000	12.50	30.00	200	1,000	5,500	—	

With Arrows Beside the Date, No Rays Around the Eagle (1854–1855)

	Mintage	Good-4	Fine-12	EF-40	AU-55	MS-63	MS-65	Proof-65
1854	12,380,000	$10.00	$25.00	$80.00	$200	$1,500	$10,000	—
1854-O combined total	1,484,000							
1854-O regular date		10.00	20.00	80.00	200	1,900	—	
1854-O with huge O		110	180	400	1,000	4,500	—	
1855	2,857,000	10.00	25.00	80.00	200	1,800	10,000	—
1855-O	176,000	35.00	100	300	600	—	—	
1855-S	396,400	30.00	60.00	250	600	4,700	—	

Arrows Removed, Without Motto (1856)

	Mintage	Good-4	Fine-12	EF-40	AU-55	MS-63	MS-65	Proof-65
1856.	7,264,000	$10.00	$20.00	$65.00	$100	$900	$3,250	$11,000
1856-O.	968,000	10.00	20.00	65.00	200	1,200	4,250	
1856-S combined total	286,000							
1856-S regular date		30.00	80.00	300	600	3,000	—	
1856-S/S		40.00	100	400	775	—	—	
1857.	9,644,000	8.00	20.00	60.00	110	1,000	3,000	10,000
1857-O.	1,180,000	8.00	20.00	60.00	225	2,000	—	
1857-S.	82,000	35.00	125	485	750	6,000	—	
1858.	7,368,000	10.00	20.00	50.00	110	900	3,000	8,500
1858-O.	520,000	11.00	22.00	60.00	275	3,000	—	
1858-S.	121,000	35.00	125	290	625	4,000	—	
1859 . . 800	1,343,200	11.00	20.00	58.00	130	1,000	—	3,300
1859-O.	260,000	12.00	35.00	65.00	250	2,500	—	
1859-S.	80,000	68.00	125	390	675	4,500	—	
1860 . . 1,000	804,400	9.00	20.00	60.00	100	1,000	—	3,500
1860-O.	388,000	12.00	30.00	70.00	350	2,000	—	
1860-S.	56,000	110	250	1,200	3,000	10,000	—	
1861 . . 1,000	4,853,600	12.00	20.00	60.00	110	1,000	2,900	3,250
1861-S.	96,000	50.00	100	300	650	—	—	3,300
1862 . . 550	932,000	10.00	20.00	60.00	100	1,000	2,900	3,300
1862-S.	67,000	50.00	80.00	280	550	—	—	
1863 . . 460	191,600	35.00	40.00	100	225	1,000	7,500	3,100
1864 . . 470	93,600	55.00	80.00	150	250	1,175	8,000	3,100
1864-S.	20,000	135	250	900	1,500	—	—	
1865 . . 500	58,800	38.00	80.00	150	250	1,000	—	4,250
1865-S.	41,000	60.00	100	250	625	3,400	—	
1866.	(unique)	—	—	—	—	—	—	

QUARTER DOLLARS (1796–PRESENT)

With Motto Above the Eagle (1866–1891)

	Mintage	Good-4	Fine-12	EF-40	AU-55	MS-63	MS-65	Proof-65
1866 . . 725	16,800	$150	$450	$550	$775	$2,500	$5,800	$3,000
1866-S	28,000	140	325	560	925	2,800	—	
1867 . . 625	20,000	100	300	400	475	1,800	—	2,400
1867-S	48,000	90.00	350	450	775	—	—	
1868 . . 600	29,400	90.00	250	275	425	2,000	4,500	2,500
1868-S	96,000	49.00	240	425	875	3,500	—	
1869 . . 600	16,000	150	425	450	675	2,200	—	2,550
1869-S	76,000	80.00	300	425	950	3,600	12,000	
1870 . . 1,000	86,400	50.00	200	225	375	1,000	4,200	2,400
1870-CC	8,340	1,100	3,500	3,900	7,000	—	—	
1871 . . 960	118,200	30.00	100	125	350	700	5,200	2,300
1871-CC	10,890	740	2,500	3,700	5,100	—	—	
1871-S	30,900	200	450	600	775	3,500	—	
1872 . . 950	182,000	25.00	80.00	100	225	1,500	—	2,300
1872-CC	22,850	250	1,800	2,300	5,000	—	—	
1872-S	83,000	200	500	600	975	3,600	—	
1873 closed 3 . . 600	40,000	69.00	300	400	475	2,200	—	2,500
1873 open 3	172,000	26.00	100	110	200	900	4,750	
1873-CC	(4 known)	—	—	—	—	—	—	

With Arrows Beside the Date (1873–1874)

	Mintage	Good-4	Fine-12	EF-40	AU-55	MS-63	MS-65	Proof-65
1873 . . 540	1,271,160	$12.00	$50.00	$200	$475	$1,600	$5,500	$5,000
1873-CC	12,462	1,200	3,000	5,000	9,000	—	—	
1873-S	156,000	18.00	50.00	200	475	2,000	—	
1874 . . 700	471,200	12.00	75.00	200	450	1,800	4,000	5,000
1874-S	392,000	15.00	80.00	200	460	1,800	4,000	

QUARTER DOLLARS (1796–PRESENT)

Arrows Removed, with Motto (1875)

	Mintage	Good-4	Fine-12	EF-40	AU-55	MS-63	MS-65	Proof-65
1875 . . *700*	4,292,800	$9.00	$20.00	$50.00	$100	$600	$1,400	$2,000
1875-CC	140,000	50.00	200	300	500	2,000	—	
1875-S	680,000	35.00	150	200	400	1,800	2,800	
1876 . . *1,150*	17,816,000	10.00	36.00	50.00	100	600	1,400	2,000
1876-CC	4,944,000	9.00	38.00	50.00	100	800	2,900	
1876-S	8,596,000	8.00	36.00	50.00	100	600	2,200	
1877 . . *510*	10,911,200	8.00	36.00	50.00	100	600	1,400	2,000
1877-CC	4,192,000	9.00	38.00	50.00	100	775	1,400	
1877-S combined total	8,996,000							
1877-S with regular mint mark		9.00	36.00	50.00	100	600	1,400	
1877-S with S struck over								
horizontal S		35.00	140	225	300	1,500	—	
1878 . . *800*	2,260,000	9.00	30.00	50.00	100	675	3,000	2,000
1878-CC	996,000	18.00	80.00	100	135	775	3,500	
1878-S		60.00	190	300	450	2,000	—	
1879 . . *1,100*	13,600	110	175	300	465	600	1,600	2,000
1880 . . *1,355*	13,600	110	185	275	350	675	1,600	2,000
1881 . . *975*	12,000	115	200	285	360	775	1,600	2,000
1882 . . *1,100*	15,200	120	200	295	360	800	1,600	2,000
1883 . . *1,039*	14,400	110	200	295	380	700	—	2,000
1884 . . *875*	8,000	110	225	295	360	700	1,600	2,000
1885 . . *930*	13,600	110	200	325	390	1,000	3,000	2,000
1886 . . *886*	5,000	190	300	400	425	1,000	3,000	2,000
1887 . . *710*	10,000	140	225	300	325	800	2,000	2,000
1888 . . *832*	10,001	140	225	300	325	700	1,500	2,000
1888-S	1,216,000	10.00	30.00	50.00	100	600	3,000	
1889 . . *711*	12,000	100	225	300	350	750	1,500	2,000
1890 . . *590*	80,000	60.00	90.00	200	275	625	1,500	2,000
1891 . . *600*	3,920,000	10.00	40.00	50.00	150	575	1,500	2,000
1891-O	68,000	100	265	475	650	4,500	—	
1891-S	2,216,000	10.00	50.00	75.00	125	575	2,000	

Barber or Liberty Head Portrait (1892-1916)

	Mintage	Good-4	Fine-12	EF-40	AU-55	MS-63	MS-65	Proof-65
1892 . . 1,245	8,236,000	$3.00	$15.00	$55.00	$110	$395	$1,800	$1,800
1892-O	2,640,000	4.00	16.00	60.00	130	395	2,000	
1892-S	964,079	12.00	35.00	100	250	750	4,000	
1893 . . 792	5,444,023	3.00	15.00	55.00	110	395	1,900	1,800
1893-O	3,396,000	4.00	18.00	60.00	130	500	2,000	
1893-S	1,454,535	5.00	22.50	90.00	250	750	6,000	
1894 . . 972	3,432,000	3.00	15.00	55.00	110	450	2,100	1,800
1894-O	2,852,000	4.00	18.00	60.00	170	1,700	3,000	
1894-S	2,648,821	4.00	17.50	60.00	150	650	4,850	
1895 . . 880	4,440,000	4.00	15.00	55.00	125	525	1,400	1,800
1895-O	2,816,000	4.00	18.00	70.00	210	700	2,300	
1895-S	1,764,681	4.00	25.00	70.00	210	750	3,000	
1896 . . 762	3,874,000	3.00	15.00	55.00	110	450	2,300	1,800
1896-O	1,484,000	5.00	40.00	300	600	1,400	6,000	
1896-S	188,039	200	550	1,250	2,700	5,000	10,000	
1897 . . 731	8,140,000	3.00	15.00	55.00	110	395	1,200	1,800
1897-O	1,414,800	7.50	50.00	300	600	1,350	4,000	
1897-S	542,229	10.00	60.00	220	600	1,500	5,500	
1898 . . 735	11,100,000	3.00	15.00	55.00	110	395	1,800	1,800
1898-O	1,868,000	5.00	30.00	140	350	950	7,000	
1898-S	1,020,592	5.00	20.00	60.00	160	750	4,500	
1899 . . 846	12,624,000	3.00	15.00	55.00	110	395	1,800	1,800
1899-O	2,644,000	5.00	20.00	75.00	225	725	4,950	
1899-S	708,000	8.00	20.00	70.00	175	750	2,800	
1900 . . 912	10,016,000	3.00	15.00	55.00	110	395	1,800	1,800
1900-O	3,416,000	5.00	25.00	85.00	215	700	3,200	
1900-S	1,858,585	5.00	18.00	60.00	110	625	4,500	
1901 . . 813	8,892,000	3.00	15.00	55.00	110	395	1,800	1,800
1901-O	1,612,000	15.00	50.00	260	550	1,100	5,500	
1901-S	72,664	1,150	2,950	6,000	8,250	17,000	50,000	

QUARTER DOLLARS (1796–PRESENT)

	Mintage	Good-4	Fine-12	EF-40	AU-55	MS-63	MS-65	Proof-65
1902 . . 777	12,196,967	3.00	15.00	55.00	110	395	1,800	1,800
1902-O	4,748,000	5.00	20.00	90.00	175	795	5,000	
1902-S	1,524,612	8.00	20.00	75.00	175	750	3,500	
1903 . . 755	9,669,309	3.00	15.00	55.00	110	395	1,800	1,800
1903-O	3,500,000	5.00	20.00	75.00	175	750	5,200	
1903-S	1,036,000	8.00	25.00	85.00	225	700	2,750	
1904 . . 670	9,588,143	3.00	15.00	55.00	110	395	1,800	1,800
1904-O	2,456,000	5.00	25.00	150	325	1,100	2,950	
1905 . . 727	4,967,523	3.00	15.00	55.00	110	395	1,800	1,800
1905-O	1,230,000	5.00	23.00	110	250	700	5,250	
1905-S	1,884,000	7.50	15.00	75.00	175	725	3,500	
1906 . . 675	3,655,760	3.00	15.00	55.00	110	395	1,300	1,800
1906-D	3,280,000	3.00	17.50	60.00	140	550	3,250	
1906-O	2,056,000	3.00	20.00	70.00	170	550	1,750	
1907 . . 575	7,192,000	3.00	15.00	55.00	110	395	1,350	1,800
1907-D	2,484,000	4.00	17.50	60.00	160	750	3,250	
1907-O	4,560,000	4.00	17.50	55.00	130	650	2,200	
1907-S	1,360,000	4.00	20.00	90.00	195	750	3,950	
1908 . . 545	4,232,000	3.00	15.00	55.00	110	395	1,600	1,800
1908-D	5,788,000	3.00	15.00	60.00	110	425	2,000	
1908-O	6,244,000	4.00	15.00	60.00	110	395	1,500	
1908-S	784,000	8.00	40.00	210	375	750	5,250	
1909 . . 650	9,268,000	3.00	15.00	55.00	110	395	1,800	1,800
1909-D	5,114,000	4.00	15.00	60.00	150	450	1,950	
1909-O	712,000	10.00	32.50	150	325	1,100	7,500	
1909-S	1,348,000	4.00	17.50	65.00	165	650	2,100	
1910 . . 551	2,244,000	3.00	15.00	55.00	110	395	1,800	1,800
1910-D	1,500,000	4.00	17.50	70.00	170	800	2,350	
1911 . . 543	3,720,000	3.00	15.00	55.00	110	395	1,800	1,800
1911-D	933,600	4.00	65.00	275	395	875	4,500	
1911-S	988,000	4.00	15.00	80.00	185	475	1,500	
1912 . . 700	4,400,000	3.00	15.00	55.00	110	395	1,500	1,800
1912-S	708,000	3.00	19.00	75.00	195	700	2,175	
1913 . . 622	484,000	3.00	50.00	330	525	1,100	3,000	1,800
1913-D	1,450,800	3.00	17.50	60.00	150	475	1,300	
1913-S	40,000	275	1,350	2,950	3,750	5,500	8,000	
1914 . . 425	6,244,230	3.00	15.00	55.00	110	395	1,800	1,900
1914-D	3,046,000	3.00	15.00	55.00	110	395	1,800	
1914-S	264,000	45.00	110	325	535	1,150	2,800	
1915 . . 450	3,480,000	3.00	15.00	55.00	110	395	1,800	1,850
1915-D	3,694,000	3.00	15.00	55.00	110	395	1,800	
1915-S	704,000	5.00	17.50	70.00	175	395	1,850	

	Mintage	Good-4	Fine-12	EF-40	AU-55	MS-63	MS-65	Proof-65
1916	1,788,000	3.00	15.00	55.00	110	395	1,800	
1916-D	6,540,800	3.00	15.00	55.00	110	395	1,800	

Standing Liberty Portrait (1916–1930)

Liberty with Bare Breast (1916–1917)

	Mintage	Good-4	Fine-12	EF-40	AU-55	MS-63	MS-65
1916	52,000	$1,000	$1,600	$2,800	$4,000	$6,350	$15,000
1917 (Type I)	8,740,000	12.00	22.00	57.00	115	270	800
1917-D (Type I)	1,509,200	16.00	26.00	85.00	120	325	1,000
1917-S (Type I)	1,952,000	15.00	18.00	125	200	340	1,275

Liberty Wearing Coat of Mail (1917–1930)

	Mintage	Good-4	Fine-12	EF-40	AU-55	MS-63	MS-65
1917 (Type 2)	13,880,000	$12.00	$17.00	$40.00	$60.00	$200	$450
1917-D (Type 2)	6,224,400	20.00	45.00	85.00	100	300	1,200
1917-S (Type 2).	5,552,000	25.00	35.00	70.00	90.00	250	1,350
1918.	14,240,000	15.00	20.00	40.00	75.00	175	500
1918-D	7,380,000	30.00	40.00	80.00	140	280	1,500
1918-S combined total	11,072,000						
1918-S regular date		15.00	25.00	50.00	80.00	300	1,500
1918/17-S overdate		1,200	1,600	4,500	8,600	22,000	56,000
1919.	11,324,000	25.00	50.00	75.00	90.00	200	475
1919-D	1,944,000	60.00	90.00	300	325	900	2,500
1919-S	1,836,000	60.00	90.00	350	450	1,200	3,250
1920.	27,860,000	15.00	20.00	30.00	60.00	200	425
1920-D	3,586,400	35.00	50.00	90.00	150	500	2,000
1920-S	6,380,000	18.00	20.00	50.00	80.00	600	2,500
1921.	1,916,000	90.00	125	240	350	725	2,100
1923.	9,716,000	15.00	25.00	35.00	60.00	200	375
1923-S	1,360,000	100	150	325	425	690	1,850
1924.	10,920,000	15.00	20.00	35.00	65.00	175	475
1924-D	3,112,000	30.00	40.00	80.00	95.00	160	475
1924-S	2,860,000	16.00	20.00	75.00	185	725	2,000

Date Recessed (1925–1930)

1925.	12,280,000	$3.00	$5.00	$30.00	$50.00	$185	$450
1926.	11,316,00	3.00	5.00	30.00	50.00	185	450
1926-D	1,716,000	6.00	12.00	40.00	75.00	175	450
1926-S	2,700,000	4.00	10.00	100	200	600	2,000
1927.	11,912,000	3.00	5.00	30.00	50.00	185	450
1927-D	976,000	6.00	12.00	75.00	125	200	465

	Mintage	Good-4	Fine-12	EF-40	AU-55	MS-63	MS-65
1927-S	396,000	10.00	50.00	950	3,000	5,250	11,000
1928.	6,336,000	3.00	5.00	30.00	60.00	175	450
1928-D	1,627,600	5.00	7.00	35.00	75.00	185	450
1928-S	2,644,000	5.00	7.00	35.00	75.00	185	450
1929.	11,140,000	5.00	7.00	35.00	75.00	185	450
1929-D	1,358,000	5.00	7.00	35.00	75.00	185	450
1929-S	1,764,000	5.00	7.00	35.00	75.00	185	450
1930.	5,632,000	5.00	7.00	35.00	75.00	185	450
1930-S	1,556,000	5.00	7.00	35.00	75.00	185	450

Washington Portrait (1932–Present)

Silver Composition (1932–1964)

	Mintage	Good-4	Fine-12	EF-40	AU-55	MS-63	MS-65	Proof-65
1932.	5,404,080	$3.00	$4.00	$8.00	$15.00	$35.00	$175	
1932-D	436,800	40.00	45.00	140	250	750	4,600	
1932-S	408,000	30.00	37.50	50.00	125	500	2,000	
1934 combined total	31,912,052							
1934 regular date		—	2.00	3.50	8.00	25.00	80.00	
1934 doubled die		20.00	50.00	100	200	300	475	
1934-D	3,527,200	4.00	5.00	9.00	40.00	100	925	
1935.	32,484,000	—	1.75	3.00	9.00	25.00	50.00	
1935-D	5,780,000	2.00	3.00	10.00	50.00	85.00	200	
1935-S	5,660,000	2.00	3.00	5.75	20.00	50.00	100	
1936 . . *3,837*	41,300,000	—	1.50	3.00	7.50	25.00	75.00	950
1936-D	5,374,000	3.00	3.25	25.00	105	350	600	
1936-S	3,828,000	2.00	2.50	9.75	25.00	70.00	90.00	
1937 . . *5,542*	19,696,000	—	1.50	2.25	12.00	25.00	70.00	300

QUARTER DOLLARS (1796-PRESENT)

	Mintage	Good-4	Fine-12	EF-40	AU-55	MS-63	MS-65	Proof-65
1937-D	7,189,600	2.00	2.25	3.75	15.00	40.00	75.00	
1937-S	1,652,000	3.00	4.00	20.00	50.00	80.00	150	
1938 . . 8,045	9,472,000	2.00	2.25	12.00	30.00	50.00	90.00	150
1938-S	2,832,000	2.00	2.25	12.00	30.00	50.00	90.00	
1939 . . 8,795	33,540,000	—	1.25	3.00	6.00	18.00	50.00	100
1939-D	7,092,000	2.00	2.25	7.00	12.00	30.00	60.00	
1939-S	2,628,000	3.00	4.00	9.00	30.00	60.00	100	
1940 . . : 11,246	35,704,000	—	1.00	1.50	5.00	15.00	50.00	90.00
1940-D	2,797,600	3.00	4.00	9.00	30.00	60.00	100	
1940-S	8,244,000	1.50	1.75	2.00	9.00	20.00	35.00	
1941 . . 15,287	79,032,000	—	—	—	4.00	7.00	20.00	90.00
1941-D	16,714,800	—	—	—	6.00	15.00	35.00	
1941-S	16,080,000	—	—	—	6.00	17.00	75.00	
1942 . . 21,123	102,096,000	—	—	—	4.00	8.00	25.00	80.00
1942-D	17,487,200	—	—	—	5.00	12.00	26.00	
1942-S	19,384,000	—	—	—	14.00	75.00	100	
1943.	99,700,000	—	—	—	3.00	8.00	26.00	
1943-D	16,095,600	—	—	—	6.00	15.00	30.00	
1943-S combined total	21,700,000							
1943-S regular strike		—	—	—	12.00	28.00	35.00	
1944.	104,956,000	—	—	—	2.75	6.00	14.00	
1944-D	14,600,800	—	—	—	4.00	12.00	24.00	
1944-S	12,560,000	—	—	—	4.75	11.50	28.00	
1945.	74,372,000	—	—	—	2.00	5.00	15.00	
1945-D	12,341,600	—	—	—	4.00	8.00	20.00	
1945-S	17,004,001	—	—	—	3.00	5.00	20.00	

	Mintage	Fine-12	EF-40	AU-55	MS-63	MS-65	Proof-65
1946	53,436,000	—	—	$2.00	$5.00	$15.00	
1946-D	9,072,800	—	—	3.00	5.00	12.00	
1946-S	4,204,000	—	—	2.00	6.00	16.00	
1947	22,556,000	—	—	3.00	7.00	12.00	
1947-D	15,338,400	—	—	3.50	7.80	12.75	
1947-S	5,532,000	—	—	2.00	6.00	15.00	
1948.	35,196,000	—	—	2.00	6.00	10.00	
1948-D	16,766,800	—	—	2.00	6.00	12.00	
1948-S	15,960,000	—	—	3.00	8.00	16.00	
1949.	9,312,000	—	—	6.00	20.00	30.00	
1949-D	10,068,400	—	—	~4.00	9.00	20.00	
1950 . . 51,386	24,920,126	—	—	3.00	8.00	12.00	80.00

QUARTER DOLLARS (1796–PRESENT)

	Mintage	Fine-12	EF-40	AU-55	MS-63	MS-65	Proof-65
1950-D combined total. . . .	21,075,600						
1950-D with regular mint							
mark		—	—	2.50	6.00	9.00	
1950-D/S		30.00	140	200	300	500	
1950-S combined total	10,284,004						
1950-S with regular mint mark			—	3.00	7.50	12.50	
1950-S/D		30.00	150	300	475	600	
1951 . . 57,500	43,448,102	—	—	2.00	5.25	6.50	40.00
1951-D	35,354,800	—	—	2.00	5.25	6.00	
1951-S	9,048,000	—	—	2.50	12.50	16.00	
1952 . . 81,980	38,780,093	—	—	2.00	3.50	4.50	35.00
1952-D	49,795,200	—	—	2.00	3.75	4.75	
1952-S	13,707,800	—	—	4.00	9.00	11.00	
1953 . . 128,800	18,536,120	—	—	2.00	3.75	4.50	30.00
1953-D	56,112,400	—	—	1.50	2.50	4.00	
1953-S	14,016,000	—	—	2.25	4.50	6.00	
1954 . . 233,300	54,412,203	—	—	1.50	2.50	3.75	18.00
1954-D	42,305,500	—	—	1.50	2.50	3.75	
1954-S	11,834,722	—	—	1.50	2.50	3.75	
1955 . . 378,200	18,180,181	—	—	1.50	2.50	3.75	15.00
1955-D	3,182,400	—	—	2.00	2.75	7.00	
1956 . . 669,384	44,144,000	—	—	1.25	2.25	3.50	8.00
1956-D	32,334,500	—	—	1.50	2.25	3.50	
1957 . . 1,247,952.	46,532,000	—	—	1.25	2.25	4.00	6.50
1957-D	77,924,160	—	—	1.25	2.25	3.50	
1958 . . 875,652	6,360,000	—	—	1.75	3.00	5.00	6.00
1958-D	78,124,900	—	—	1.25	2.25	3.50	
1959 . . 1,149,291.	24,384,000	—	—	1.25	2.25	3.50	4.00
1959-D	62,054,232	—	—	1.25	2.25	3.50	
1960 . . 1,691,602.	29,164,000	—	—	1.25	2.50	3.75	3.90
1960-D	63,000,324	—	—	1.25	2.25	3.50	
1961 . . 3,028,244.	37,036,000	—	—	1.25	2.25	3.50	3.80
1961-D	88,656,928	—	—	1.25	2.25	3.50	
1962 . . 3,218,019.	36,156,000	—	—	1.25	2.25	3.50	3.80
1962-D	127,554,756	—	—	1.25	2.25	3.50	
1963 . . 3,075,645.	74,316,000	—	—	1.25	2.25	3.50	3.80
1963-D	135,288,184	—	—	1.25	2.25	3.50	
1964 . . 3,950,762.	560,390,585	—	—	1.25	2.25	3.50	3.80
1964-D	704,135,528	—	—	1.25	2.25	3.50	

Copper-Nickel Clad Composition (1965–Present)

	Mintage	EF-40	MS-65	Proof-65
1965	1,819,717,540	—	$.60	
1966	821,101,500	—	.60	
1967	1,524,031,848	—	.75	
1968	220,731,500	—	.60	
1968-D	101,534,000	—	.75	
1968-S (proof only)	3,041,506	—	—	$1.20
1969	176,212,000	—	.75	
1969-D	114,372,000	—	.75	
1969-S (proof only)	2,934,631	—	—	1.20
1970	136,420,000	—	.40	
1970-D	417,341,364	—	.35	
1970-S (proof only)	2,632,810	—	—	1.90
1971	109,284,000	—	.45	
1971-D	258,634,428	—	.35	
1971-S (proof only)	3,220,733	—	—	1.20
1972	215,048,000	—	.35	
1972-D	311,067,732	—	.35	
1972-S (proof only)	3,260,996	—	—	—
1973	346,924,000	—	.35	
1973-D	232,977,400	—	.35	
1973-S (proof only)	2,760,339	—	—	1.35
1974	801,456,000	—	.35	
1974-D	353,160,300	—	.35	
1974-S (proof only)	2,612,568	—	—	1.50

Bicentennial Portrait (1975–1976)

	Mintage	EF-40	MS-65	Proof-65
1776–1976 copper-nickel clad	809,784,016	—	$.40	
1776–1976-D copper-nickel clad	860,118,839	—	.40	
1776–1976-S copper-nickel clad (proof only; includes coins from both 1975 and 1976 proof sets)	6,968,506	—	—	1.60
1776–1976-S silver clad . . 3,998,621	4,908,319	—	1.50	2.25

Regular Design Returns (1977)

	Mintage	EF-40	MS-65	Proof-65
1977	468,556,000	—	.35	
1977-D	256,524,978	—	.35	
1977-S (proof only)	3,251,152	—	—	1.75
1978	521,452,000	—	.35	
1978-D	287,373,152	—	.35	
1978-S (proof only)	3,127,781	—	—	1.80
1979	515,708,000	—	.40	
1979-D	489,789,780	—	.40	
1979-S combined total (proof only)	3,677,175			
1979-S with clear S		—	—	14.50
1979-S with clogged S		—	—	1.65
1980-P	635,832,000	—	.40	
1980-D	518,327,487	—	.40	
1980-S (proof only)	3,554,806	—	—	1.80
1981-P	601,716,000	—	.40	
1981-D	575,722,833	—	.40	
1981-S (proof only)	4,063,083	—	—	1.60
1982-P	500,931,000	—	3.50	
1982-D	480,042,788	—	2.25	
1982-S (proof only)	3,857,479	—	—	1.65
1983-P	673,535,000	—	4.50	
1983-D	617,806,446	—	6.00	
1983-S (proof only)	3,279,126	—	—	1.75
1984-P	676,545,000	—	.60	
1984-D	546,483,064	—	1.25	
1984-S (proof only)	3,065,110	—	—	3.00
1985-P	775,818,962	—	.90	
1985-D	519,962,888	—	2.00	
1985-S (proof only)	3,362,821	—	—	1.80
1986-P	551,199,333	—	2.50	
1986-D	504,298,660	—	2.50	
1986-S (proof only)	3,010,497	—	—	5.50
1987-P	582,499,481	—	.40	
1987-D	655,594,696	—	.40	
1987-S (proof only)	3,792,233	—	—	1.65
1988-P	562,052,000	—	.40	
1988-D	596,810,688	—	.40	
1988-S (proof only)	3,262,948	—	—	3.00
1989-P	512,868,000	—	.40	
1989-D	896,535,597	—	.40	
1989-S (proof only)	3,215,728	—	—	2.40

	Mintage	EF-40	MS-65	Proof-65
1990-P	613,792,000	—	.40	
1990-D	927,638,181	—	.40	
1990-S (proof only)	*3,299,559*	—	—	4.00
1991-P	570,968,000	—	.40	
1991-D	630,966,693	—	.40	
1991-S (proof only)	*2,867,787*	—	—	3.00
1992-P	384,764,000	—	.40	
1992-D	389,777,107	—	.40	
1992-S (proof only) clad . . .	*4,176,544**	—	—	3.00
1993-P	639,276,000	—	.40	
1993-D	645,476,128	—	.40	
1993-S (proof only) clad . . .	*3,360,876**	—	—	3.00
1994-P	827,010,896	—	.40	
1994-D	881,245,006	—	.40	
1994-S (proof only) clad . . .	*3,212,792**	—	—	3.00
1995-P	—	—	.40	
1995-D	—	—	.40	
1995-S (proof only) clad . . .	—	—	—	3.00

* Includes 90% silver issue

HALF DOLLARS (1794–PRESENT)

Flowing Hair Portrait (1794–1795)

	Mintage	Good-4	Fine-12	EF-40
1794	23,464	$950	$2,750	$8,500
1795 combined total	299,680			
1795 with 2 leaves under each wing		375	750	3,300
1795 with 3 leaves under each wing		1,050	2,400	7,000

Draped Bust Portrait with Small Eagle on Reverse (1796–1797)

	Mintage	Good-4	Fine-12	EF-40
1796 combined total	934			
1796 with 15 stars		$9,250	$15,000	$39,000
1796 with 16 stars		10,500	17,000	41,000
1797	2,984	10,300	16,000	40,000

Draped Bust Portrait with Heraldic Eagle on Reverse (1801–1807)

	Mintage	Good-4	Fine-12	EF-40
1801	30,289	$180	$500	$2,000
1802	29,890	165	420	1,800
1803 combined total	188,234			
1803 with small 3		120	290	900
1803 with large 3		100	205	800
1805 combined total	211,722			

	Mintage	Good-4	Fine-12	EF-40
1805 with regular date		95	200	850
1805/4 overdate		175	425	1,600
1806 combined total	839,576			
1806/5 overdate		110	220	750
1806 with horizontal 0 in date. . . .		150	450	1,500
1806 with knob-top 6 and no stem through eagle's claw	(4 known)	16,000	30,000	58,500
1806, all others		95.00	185	550
1807	301,076	95.00	185	550

Capped Bust Portrait, Lettered Edge (1807–1836)

	Mintage	Good-4	Fine-12	EF-40	AU-55	MS-63
1807 combined total	750,500					
1807 with small stars		$60.00	$190	$750	$2,600	$7,000
1807 with large stars.		50.00	170	750	2,600	5,000
1807 with 50c. over 20c. . . .		36.00	105	550	2,100	5,500
1808 combined total	1,368,600					
1808 regular date		30.00	60.00	210	600	1,600
1808/7 overdate		34.00	80.00	285	900	3,250
1809	1,405,810	30.00	60.00	200	900	3,400
1810	1,276,276	28.00	45.00	175	550	2,000
1811 combined total	1,203,644					
1811 with small 8		27.00	46.00	150	375	1,900
1811 with large 8		27.00	46.00	175	425	2,000
1811/10 overdate		30.00	70.00	280	600	—
1812 combined total	1,628,059					
1812 regular date		26.00	44.00	150	450	1,900
1812/11 with small 8.		35.00	80.00	300	1,000	3,000
1812/11 with large 8.		1,500	3,000	7,500	—	—

	Mintage	Good-4	Fine-12	EF-40	AU-55	MS-63
1813 combined total	1,241,903					
1813 regular date		26.00	44.00	150	450	1,400
1813 with 50c. over UNI		30.00	70.00	250	1,100	—
1814 combined total	1,039,075					
1814 regular date		25.00	42.00	175	600	1,400
1814/3 overdate		42.00	70.00	340	850	—
1815/2 overdate	47,150	600	1,100	2,600	6,500	—
1817 combined total	1,215,567					
1817 regular date		25.00	42.00	150	450	1,400
1817/3 overdate		70.00	160	510	1,700	—
1817/4 overdate		25,000	50,000	—	—	—
1818 combined total	1,960,322					
1818 regular date		25.00	42.00	125	400	1,300
1818/7 overdate		28.00	44.00	180	550	—
1819 combined total	2,208,000					
1819 regular date		23.00	36.00	125	375	1,300
1819/8 overdate		28.00	55.00	140	450	1,300
1820	751,122	28.00	50.00	210	600	2,000
1821	1,305,797	25.00	42.00	125	375	1,300
1822 combined total	1,559,573					
1822 regular date		25.00	38.00	125	375	1,300
1822/1 overdate		45.00	70.00	275	900	2,850
1823 combined total	1,694,200					
1823 regular date		23.00	35.00	120	375	1,300
1823 with broken 3		40.00	70.00	300	800	2,500
1824 combined total	3,504,954					
1824 regular date		23.00	35.00	100	350	1,300
1824/1 overdate		26.00	42.00	160	450	1,800
1824/4 overdate		27.00	48.00	160	1,400	1,500
1825	2,943,166	23.00	30.00	85.00	300	1,200
1826	4,004,180	23.00	30.00	85.00	300	1,200
1827 combined total	5,493,400					
1827 with square-base 2		23.00	30.00	85.00	300	1,200
1827 with curl-base 2		26.00	38.00	115	325	1,300
1827/6 overdate		27.00	40.00	150	450	1,675
1828 combined total	3,075,200					
1828 with small 8's		23.00	30.00	75.00	300	1,200
1828 with large 8's		25.00	32.00	90.00	375	1,350
1828, all others		23.00	30.00	75.00	300	1,200
1829 combined total	3,712,156					
1829 regular date		23.00	30.00	75.00	300	1,200
1829/7 overdate		26.00	42.00	110	400	1,800

	Mintage	Good-4	Fine-12	EF-40	AU-55	MS-63
1830 combined total	4,764,800					
1830 with small 0		23.00	30.00	75.00	300	1,200
1830 with large 0		23.00	30.00	75.00	300	1,200
1831.	5,873,660	23.00	30.00	75.00	300	1,200
1832 combined total	4,797,000					
1832 with regular letters on reverse.		25.00	35.00	80.00	250	1,200
1832 with large letters		25.00	35.00	80.00	250	1,200
1833.	5,206,000	25.00	35.00	80.00	200	1,200
1834.	6,412,004	25.00	35.00	80.00	225	1,200
1835.	5,352,006	25.00	35.00	80.00	200	1,200
1836 combined total	6,545,000					
1836 with regular 50c.		25.00	35.00	80.00	200	1,200
1836 with 50c. over 00 c.. . .		30.00	50.00	150	625	2,175

Capped Bust Portrait, Reeded Edge (1836–1839)

"50 CENTS" on Reverse (1836–1837)

		Good-4	Fine-12	EF-40	AU-55	MS-63
1836.	1,200	$700	$975	$1,800	$3,800	$9,500
1837.	3,629,820	30.00	50.00	150	350	1,750

"HALF DOL." on Reverse (1838–1839)

		Good-4	Fine-12	EF-40	AU-55	MS-63
1838.	3,546,000	$35.00	$45.00	$200	$300	$1,700
1838-O (proof only)	20	—	—	—	—	—
1839.	1,392,976	35.00	45.00	200	300	1,700
1839-O.	178,976	125	225	575	—	5,500

Seated Liberty Portrait (1839–1891)

	Mintage	Good-4	Fine-12	EF-40	AU-55	MS-63	MS-65
1839 combined total	1,972,400						
1839 with no drapery hanging from elbow. . . .		$40.00	$100	$675	$1,200	$5,200	$92,500
1839 with drapery from elbow		25.00	45.00	100	250	1,500	—
1840 with small letters	1,435,008	30.00	45.00	100	300	1,000	—

	Mintage	Good-4	Fine-12	EF-40	AU-55	MS-63	MS-65
1840 with medium letters (struck at New Orleans without mint mark)		125	240	350	790	4,600	—
1840-O	855,100	25.00	45.00	125	250	1,400	—
1841	310,000	30.00	75.00	210	325	2,200	—
1841-O	401,000	20.00	35.00	110	200	1,175	—
1842 combined total	2,012,764						
1842 small date		25.00	75.00	120	190	1,100	—
1842 medium date		20.00	45.00	110	250	800	—
1842-O combined total	754,000						
1842-O small date		600	900	1,150	3,800	6,000	—
1842-O large date		25.00	35.00	110	240	—	—
1843	3,844,000	22.00	35.00	75.00	150	775	—
1843-O	2,268,000	22.00	35.00	80.00	175	1,150	—
1844	1,766,000	22.00	35.00	75.00	160	775	—
1844-O combined total	2,005,000						
1844-O regular date		22.00	32.00	75.00	140	—	—
1844-O with doubled date		—	800	2,400	4,000	—	—
1845	589,000	30.00	55.00	175	300	1,600	—
1845-O combined total	2,094,000						
1845-O with drapery		20.00	35.00	75.00	180	775	—
1845-O with no drapery . . .		30.00	65.00	175	350	—	—
1846 combined total	2,210,000						
1846 small date		20.00	35.00	85.00	150	1,400	—
1846 tall date		20.00	35.00	125	200	2,000	—
1846/horizontal 6 overdate		150	225	400	1,000	—	—
1846-O combined total	2,304,000						
1846-O medium date		25.00	35.00	100	300	—	—
1846-O tall date		150	300	750	1,500	—	—
1847 combined total	1,156,000						
1847 regular date		20.00	35.00	80.00	150	775	—
1847/6 overdate		1,200	3,000	4,500	9,000	—	—
1847-O	2,584,000	20.00	35.00	80.00	150	1,000	—
1848	580,000	30.00	65.00	200	450	1,600	—
1848-O	3,180,000	20.00	35.00	75.00	225	1,600	—
1849	1,252,000	25.00	50.00	150	300	1,200	—
1849-O	2,310,000	25.00	35.00	100	225	2,000	—
1850	227,000	175	300	550	800	—	—
1850-O	2,456,000	25.00	35.00	100	225	775	4,500
1851	200,750	190	300	450	525	2,100	—
1851-O	402,000	25.00	50.00	140	200	775	4,500
1852	77,130	250	400	625	700	1,600	—

HALF DOLLARS (1794–PRESENT)

	Mintage	Good-4	Fine-12	EF-40	AU-55	MS-63	MS-65	
1852-O	144,000	40.00	140	300	600	2,200	9,750	
1853-O without arrows or rays (3 known)	170,000	—	—	—	—	—	—	

With Arrows Beside the Date, Rays Around the Eagle (1853)

	Mintage	Good-4	Fine-12	EF-40	AU-55	MS-63	MS-65	Proof-65
1853	3,532,708	$20.00	$40.00	$200	$600	$2,500	$18,500	—
1853-O	1,328,000	25.00	50.00	250	650	5,000	—	

With Arrows Beside the Date, No Rays Around the Eagle (1854–1855)

	Mintage	Good-4	Fine-12	EF-40	AU-55	MS-63	MS-65	Proof-65
1854	2,982,000	$20.00	$40.00	$125	$250	$1,800	$7,500	—
1854-O	1,328,000	20.00	40.00	125	250	1,800	7,500	
1855 combined total	759,500							
1855 regular date		25.00	40.00	110	250	2,250	9,250	
1855/4 overdate		60.00	160	350	500			
1855-O	3,688,000	20.00	35.00	120	240	1,600	7,500	
1855-S	129,950	390	600	2,500	3,500	—	—	

Arrows Removed (1856)

	Mintage	Good-4	Fine-12	EF-40	AU-55	MS-63	MS-65	Proof-65
1856	938,000	$20.00	$35.00	$80.00	$150	$975	$6,800	—
1856-O	2,658,000	20.00	35.00	80.00	150	975	—	
1856-S	211,000	45.00	85.00	325	600	—	—	
1857	1,988,000	20.00	40.00	80.00	140	950	5,800	14,500
1857-O	818,000	20.00	40.00	75.00	160	1,650	—	
1857-S	158,000	45.00	110	350	450	—	—	
1858	4,226,000	20.00	40.00	80.00	150	1,200	6,000	12,500
1858-O	7,294,000	20.00	40.00	80.00	160	1,450	—	

HALF DOLLARS (1794–PRESENT)

	Mintage	Good-4	Fine-12	EF-40	AU-55	MS-63	MS-65	Proof-65
1858-S	476,000	20.00	45.00	200	350	1,650		
1859 . . 800	747,200	30.00	55.00	85.00	170	1,100	5,000	5,250
1859-O	2,834,000	20.00	40.00	80.00	150	1,100	5,000	
1859-S	566,000	20.00	50.00	150	275	1,400	—	
1860 . . 1,000	302,700	20.00	40.00	75.00	300	900	5,000	5,250
1860-O	1,290,000	18.00	35.00	80.00	150	1,025	5,000	
1860-S	472,000	20.00	40.00	85.00	165	2,000	—	
1861 . . 1,000	2,887,400	18.00	35.00	85.00	145	925	5,000	5,250
1861-O	2,532,633	18.00	35.00	85.00	145	925	5,000	
1861-S	939,500	19.00	40.00	90.00	165	1,000	8,250	
1862 . . 550	253,000	30.00	50.00	140	250	1,075	5,000	5,250
1862-S	1,352,000	18.00	35.00	80.00	150	1,000	—	
1863 . . 460	503,200	20.00	40.00	90.00	200	1,000	5,000	5,300
1863-S	916,000	18.00	35.00	80.00	150	1,000	—	
1864 . . 470	379,100	21.00	45.00	150	200	1,000	5,000	5,400
1864-S	658,000	20.00	30.00	80.00	150	1,175	—	
1865 . . 500	511,400	20.00	50.00	150	225	885	5,000	5,250
1865-S	675,000	15.00	35.00	80.00	175	1,175	—	
1866	(unique)	—	—	—	—	—	215,000	

With Motto Above the Eagle (1866–1891)

	Mintage	Good-4	Fine-12	EF-40	AU-55	MS-63	MS-65	Proof-65
1866 . . . 725	744,900	$20.00	$45.00	$100	$190	$1,000	$4,000	$4,000
1866-S	994,000	20.00	35.00	75.00	150	1,250	—	
1867 . . 625	449,300	20.00	55.00	140	250	950	4,000	4,200
1867-S	1,196,000	20.00	35.00	75.00	135	1,500	—	
1868 . . 600	417,600	35.00	70.00	175	225	1,100	—	3,900
1868-S	1,160,000	20.00	40.00	125	200	1,100	—	
1869 . . 600	795,300	25.00	42.00	130	175	1,050	3,600	3,500
1869-S	656,000	18.00	35.00	150	190	1,200	—	
1870 . . 1,000	633,900	20.00	35.00	140	175	950	—	3,200
1870-CC	54,617	475	1,175	4,000	6,250	—	—	
1870-S	1,004,000	18.00	40.00	90.00	225	1,200	—	
1871 . . 960	1,203,600	20.00	35.00	80.00	140	975	3,800	3,200
1871-CC	153,950	140	210	750	1,250	—	—	
1871-S	2,178,000	16.00	35.00	80.00	190	950	4,600	
1872 . . 950	880,600	16.00	35.00	80.00	190	950	4,000	3,100
1872-CC	257,000	50.00	135	340	900	—	—	
1872-S	580,000	30.00	60.00	165	375	1,200	—	
1873 closed 3 . . 600 . . .	587,000	25.00	65.00	125	200	950	4,000	3,100
1873 open 3	214,200	2,250	3,500	6,000	7,800	—	—	
1873-CC	122,500	110	225	650	1,900	—	—	

With Arrows Beside the Date (1873–1874)

	Mintage	Good-4	Fine-12	EF-40	AU-55	MS-63	MS-65	Proof-65
1873 . . _540_	1,815,150	$20.00	$35.00	$200	$475	$2,000	$21,000	$10,000
1873-CC	214,560	110	250	1,000	2,500	—	—	
1873-S	228,000	40.00	100	400	675	—		
1874 . . _700_	2,359,600	20.00	30.00	175	450	2,000	21,000	10,500
1874-CC	59,000	210	525	1,650	3,000	—	—	
1874-S	394,000	32.00	60.00	375	500	3,250	—	

Arrows Removed (1875), with Motto

	Mintage	Good-4	Fine-12	EF-40	AU-55	MS-63	MS-65	Proof-65
1875 . . _700_	6,026,800	$20.00	$35.00	$75.00	$150	$750	$3,500	$3,000
1875-CC	1,008,000	21.00	50.00	125	225	1,100	—	
1875-S	3,200,000	20.00	45.00	100	125	750	3,300	
1876 . . _1,150_	8,418,000	20.00	35.00	75.00	150	750	2,800	3,000
1876-CC	1,956,000	20.00	38.00	90.00	190	900	3,000	
1876-S	4,528,000	20.00	35.00	75.00	175	750	3,600	
1877 . . _510_	8,304,000	20.00	35.00	80.00	175	750	2,500	3,400
1877-CC	1,420,000	22.00	45.00	110	190	875	3,000	

	Mintage	Good-4	Fine-12	EF-40	AU-55	MS-63	MS-65	Proof-65
1877-S	5,356,000	20.00	35.00	.100	130	775	3,500	3,250
1878 . . 800	1,377,600	22.00	45.00	110	135	900	3,900	4,300
1878-CC	62,000	275	360	1,250	2,900	7,800	—	
1878-S	12,000	6,800	7,000	12,000	15,000	50,000	—	
1879 . . 1,100	4,800	200	300	400	480	900	2,500	3,000
1880 . . 1,355	8,400	200	250	300	380	900	3,000	3,000
1881 . . 975	10,000	190	240	300	380	900	3,000	3,000
1882 . . 1,100	4,400	200	340	375	410	900	3,000	3,000
1883 . . 1,039	8,000	190	300	350	400	900	3,000	3,000
1884 . . 875	4,400	210	360	425	485	900	3,000	3,000
1885 . . 930	5,200	200	240	325	410	900	3,000	3,000
1886 . . 886	5,000	210	310	360	490	900	3,000	3,000
1887 . . 710	5,000	225	400	500	575	900	3,000	3,000
1888 . . 832	12,001	190	250	300	400	900	3,000	3,000
1889 . . 711	12,000	190	250	325	360	900	3,000	3,000
1890 . . 590	12,000	200	225	335	400	900	3,000	3,000
1891 . . 600	200,000	60.00	100	135	245	900	3,000	3,000

Barber or Liberty Head Portrait (1892–1915)

	Mintage	Good-4	Fine-12	EF-40	AU-55	MS-63	MS-65	Proof-65
1892 . . 1,245	934,000	$12.50	$35.00	$170	$275	$895	$2,000	$2,800
1892-O	390,000	70.00	150	390	475	1,150	5,500	
1892-S	1,029,028	95.00	165	375	550	1,550	5,000	
1893 . . 792	1,826,000	10.00	35.00	150	300	850	3,250	2,800
1893-O	1,389,000	15.00	45.00	250	325	1,150	7,600	
1893-S	740,000	50.00	110	325	450	1,800	7,250	
1894 . . 972	1,148,000	10.00	45.00	170	295	925	3,750	2,800
1894-O	2,138,000	9.00	43.00	240	325	1,100	4,500	
1894-S	4,048,690	9.00	40.00	185	300	925	9,500	

HALF DOLLARS (1794–PRESENT)

	Mintage	Good-4	Fine-12	EF-40	AU-55	MS-63	MS-65	Proof-65
1895 . . 880	1,834,338	8.00	35.00	170	285	950	2,800	2,800
1895-O	1,766,000	8.00	40.00	210	325	1,100	5,000	
1895-S	1,108,086	15.00	50.00	235	325	950	6,800	
1896 . . 762	950,000	10.00	35.00	175	275	895	4,500	2,800
1896-O	924,000	15.00	70.00	325	600	2,100	9,500	
1896-S	1,140,948	50.00	90.00	340	525	1,950	8,500	
1897 . . 731	2,480,000	5.00	25.00	110	275	850	3,250	2,800
1897-O	632,000	40.00	225	725	950	2,100	4,000	
1897-S	933,900	70.00	225	600	900	2,050	7,500	
1898 . . 735	2,956,000	5.00	25.00	110	275	850	2,000	2,800
1898-O	874,000	15.00	55.00	285	425	1,900	5,500	
1898-S	2,358,550	10.00	30.00	190	325	1,450	7,500	
1899 . . 846	5,538,000	5.00	25.00	110	275	850	3,250	
1899-O	1,724,000	10.00	40.00	210	310	1,250	5,500	
1899-S	1,686,411	10.00	35.00	175	300	1,250	5,750	
1900 . . 912	4,762,000	5.00	25.00	110	275	850	3,250	2,800
1900-O	2,744,000	10.00	35.00	225	325	1,425	8,500	
1900-S	2,560,322	10.00	30.00	175	300	1,250	6,500	
1901 . . 813	4,268,000	5.00	25.00	110	275	850	3,250	2,800
1901-O	1,124,000	10.00	40.00	250	425	1,750	9,500	
1901-S	847,044	15.00	80.00	500	825	2,500	9,500	
1902 . . 777	4,922,000	5.00	25.00	110	275	850	3,250	2,800
1902-O	2,526,000	8.00	35.00	170	325	1,250	7,500	
1902-S	1,460,670	8.00	40.00	180	350	1,400	4,900	
1903 . . 755	2,278,000	8.00	28.00	135	275	1,050	4,500	2,800
1903-O	2,100,000	8.00	35.00	170	325	950	5,500	
1903-S	1,920,772	7.50	35.00	200	330	1,250	6,500	
1904 . . 670	2,992,000	5.00	25.00	110	275	850	3,250	2,800
1904-O	1,117,000	10.00	45.00	275	450	1,350	7,500	
1904-S	553,038	12.50	75.00	450	750	2,500	9,500	
1905 . . 727	662,000	10.00	40.00	175	350	1,150	4,950	2,800
1905-O	505,000	10.00	25.00	200	350	1,150	5,000	
1905-S	2,494,000	7.50	35.00	175	325	1,450	6,500	
1906 . . 675	2,638,000	5.00	25.00	110	275	850	3,250	2,800
1906-D	4,028,000	6.00	25.00	135	275	900	3,950	
1906-O	2,446,000	6.00	30.00	150	280	950	5,500	
1906-S	1,740,154	6.00	35.00	175	325	1,000	4,500	
1907 . . 575	2,598,000	5.00	25.00	110	275	850	2,000	2,800
1907-D	3,856,000	5.00	25.00	110	275	850	2,000	
1907-O	3,946,600	5.00	25.00	110	275	850	3,500	
1907-S	1,250,000	6.00	35.00	250	350	2,000	9,500	
1908 . . 545	1,354,000	5.00	25.00	110	275	850	3,750	2,800

	Mintage	Good-4	Fine-12	EF-40	AU-55	MS-63	MS-65	Proof-65
1908-D	3,280,000	5.00	25.00	110	275	850	2,000	
1908-O	5,360,000	5.00	25.00	110	275	850	2,000	
1908-S	1,644,828	6.00	35.00	175	300	1,300	5,750	
1909 . . 650	2,368,000	5.00	25.00	110	275	850	2,000	2,800
1909-O	925,400	10.00	35.00	250	425	1,600	5,500	
1909-S	1,764,000	6.00	25.00	165	300	1,000	3,950	
1910 . . 551	418,000	10.00	50.00	250	350	950	4,250	2,800
1910-S	1,948,000	6.00	26.00	160	290	1,200	4,000	
1911 . . 543	1,406,000	5.00	25.00	110	275	850	2,000	2,800
1911-D	695,080	6.00	30.00	150	300	850	2,000	
1911-S	1,272,000	6.00	30.00	150	300	1,000	5,500	
1912 . . 700	1,550,000	5.00	25.00	130	300	850	3,250	2,800
1912-D	2,300,800	6.00	25.00	120	275	850	2,500	
1912-S	1,370,000	6.00	27.50	150	290	1,000	4,500	
1913 . . 627	188,000	14.00	75.00	300	625	1,250	3,000	3,100
1913-D	534,800	6.00	35.00	170	300	900	4,000	
1913-S	604,000	6.00	35.00	170	350	1,100	4,200	
1914 . . 380	124,230	18.00	150	425	700	1,500	7,500	3,200
1914-S	992,000	6.00	30.00	170	350	1,100	3,500	
1915 . . 450	138,000	15.00	80.00	325	650	1,700	5,000	3,100
1915-D	1,170,400	5.00	25.00	110	275	850	2,000	
1915-S	1,604,000	-5.00	25.00	110	275	850	2,000	

Walking Liberty Portrait (1916–1947)

	Mintage	Good-4	Fine-12	EF-40	AU-55	MS-63	MS-65	Proof-65
1916	608,080	$23.00	$52.50	$105	$190	$300	$975	
1916-D	1,014,400	17.50	29.00	80.00	150	330	1,250	
1916-S	508,000	44.00	95.00	400	580	1,050	2,800	
1917	12,292,000	6.50	8.00	30.00	60.00	140	700	

	Mintage	Good-4	Fine-12	EF-40	AU-55	MS-63	MS-65	Proof-65
1917-D, with D on obverse	765,400	8.00	28.00	110	270	750	4,900	
1917-D, with D on reverse	1,940,000	6.00	17.50	115	350	1,400	7,300	
1917-S, with S on obverse	952,000	9.00	30.00	430	600	2,800	6,900	
1917-S, with S on reverse. . .	5,554,000	4.00	11.00	40.00	140	800	6,700	
1918.	6,634,000	4.00	15.00	100	420	650	2,700	
1918-D.	3,853,040	5.00	18.00	120	350	1,250	13,000	
1918-S.	10,282,000	4.00	12.50	50.00	140	1,050	10,000	
1919.	962,000	9.00	28.00	300	625	1,825	3,700	
1919-D.	1,165,000	7.00	29.00	370	1,100	4,000	40,000	
1919-S.	1,552,000	8.00	24.00	500	1,000	4,200	7,500	
1920.	6,372,000	5.00	11.00	50.00	115	475	4,300	
1920-D.	1,551,000	6.00	24.00	275	625	2,200	7,000	
1920-S.	4,624,000	7.00	15.00	140	400	1,250	6,000	
1921.	246,000	40.00	170	1,200	1,200	2,800	8,300	
1921-D.	208,000	60.00	200	1,700	1,700	3,500	8,500	
1921-S.	548,000	15.00	65.00	3,400	4,600	10,000	30,000	
1923-S.	2,178,000	6.00	17.50	170	625	2,050	8,800	
1927-S.	2,392,000	3.00	9.00	65.00	375	1,000	6,500	
1928-S.	1,940,000	4.00	10.50	85.00	325	1,400	4,000	
1929-D.	1,001,200	4.00	8.50	55.00	165	400	1,600	
1929-S.	1,902,000	3.00	8.50	50.00	135	400	1,800	
1933-S.	1,786,000	4.00	8.00	45.00	225	750	2,300	
1934.	6,964,000	2.25	2.75	10.00	26.00	165	300	
1934-D.	2,361,400	3.50	4.75	23.00	58.00	450	850	
1934-S.	3,652,000	2.75	3.50	22.50	125	450	1,600	
1935.	9,162,000	2.25	2.75	6.50	23.00	50.00	220	
1935-D.	3,003,800	3.50	3.75	23.00	55.00	225	850	
1935-S.	3,854,000	3.00	3.25	22.50	75.00	210	120	
1936 . . 3,901	12,614,000	2.25	3.50	6.50	24.00	50.00	125	1,900
1936-D. . . . ~.	4,252,400	2.75	5.00	15.00	46.00	90.00	230	
1936-S.	3,884,000	2.75	5.50	15.50	52.00	130	400	
1937 . . 5,728	9,522,000	2.25	3.75	6.75	22.50	45.00	125	650
1937-D.	1,676,000	4.75	7.00	29.00	72.50	150	380	
1937-S.	2,090,000	4.75	5.00	16.00	58.00	130	360	
1938 . . 8,152	4,110,000	2.75	5.50	12.00	33.00	70.00	155	460
1938-D.	491,600	16.50	17.00	35.00	90.00	375	700	
1939 . . 8,808	6,812,000	2.25	4.75	9.00	40.00	40.00	120	440
1939-D.	4,267,800	2.75	4.75	9.25	23.00	40.00	100	
1939-S.	2,552,000	5.50	4.00	7.00	25.00	95.00	170	
1940 . . 11,279	9,156,000	2.25	3.75	6.00	15.00	30.00	85.00	360
1940-S.	4,550,000	2.50	3.00	10.00	24.00	32.50	285	
1941 . . 15,412	24,192,000	2.25	3.75	5.50	15.00	30.00	80.00	360

	Mintage	Good-4	Fine-12	EF-40	AU-55	MS-63	MS-65	Proof-65
1941-D	11,248,400	2.50	3.75	5.75	25.00	35.00	75.00	
1941-S	8,098,000	2.75	5.00	8.00	43.00	85.00	700	
1942 . . . 21,120	47,818,000	2.25	2.75	6.00	15.00	35.00	80.00	325
1942-D combined total. . . .	10,973,800							
1942-D regular mint mark		2.50	4.10	7.50	20.00	50.00	125	
1942-D/S		25.00	45.00	325	800	1,600	3,000	
1942-S	12,708,000	2.50	4.10	6.75	25.00	40.00	275	
1943	53,190,000	2.25	2.75	6.25	15.00	35.00	85.00	
1943-D	11,346,000	2.50	4.10	6.25	24.00	45.00	120	
1943-S	13,450,000	2.50	4.45	6.50	25.00	40.00	230	
1944	28,206,000	2.25	2.75	6.00	15.00	30.00	85.00	
1944-D	9,769,000	2.50	4.10	6.25	20.00	35.00	85.00	
1944-S	8,904,000	2.50	4.10	6.25	24.00	35.00	400	
1945	31,502,000	2.25	2.75	6.00	15.00	35.00	85.00	
1945-D	9,966,800	2.75	4.00	6.25	22.50	35.00	95.00	
1945-S	10,156,000	2.75	4.10	6.25	24.00	35.00	145	
1946	12,118,000	2.25	2.75	6.25	18.00	35.00	100	
1946-D	2,151,000	2.75	6.25	12.50	29.00	35.00	85.00	
1946-S	3,724,000	2.75	3.00	6.25	23.00	35.00	85.00	
1947	4,094,000	2.75	3.20	7.50	24.00	35.00	90.00	
1947-D	3,900,600	2.75	3.20	7.50	23.00	35.00	90.00	

Franklin Portrait (1948-1963)

	Mintage	Fine-12	EF-40	AU-55	MS-60	MS-63	MS-65	Proof-65
1948	3,006,814	$3.00	$5.00	$4.00	$15.00	$18.00	$55.00	
1948-D	4,028,600	2.00	3.50	4.00	7.50	12.50	100	
1949	5,614,000	2.00	4.00	9.00	32.50	35.00	60.00	
1949-D	4,120,600	2.00	6.00	11.00	32.50	33.00	600	
1949-S	3,744,000	2.00	9.00	18.00	41.00	50.00	125	

HALF DOLLARS (1794–PRESENT)

	Mintage	Fine-12	EF-40	AU-55	MS-60	MS-63	MS-65	Proof-65
1950 . . 51,386	7,742,123	2.00	4.00	17.00	34.00	40.00	70.00	215
1950-D	8,031,600	2.00	4.00	12.50	21.00	24.00	320	
1951 . . 57,500	16,802,102	1.85	3.25	8.00	10.00	16.00	55.00	150
1951-D	9,475,200	1.85	5.25	15.00	31.00	35.00	110	
1951-S	13,696,000	1.85	4.00	8.00	20.00	30.00	45.00	
1952 . . 81,980	21,192,093	1.85	4.00	5.00	6.50	12.50	40.00	75.00
1952-D	25,395,600	1.85	3.50	5.00	6.50	12.50	95.00	
1952-S	5,526,000	1.85	3.25	12.50	28.00	36.00	35.00	
1953 . . 128,800	2,668,120	4.00	6.00	9.00	18.00	23.00	110	50.00
1953-D	20,900,400	1.85	4.00	5.00	6.25	12.50	110	
1953-S	4,148,000	1.85	3.25	8.00	12.00	16.00	50.00	
1954 . . 233,300	13,188,203	1.85	3.25	3.50	4.50	10.00	70	35.00
1954-D	25,445,580	1.85	3.25	3.50	4.50	10.00	110	
1954-S	4,993,400	1.85	3.25	3.50	5.00	11.00	32.00	
1955 . . 378,200	2,498,181	4.00	4.50	5.00	6.00	11.00	28.00	30.00
1956 . . 669,384	4,032,000	1.85	3.50	4.00	5.25	9.00	28.00	11.00
1957 . . 1,247,952	5,114,000	1.85	3.50	4.50	5.75	11.00	28.00	10.00
1957-D	19,966,850	1.65	1.70	1.80	4.50	10.00	28.00	
1958 . . 875,652	4,042,000	1.65	1.70	1.75	4.00	10.00	28.00	10.00
1958-D	23,962,412	1.65	1.70	1.75	3.00	8.00	28.00	
1959 . . 1,149,291	6,200,000	1.65	1.70	1.75	3.75	9.00	50.00	10.00
1959-D	13,053,750	1.65	1.70	1.75	3.75	7.50	50.00	
1960 . . 1,691,602	6,024,000	2.00	3.00	3.25	4.00	6.25	100	10.00
1960-D	18,215,812	2.00	3.00	3.25	4.00	6.00	530	
1961 . . 3,028,244	8,290,000	2.00	3.00	3.25	4.00	6.00	150	11.00
1961-D	20,276,442	2.00	3.00	3.25	4.00	6.00	370	
1962 . . 3,218,019	9,714,000	2.00	3.00	3.25	4.00	6.00	145	10.00
1962-D	35,473,281	2.00	3.00	3.25	4.00	5.00	280	
1963 . . 3,075,645	22,164,000	2.00	3.00	3.25	3.50	5.00	70.00	10.00
1963-D	67,069,292	2.00	3.00	3.25	3.50	5.00	70.00	

Kennedy Portrait (1964–Present)

Silver Composition (1964)

	Mintage	EF-40	MS-65	Proof-65
1964 . . *3,950,762.*	273,304,004	$1.75	$8.00	$7.00
1964-D.	156,205,446	1.75	8.00	

Silver Clad Composition (1965–1970)

1965.	65,879,366	$1.00	$5.00	
1966.	108,984,932	1.00	5.00	
1967.	295,046,978	1.00	7.00	
1968-D.	246,951,930	1.00	5.00	
1968-S (proof only)	*3,041,506*	—	—	3.00
1969-D.	129,881,800	1.00	4.00	
1969-S (proof only)	*2,934,631*	—	—	3.00
1970-D.	2,150,000	10.00	36.00	
1970-S (proof only)	*2,632,810*	—	—	3.00

Copper-Nickel Clad Composition (1971–Present)

1971.	155,164,000	—	$3.50	
1971-D.	302,097,424	—	2.00	
1971-S (proof only)	*3,220,733*	—	—	3.00
1972.	153,180,000	—	3.00	
1972-D.	141,890,000	—	3.00	
1972-S (proof only)	*3,260,996*	—	—	3.00
1973.	64,964,000	—	3.00	
1973-D.	83,171,400	—	3.00	
1973-S (proof only)	*2,760,339*	—	—	3.00
1974.	201,596,000	—	1.75	

HALF DOLLARS (1794–PRESENT)

	Mintage	EF-40	MS-65	Proof-65
1974-D	79,066,300	—	.75	
1974-S (proof only)	2,612,568	—	—	2.00

Bicentennial Portrait (1975–1976)

	Mintage	EF-40	MS-65	Proof-65
1776–1976 copper-nickel clad	234,308,000	—	$.75	
1776–1976-D copper-nickel clad	287,565,248	—	.75	
1776–1976-S copper-nickel clad (proof only; includes coins from both 1975 and 1976 proof sets)	6,995,180	—	—	2.00
1776–1976-S silver clad . . 3,998,621	4,908,319	—	2.50	3.50

Regular Design Returns (1977–Present)

	Mintage	EF-40	MS-65	Proof-65
1977	43,598,000	—	$.75	
1977-D	31,449,106	—	1.00	
1977-S (proof only)	3,251,152	—	—	2.00
1978	14,350,000	—	1.00	
1978-D	13,765,799	—	1.25	
1978-S (proof only)	3,127,781	—	—	2.25
1979	68,312,000	—	.75	
1979-D	15,815,422	—	1.00	
1979-S combined total (proof only)	3,677,175			
1979-S with clear S		—	—	18.00
1979-S with clogged S		—	—	2.00
1980-P	44,134,000	—	.75	
1980-D . . . . . . :	33,456,449	—	.75	
1980-S (proof only)	3,554,806	—	—	2.00
1981-P	29,544,000	—	.75	
1981-D	27,839,533	—	.75	
1981-S (proof only)	4,063,083	—	—	2.00
1982-P	10,819,000	—	.75	
1982-D	13,140,102	—	.75	
1982-S (proof only)	3,857,479	—	—	2.25
1983-P	34,139,000	—	.75	
1983-D	32,472,244	—	1.00	
1983-S (proof only)	3,279,126	—	—	2.50
1984-P	26,029,000	—	1.25	
1984-D	26,262,158	—	.75	

HALF DOLLARS (1794–PRESENT)

	Mintage	EF-40	MS-65	Proof-65
1984-S (proof only)	3,065,110	—	—	4.00
1985-P	18,706,962	—	1.25	
1985-D	19,814,034	—	1.25	
1985-S (proof only)	3,362,821	—	—	2.50
1986-P	13,107,633	—	.75	
1986-D	15,336,145	—	1.00	
1986-S (proof only)	3,010,497	—	—	6.50
1987-P	2,890,758	—	1.50	
1987-D	2,890,758	—	1.50	
1987-S (proof only)	3,792,233	—	—	2.50
1988-P	13,626,000	—	.75	
1988-D	12,000,096	—	.75	
1988-S (proof only)	3,262,948	—	—	3.75
1989-P	24,542,000	—	.75	
1989-D	23,000,216	—	.75	
1989-S (proof only)	3,215,728	—	—	3.25
1990-P	22,278,000	—	.75	
1990-D	20,096,242	—	.75	
1990-S (proof only)	3,299,559	—	—	5.25
1991-P	14,874,000	—	.75	
1991-D	15,054,678	—	.75	
1991-S (proof only)	2,867,787	—	—	4.00
1992-P	17,628,000	—	.75	
1992-D	17,000,106	—	.75	
1992-S (proof only) clad	4,176,544*	—	—	4.00
1993-P	15,510,000	—	.75	
1993-D	15,000,006	—	.75	
1993-S (proof only) clad	3,360,876*	—	—	4.00
1994-P	24,928,896	—	.75	
1994-D	25,039,006	—	.75	
1994-S (proof only) clad	3,212,792*	—	—	4.00
1995-P	—	—	.75	
1995-D	—	—	.75	
1995-S (proof only) clad	—	—	—	4.00

* Includes 90% silver issue

SILVER DOLLARS (1794–1935)

Flowing Hair Portrait (1794–1795)

	Mintage	Good-4	Fine-12	EF-40
1794	1,758	$8,500	$20,000	$50,000
1795 combined total . .	160,295			
1795 with 2 leaves				
under each wing . .		750	1,300	4,000
1795 with 3 leaves				
under each wing . .		750	1,300	4,000

Draped Bust Portrait with Small Eagle on Reverse (1795–1798)

	Mintage	Good-4	Fine-12	EF-40
1795	42,738	$600	$1,100	$3,750
1796 combined total . . .	72,920			
1796 with small date and small letters . . .		600	1,100	3,250
1796 with small date and large letters . . .		600	1,100	3,250
1796 with large date and small letters . . .		600	1,000	3,250
1797 combined total	7,776			
1797 with 9 stars left, 7 right and small letters		1,100	2,100	8,500
1797 with 9 stars left, 7 right and large letters		550	1,000	3,250
1797 with 10 stars left, 6 right		550	1,000	3,250
1798 combined total	327,536			
1798 with 13 stars . . .		950	1,750	4,250
1798 with 15 stars . . .		950	1,800	4,250

Draped Bust Portrait with Heraldic Eagle on Reverse (1798–1804)

	Mintage	Good-4	Fine-12	EF-40	Proof
1798 (mintage included above)		$350	$600	$1,850	
1799 combined total . .	423,515				
1799 regular date. . . .		325	500	1,400	
1799 with 8 stars left, 5 right		350	600	1,500	
1799/8 overdate		400	700	1,500	
1800	220,920	325	475	1,400	
1801	54,454	325	475	1,400	
1802 combined total	41,650				
1802 regular date. . . .		325	475	1,400	
1802/1 overdate		325	475	1,400	
1803 combined total . .	85,634				
1803 with small 3 . . .		350	500	1,650	
1803 with large 3. . . .		325	475	1,600	
1804 original. . . . . . (8 proofs)		—	—	—	1,250,000
1804 restrike . . . . . . (7 proofs)		—	—	—	300,000

(NOTE: All silver dollars dated 1804 were actually minted decades later, and all are extremely rare. The so-called "original" specimens were struck in the 1830s as presentation pieces intended as gifts for monarchs in the Far and Middle East. The restrikes were produced in 1859 to fill demand from collectors who wanted examples of this great rarity. All 15 known examples are accounted for, and all bring enormous premiums whenever they're offered for sale.

In 1989, one of the eight known original examples changed hands for $990,000 at a major auction. As this book goes to press, that remains the all-time highest price ever paid at auction for any U.S. coin.)

Gobrecht Dollars (1836–1839)

	Mintage	Fine-12	EF-40	AU-55	MS-65	Proof-65
1836 pattern . . . . (unknown)		—	—	—	—	$150,000
1836 circulation strike with						
416 grains of silver	1,000	3,000	4,250	9,000	35,000	45,000
1836 circulation strike with						
412½ grains of silver . . .	600	3,000	4,750	9,500	48,000	47,500
1838 pattern . . . . (unknown)		3,250	5,250	17,000	60,000	55,000
1839 circulation strike	300	3,500	5,000	12,000	45,000	47,500

Seated Liberty Portrait (1840–1873)

	Mintage	Good-4	Fine-12	EF-40	AU-55	MS-63	MS-65	Proof-65
1840.	61,005	$140	$200	$400	$850	$3,000	$65,000	—
1841.	173,000	110	190	350	750	3,000	20,000	—
1842.	184,618	100	180	350	750	3,000	20,000	—
1843.	165,100	100	180	350	750	3,500	20,000	—
1844.	20,000	175	250	550	1,000	4,500	25,000	—
1845.	24,500	175	250	500	900	8,500	45,000	—
1846.	110,600	100	175	350	750	3,500	20,000	—
1846-O.	59,000	175	250	600	900	5,500	25,000	—
1847.	140,750	100	190	400	750	3,500	20,000	—
1848.	15,000	250	500	800	1,250	3,750	25,000	—
1849.	62,600	125	225	350	750	3,500	20,000	—
1850.	7,500	300	600	900	1,350	7,500	35,000	—
1850-O.	40,000	250	350	1,200	2,250	11,500	25,000	—
1851 original	1,300	3,000	8,000	10,000	12,500	20,000	50,000	—
1851 restrike	(unknown)	—	—	—	—	—	—	—
1852 original	1,100	1,500	7,500	9,500	12,000	15,000	35,000	—
1852 restrike	(unknown)	—	—	—	—	—	—	—
1853.	46,118	135	300	600	850	3,500	20,000	—
1854.	33,140	650	1,250	2,750	4,000	7,500	35,000	—
1855.	26,000	600	1,250	2,750	3,500	11,000	25,000	—
1856.	63,500	180	340	765	1,150	3,750	20,000	—
1857.	94,000	190	350	600	1,100	3,500	20,000	—
1858 (proof only)	(about 80)	—	—	—	—	—	—	35,000
1859 . . 800	255,700	—	—	—	—	3,250	25,000	20,000
1859-O.	360,000	200	400	650	800	2,250	20,000	—
1859-S.	20,000	300	400	650	1,500	3,250	20,000	—
1860 . . 1,330	217,600	275	375	675	800	3,000	20,000	20,000

SILVER DOLLARS (1794–1935)

	Mintage	Good-4	Fine-12	EF-40	AU-55	MS-63	MS-65	Proof-65
1860-O	515,000	95.00	175	375	475	2,250	50,000	
1861 . . *1,000*	77,500	325	550	1,100	2,200	3,500	20,000	17,500
1862 . . *550*	11,540	350	550	1,100	2,000	2,500	20,000	20,000
1863 . . *460*	27,200	200	300	650	1,000	2,500	16,000	15,000
1864 . . *470*	30,700	180	250	600	1,100	2,500	8,000	12,500
1865 . . *500*	46,500	180	250	550	1,000	2,500	20,000	15,000
1866 with no motto above the eagle . . . . *(2 known)*		—	—	—	—	—	—	—

With Motto Above the Eagle (1866–1873)

	Mintage	Good-4	Fine-12	EF-40	AU-55	MS-63	MS-65	Proof-65
1866 . . *725*	48,900	$110	$250	$550	$600	$2,250	$27,500	$9,000
1867 . . *625*	46,900	110	260	600	700	2,500	27,500	9,000
1868 . . *600*	162,100	110	250	550	700	2,500	30,000	9,000
1869 . . *600*	423,700	100	225	500	600	2,250	27,500	9,000
1870 . . *1,000*	415,000	100	200	400	500	2,250	27,500	9,000
1870-CC	12,462	250	475	1,100	2,350	15,000	50,000	
1870-S . . . . *(about 10)*		—	—	85,000	90,000	—	—	
1871 . . *960*	1,073,800	100	175	375	500	2,250	27,500	9,000
1871-CC	1,376	2,000	3,300	8,500	15,000	25,000	65,000	
1872 . . *950*	1,105,500	100	175	375	500	2,250	27,500	9,000
1872-CC	3,150	650	1,400	3,800	6,000	20,000	45,000	
1872-S	9,000	180	410	900	1,500	12,500	35,000	
1873 . . *600*	293,000	110	225	400	500	2,250	27,500	11,500
1873-CC	2,300	2,250	4,750	12,500	17,500	50,000	100,000	
1873-S	700				(no examples known to exist)			

Morgan or Liberty Head Portrait (1878–1921)

(NOTE: Values shown for MS-65 examples apply only to coins which have been certified in that grade by the Professional Coin Grading Service or the Numismatic Guaranty Corporation of America.)

	Mintage	Fine-12	EF-40	AU-55	MS-63	MS-65	Proof-65
1878 with 8 tail feathers . . *500*	749,500	$11.00	$22.00	$30.00	$85.00	$900	$6,500
1878 with 7 tail feathers, combined total . . *250*	9,759,300						
1878 with 7 tail feathers, reverse of 1878		11.00	14.00	20.00	75.00	850	
1878 with 7 tail feathers, reverse of 1879		11.00	25.00	28.00	225	1,650	8,500
1878 with 7 tail feathers over 8		14.00	36.00	45.00	125	1,700	
1878-CC	2,212,000	30.00	38.00	48.00	150	1,500	
1878-S	9,774,000	14.00	15.00	18.00	40.00	250	
1879 . . *1,100*	14,806,000	10.00	13.00	16.00	50.00	1,500	4,500
1879-CC combined total . . .	756,000						
1879-CC with regular mint mark		30.00	185	550	2,750	12,500	
1879-CC with muddled mint mark		28.00	210	450	2,500	13,000	
1879-O	2,887,000	9.00	12.00	22.00	215	3,500	
1879-S combined total	9,110,000						
1879-S with reverse of 1878		18.00	23.00	38.00	350	4,250	
1879-S with reverse of 1879		9.00	14.00	16.00	35.00	115.00	

SILVER DOLLARS (1794–1935)

	Mintage	Fine-12	EF-40	AU-55	MS-63	MS-65	Proof-65
1880 . . *1,355*	12,600,000	9.00	12.00	16.00	45.00	1,100	3,500
1880-CC	591,000	50.00	90.00	130	180	575	
1880-O	5,305,000	9.00	14.00	22.00	400	15,000	
1880-S	8,900,000	9.00	13.00	16.00	30.00	115	
1881 . . *975*	9,163,000	9.00	12.00	16.00	45.00	1,250	3,500
1881-CC	296,000	85.00	120	140	200	400	
1881-O	5,708,000	9.00	12.00	16.00	45.00	1,500	
1881-S	12,760,000	9.00	12.00	16.00	30.00	115	
1882 . . *1,100*	11,100,000	9.00	12.00	17.00	35.00	590	3,500
1882-CC	1,133,000	30.00	45.00	55.00	85.00	225	
1882-O	6,090,000	9.00	12.00	15.00	38.00	1,100	
1882-S	9,250,000	10.00	17.00	18.00	30.00	115	
1883 . . *1,039*	12,290,000	9.00	12.00	14.00	32.00	175	3,500
1883-CC	1,204,000	30.00	45.00	55.00	80.00	200	
1883-O	8,725,000	9.00	12.00	14.00	30.00	115	
1883-S	6,250,000	15.00	22.00	100.00	1,300	22,500	
1884 . . *875*	14,070,000	9.00	12.00	17.00	38.00	275	3,500
1884-CC	1,136,000	45.00	55.00	70.00	75.00	210	
1884-O	9,730,000	9.00	12.00	14.00	30.00	115	
1884-S	3,200,000	15.00	30.00	225	17,000	125,000	
1885 . . *930*	17,786,837	9.00	12.00	16.00	30.00	130	3,500
1885-CC	228,000	175	195	210	235	475	
1885-O	9,185,000	9.00	12.00	14.00	30.00	115	
1885-S	1,497,000	15.00	22.00	45.00	225	1,650	
1886 . . *886*	19,963,000	9.00	12.00	14.00	29.00	115	3,500
1886-O	10,710,000	12.00	18.00	50.00	1,600	45,000	
1886-S	750,000	15.00	35.00	55.00	285	2,000	
1887 combined							
total . . *710*	20,290,000						
1887 with regular date		9.00	12.00	14.00	30.00	115	3,500
1887/6 overdate		15.00	28.00	43.00	2,100	4,000	3,500
1887-O combined total. . . .	11,550,000						
1887-O with regular date . . .		9.00	14.00	25.00	160	4,750	
1887/6-O overdate		15.00	25.00	43.00	2,750	10,000	
1887-S	1,771,000	15.00	20.00	32.00	210	3,500	
1888 . . *832*	19,183,000	9.00	12.00	15.00	30.00	200	3,500
1888-O	12,150,000	9.00	13.00	17.00	36.00	595	
1888-S	657,000	20.00	27.00	50.00	280	2,500	
1889 . . *811*	21,726,000	9.00	12.00	14.00	30.00	395	3,500
1889-CC	350,000	175	750	2,700	15,000	110,000	
1889-O	11,875,000	11.00	17.00	35.00	210	4,000	
1889-S	700,000	15.00	30.00	50.00	200	1,100	

SILVER DOLLARS (1794–1935)

	Mintage	Fine-12	EF-40	AU-55	MS-63	MS-65	Proof-65
1890 . . *590*	16,802,000	9.00	12.00	17.00	50.00	3,300	4,000
1890-CC	2,309,041	30.00	40.00	85.00	375	4,000	
1890-O	10,701,000	10.00	13.00	30.00	80.00	2,000	
1890-S	8,230,373	10.00	13.00	30.00	80.00	700	
1891 . . *650*	8,693,556	9.00	12.00	28.00	130	4,500	4,000
1891-CC	1,618,000	25.00	45.00	75.00	300	2,250	
1891-O	7,954,529	12.00	20.00	32.00	190	5,500	
1891-S	5,296,000	12.00	15.00	25.00	85.00	900	
1892 . . *1,245*	1,036,000	15.00	20.00	50.00	290	2,250	4,000
1892-CC	1,352,000	35.00	85.00	190	750	3,500	
1892-O	2,744,000	15.00	20.00	50.00	210	4,250	
1892-S	1,200,000	20.00	140	1,600	30,000	50,000	
1893 . . *792*	389,000	45.00	75.00	150	500	4,000	4,000
1893-CC	677,000	60.00	425	700	2,500	35,000	
1893-O	300,000	60.00	160	400	4,500	100,000	
1893-S	100,000	1,000	2,750	12,500	50,000	200,000	
1894 . . *972*	110,000	225	300	500	2,250	11,000	3,500
1894-O	1,723,000	20.00	30.00	140	2,500	25,000	
1894-S	1,260,000	30.00	85.00	180	650	4,000	
1895 . . *880*	12,000*	8,500	10,000	11,000	17,500	25,000	18,000
1895-O	450,000	65.00	180	800	20,000	150,000	
1895-S	400,000	100	400	650	2,250	15,000	
1896 . . *762*	9,976,000	9.00	12.00	14.00	35.00	200	4,000
1896-O	4,900,000	12.00	18.00	110.00	5,000	43,000	
1896-S	5,000,000	17.00	95.00	295	1,100	6,500	
1897 . . *731*	2,822,000	9.00	12.00	16.00	33.00	300	4,500
1897-O	4,004,000	12.00	16.00	65.00	3,250	25,000	
1897-S . . . . / . .	5,825,000	12.00	14.00	22.00	75.00	525	
1898 . . *735*	5,884,000	9.00	12.00	16.00	33.00	275	4,000
1898-O	4,440,000	13.00	14.00	25.00	33.00	125	
1898-S	4,102,000	14.00	24.00	55.00	285	1,250	
1899 . . *846*	330,846	35.00	45.00	70.00	115	1,000	4,300
1899-O	12,290,000	9.00	14.00	16.00	33.00	130	
1899-S	2,562,000	15.00	26.00	70.00	260	1,200	
1900 . . *912*	8,830,000	9.00	12.00	16.00	30.00	200	4,300
1900-O combined total. . . .	12,590,000						
1900-O with regular mint mark		9.00	12.00	16.00	30.00	120	
1900-O/CC		20.00	30.00	90.00	350	1,750	
1900-S	3,540,000	15.00	25.00	55.00	265	1,750	
1901 . . *813*	6,962,000	20.00	40.00	175	7,500	125,000	6,000
1901-O	13,320,000	9.00	12.00	16.00	33.00	200	

	Mintage	Fine-12	EF-40	AU-55	MS-63	MS-65	Proof-65
1901-S	2,284,000	20.00	45.00	100	390	3,500	
1902 . . *777*	7,994,000	10.00	14.00	28.00	65.00	650	4,000
1902-O.	8,636,000	10.00	12.00	17.00	32.00	135	
1902-S	1,530,000	30.00	65.00	90.00	310	2,000	
1903 . . *755*	4,652,000	12.00	17.00	22.00	50.00	250	3,750
1903-O.	4,450,000	125	140	165	180	325	
1903-S	1,241,000	25.00	165	675	3,000	5,500	
1904 . . *650*	2,788,000	9.00	17.00	35.00	170	3,250	3,750
1904-O.	3,720,000	10.00	12.00	15.00	30.00	110	
1904-S	2,304,000	30.00	115	425	1,450	5,000	
1921.	44,690,000	7.00	8.00	9.00	22.00	115	
1921-D	20,345,000	7.00	8.00	11.00	33.00	300	
1921-S	21,695,000	7.00	8.00	11.00	36.00	1,100	

* Only proofs are known to exist for 1895 silver dollars from the Philadelphia Mint.

Peace Portrait (1921–1935)

	Mintage	Fine-12	EF-40	AU-55	MS-63	MS-65	Proof-65
1921.	1,006,473	$30.00	$45.00	$80.00	$260	$1,500	—
1922.	51,737,000	7.00	8.00	9.00	20.00	150	—
1922-D	15,063,000	7.00	8.00	11.00	50.00	650	
1922-S	17,475,000	7.00	8.00	11.00	70.00	1,850	
1923.	30,800,000	7.00	8.00	9.00	20.00	145	
1923-D	6,811,000	7.00	9.00	13.00	80.00	1,900	
1923-S	19,020,000	7.00	9.00	13.00	80.00	5,000	

TRADE DOLLARS (1873–1885)

	Mintage	Fine-12	EF-40	AU-55	MS-63	MS-65	Proof-65
1924	11,811,000	7.00	10.00	14.00	28.00	175	
1924-S	1,728,000	12.00	20.00	55.00	400	5,500	
1925	10,198,000	7.00	10.00	14.00	25.00	150	
1925-S	1,610,000	11.00	17.00	30.00	170	6,750	
1926	1,939,000	8.00	14.00	20.00	43.00	500	
1926-D	2,348,700	10.00	15.00	30.00	125	950	
1926-S	6,980,000	9.00	13.00	20.00	80.00	1,450	
1927	848,000	17.00	25.00	35.00	130	5,000	
1927-D	1,268,900	17.00	22.00	75.00	375	5,250	
1927-S	866,000	15.00	20.00	60.00	185	5,900	
1928	360,649	95.00	125	155	300	2,400	
1928-S	1,632,000	15.00	19.00	50.00	375	10,000	
1934	954,057	18.00	22.00	35.00	150	1,500	
1934-D	1,569,500	16.00	19.00	38.00	190	1,750	
1934-S	1,011,000	20.00	150	450	2,500	5,500	
1935	1,576,000	15.00	19.00	25.00	90.00	1,000	
1935-S	1,964,000	15.00	18.00	65.00	275	1,100	

TRADE DOLLARS (1873–1885)

	Mintage	Fine-12	EF-40	AU-55	MS-63	MS-65	Proof-65
1873 . . *865*	396,635	$110.00	$225	$400	$1,300	$10,000	$7,500
1873-CC	124,500	175	450	750	3,500	20,000	
1873-S	703,000	110.00	250	425	1,750	10,000	
1874 . . *700*	987,100	110.00	225	400	1,300	10,000	7,500
1874-CC	1,373,200	120.00	225	450	1,750	20,000	
1874-S	2,549,000	90.00	185	350	2,250	10,250	

TRADE DOLLARS (1873–1885)

	Mintage	Fine-12	EF-40	AU-55	MS-63	MS-65	Proof-65
1875 . . *700*	218,200	275	550	850	2,000	12,500	7,000
1875-CC	1,573,700	85.00	225	400	2,000	16,000	
1875-S combined total	4,487,000						
1875-S with regular mint mark		75.00	140	325	1,300	8,000	
1875-S/CC		600	1,700	2,200	3,000	30,000	
1876 . . *1,150*	455,000	75.00	150	350	1,300	8,000	7,000
1876-CC	509,000	110.00	290	425	3,000	20,000	
1876-S	5,227,000	90.00	150	325	1,300	8,000	
1877 . . *510*	3,039,200	90.00	150	350	1,500	8,000	7,000
1877-CC	534,000	185	350	600	1,550	20,000	
1877-S	9,519,000	80.00	150	325	1,300	8,000	
1878 (proof only)	*900*	—	—	—	—	—	8,500
1878-CC	97,000	500	1,400	2,750	17,500	35,000	
1878-S	4,162,000	90.00	150	325	1,300	8,000	
1879 (proof only)	*1,541*	—	—	—	—	—	6,500
1880 (proof only)	*1,987*	—	—	—	—	—	6,500
1881 (proof only)	*960*	—	—	—	—	—	6,500
1882 (proof only)	*1,097*	—	—	—	—	—	6,500
1883 (proof only)	*979*	—	—	—	—	—	6,500
1884 (proof only)	*10*	—	—	—	—	—	75,000
1885 (proof only)	*5*	—	—	—	—	—	175,000

CLAD DOLLARS (1971–1981)

Eisenhower Portrait (1971–1978)

	Mintage	MS-65	Proof-65
1971 copper-nickel clad	47,799,000	$3.00	
1971-D copper-nickel clad	68,587,424	2.00	
1971-S silver clad . . *4,265,234*	6,868,530	3.50	$4.00
1972 copper-nickel clad	75,890,000	2.00	
1972-D copper-nickel clad	92,548,511	2.00	
1972-S silver clad . . *1,811,631*	2,193,056	4.00	4.00
1973 copper-nickel clad	2,000,056	4.00	
1973-D copper-nickel clad	2,000,000	3.00	
1973-S copper-nickel clad (proof only)	*2,760,339*	—	4.00
1973-S silver clad . . *1,013,646*	1,883,140	4.00	20.00
1974 copper-nickel clad	27,366,000	2.00	
1974-D copper-nickel clad	45,517,000	2.00	
1974-S copper-nickel clad (proof only)	*2,612,568*	—	5.00
1974-S silver clad . . *1,306,579*	1,900,156	6.00	7.00

Bicentennial Portrait (1975–1976)

	Mintage	MS-65	Proof-65
1776–1976 copper-nickel clad with thick lettering on reverse	4,019,000	4.50	
1776–1976 copper-nickel clad with thin lettering	113,318,000	2.00	
1776–1976-D copper-nickel clad with thick lettering	21,048,710	3.00	

	Mintage	MS-65	Proof-65
1776–1976-D copper-nickel clad with thin lettering	82,179,564	2.00	
1776–1976-S copper-nickel clad (proof only; includes coins from both 1975 and 1976 proof sets)	6,995,180	—	5.50
1776–1976-S silver clad . . 3,998,621	4,908,319	—	5.50

Regular Design Returns (1977–1978)

	Mintage	MS-65	Proof-65
1977 copper-nickel clad	12,596,000	2.00	
1977-D copper-nickel clad	32,983,006	2.00	
1977-S copper-nickel clad (proof only)	3,251,152	—	4.50
1978 copper-nickel clad	25,702,000	2.00	
1978-D copper-nickel clad	33,012,890	2.00	
1978-S copper-nickel clad (proof only)	3,127,781	—	4.50

Susan B. Anthony Portrait (1979–1981)

	Mintage	MS-65	Proof-65
1979-P	360,222,000	$2.00	
1979-D	288,015,744	2.00	
1979-S combined total . . 3,677,175	109,576,000		
1979-S with clear S		2.00	55.00
1979-S with clogged S		2.00	5.00
1980-P	27,610,000	2.00	
1980-D	41,628,708	2.00	
1980-S . . 3,554,806	20,422,000	2.00	5.00
1981-P	3,000,000	3.00	

	Mintage	MS-65	Proof-65
1981-D.	3,250,000	3.00	
1981-S combined total . . *4,063,083*	3,492,000		
1981-S with clear S		3.00	65.00
1981-S with clogged S		3.00	7.00

GOLD DOLLARS (1849–1889)

Liberty Head Portrait (1849–1854)

	Mintage	Fine-12	EF-40	AU-55	MS-65	Proof-65
1849 combined total	688,567					
1849 with open wreath . . .		$110	$150	$200	$5,500	
1849 with closed wreath . . .		110	150	200	5,000	
1849-C combined total. . . .	11,634					
1849-C with open wreath. . .	-	—	—	—	—	
1849-C with closed wreath		275	925	2,000	—	
1849-D	21,588	250	610	1,000	—	
1849-O	215,000	125	210	400	—	
1850	481,953	100	150	200	5,000	
1850-C	6,966	325	805	2,000	—	
1850-D	8,382	300	950	2,000	—	
1850-O	14,000	200	300	775	—	
1851	3,317,671	100	150	200	5,000	
1851-C	41,267	250	600	900	—	
1851-D	9,882	225	700	1,500	—	
1851-O	290,000	110	175	200	—	
1852	2,045,351	100	150	200	5,250	
1852-C	9,434	240	785	1,475	—	
1852-D	6,360	300	1,200	1,500	—	
1852-O	140,000	125	185	260	—	
1853	4,076,051	100	200	225	4,800	
1853-C	11,515	200	850	1,500	—	
1853-D	6,583	300	875	2,150	—	

	Mintage	Fine-12	EF-40	AU-55	MS-65	Proof-65
1853-O	290,000	140	175	195	5,600	
1854	855,502	110	175	185	4,800	—
1854-D	2,935	515	1,740	6,000	—	
1854-S	14,632	240	385	650	—	

Indian Head Portrait with Small Head (1854–1856)

	Mintage	Fine-12	EF-40	AU-55	MS-65	Proof-65
1854	783,943	$200	$500	$700	$24,800	—
1855	758,269	200	500	700	24,800	160,000
1855-C	9,803	600	2,000	4,000	—	
1855-D	1,811	1,600	4,000	8,000	—	
1855-O	55,000	300	710	1,500	—	
1856-S	24,600	400	910	2,240	—	

Indian Head Portrait with Large Head (1856–1889)

	Mintage	Fine-12	EF-40	AU-55	MS-65	Proof-65
1856 combined total	1,762,936					
1856 with upright 5		$125	$200	$300	$3,000	
1856 with slanted 5		100	110	160	2,875	—
1856-D	1,460	2,500	6,000	10,250	—	
1857	774,789	90.00	135	150	2,875	—
1857-C	13,280	290	950	2,750	—	
1857-D	3,533	275	1,600	3,000	—	
1857-S	10,000	250	775	1,685	—	
1858	117,995	105	140	160	3,000	22,500
1858-D	3,477	400	1,100	2,400	—	
1858-S	10,000	250	525	1,575	—	
1859 . . *80*	168,164	100	140	160	2,800	—
1859-C	5,235	250	1,175	2,150	—	
1859-D	4,952	400	1,310	2,450	—	
1859-S	15,000	240	500	1,700	—	
1860 . . *154*	36,514	100	140	170	5,000	8,775
1860-D	1,566	2,000	3,800	6,500	—	
1860-S	13,000	300	400	700	—	
1861 . . *349*	527,150	100	140	200	3,000	13,000
1861-D	(unknown)	4,000	9,000	12,500	—	
1862 . . *35*	1,361,355	100	140	160	2,900	14,500
1863 . . *50*	6,200	325	750	1,600	—	—
1864 . . *50*	5,900	250	400	600	6,000	22,500
1865 . . *25*	3,700	250	400	600	8,000	10,000
1866 . . *30*	7,100	275	400	675	4,200	9,750
1867 . . *50*	5,200	300	500	600	3,000	—
1868 . . *25*	10,500	250	400	500	3,000	—
1869 . . *25*	5,900	300	500	700	5,000	—
1870 . . *35*	6,300	250	400	500	5,000	—
1870-S	3,000	300	700	1,400	—	
1871 . . *30*	3,900	275	400	500	4,750	—
1872 . . *30*	3,500	250	400	500	4,775	16,500
1873 closed 3 . . *25*	1,800	300	700	1,000	—	—

GOLD DOLLARS (1849–1889)

	Mintage	Fine-12	EF-40	AU-55	MS-65	Proof-65
1873 open 3	123,300	100	150	200	—	
1874 . . 20	198,800	100	150	200	2,900	—
1875 . . 20	400	1,600	3,500	5,000	20,000	36,500
1876 . . 45	3,200	200	300	400	5,000	15,000
1877 . . 20	3,900	150	300	425	5,375	20,000
1878 . . 20	3,000	175	310	395	3,000	—
1879 . . 30	3,000	140	250	375	3,400	—
1880 . . 36	1,600	140	175	210	2,900	—
1881 . . 87	7,620	140	175	195	2,800	—
1882 . . 125	5,000	135	190	210	2,800	8,600
1883 . . 207	10,800	115	175	210	2,800	8,600
1884 . . 1,006	5,230	115	175	210	2,800	8,600
1885 . . 1,105	11,156	115	175	210	2,800	8,600
1886 . . 1,016	5,000	115	175	210	2,800	8,600
1887 . . 1,043	7,500	115	175	210	2,800	8,600
1888 . . 1,079	15,501	115	175	210	2,800	8,600
1889 . . 1,779	28,950	115	175	210	2,800	8,600

QUARTER EAGLES, OR $2.50 GOLD PIECES (1796–1929)

Capped Bust Portrait Facing Right (1796–1807)

	Mintage	Fine-12	EF-40	MS-60
1796 with no stars.	963	$9,500	$26,000	$78,000
1796 with stars	432	8,000	18,000	58,250
1797.	427	7,750	15,000	30,000
1798.	1,094	3,000	4,000	11,000
1802/1 overdate.	3,035	3,000	4,000	11,000
1804 combined total	3,327			
1804 with 13 stars.		13,000	28,000	—
1804 with 14 stars.		3,250	4,800	16,000
1805.	1,781	2,800	4,000	13,750
1806/4 overdate.	1,136	3,000	5,000	13,750
1806/5 overdate.	480	5,000	9,000	—
1807.	6,812	3,000	4,000	11,000

Capped Bust Portrait Facing Left (1808)

	Mintage	Fine-12	EF-40	MS-60
1808.	2,710	$8,000	$16,000	$31,500

Capped Head Portrait (1821–1834)

	Mintage	Fine-12	EF-40	AU-55	MS-60	MS-63
1821	6,448	$3,000	$4,800	$6,000	$12,000	$24,000
1824/1 overdate	2,600	3,200	4,000	5,000	10,000	20,000
1825	4,434	3,000	4,000	5,000	9,000	18,000
1826	760	3,000	5,000	7,000	20,000	30,000
1827	2,800	4,000	6,000	7,000	13,000	25,000

Size Reduced (1829–1834)

	Mintage	Fine-12	EF-40	AU-55	MS-60	MS-63
1829	3,403	3,000	4,000	4,850	7,250	12,500
1830	4,540	3,000	4,000	4,850	7,250	12,500
1831	4,520	3,000	4,000	4,850	7,250	12,500
1832	4,400	3,000	4,000	4,850	7,250	15,000
1833	4,160	3,000	4,000	4,850	7,750	—
1834 (E PLURIBUS UNUM on reverse)	4,000	6,000	15,000	22,000	28,000	—

Classic Head Portrait (1834–1839)

	Mintage	Fine-12	EF-40	AU-55	MS-60	MS-63
1834 (no motto on reverse)	112,234	$200	$425	$700	$2,000	$5,000
1835	131,402	200	425	700	2,800	6,000

QUARTER EAGLES, OR $2.50 GOLD PIECES

	Mintage	Fine-12	EF-40	AU-55	MS-60	MS-63
1836	547,986	200	425	700	2,000	5,000
1837	45,080	200	425	800	3,000	6,000
1838	47,030	200	425	800	2,900	5,000
1838-C	7,880	500	1,425	4,000	20,000	—
1839	27,021	200	600	2,000	6,000	12,850
1839-C	18,140	400	1,600	4,000	14,000	25,000
1839-D	13,674	475	2,600	5,000	18,000	—
1839-O	17,781	400	1,000	2,200	5,800	14,750

Coronet Portrait (1840–1907)

	Mintage	Fine-12	EF-40	AU-55	MS-60	MS-63	Proof-65
1840	18,859	$100	$500	$1,500	$4,000	$9,500	
1840-C	12,822	300	1,000	4,000	14,000	30,000	
1840-D	3,532	1,000	3,500	8,000	25,000	—	
1840-O	33,580	300	800	1,800	7,500	20,000	
1841 (proof only)	(very rare)	12,000	20,000	30,000	—	—	—
1841-C	10,281	300	1,000	3,000	16,000	32,000	
1841-D	4,164	1,400	3,000	6,000	16,000	35,000	
1842	2,823	600	2,500	5,500	14,000	32,000	
1842-C	6,729	1,100	2,500	4,500	15,000	32,750	
1842-D	4,643	1,000	3,000	7,500	15,500	42,500	
1842-O	19,800	275	1,200	2,800	11,000	28,500	
1843	100,546	120	225	275	725	2,600	
1843-C small date	2,988	2,500	5,000	11,000	22,000	40,000	
1843-C large date	23,076	500	900	2,650	7,000	24,000	
1843-D	36,209	600	1,000	2,000	7,000	24,350	
1843-O small date	288,002	225	300	400	1,200	4,000	
1843-O large date	76,000	200	325	900	2,500	—	
1844	6,784	375	900	2,500	7,600	20,000	
1844-C	11,622	600	1,300	3,500	14,000	40,000	
1844-D	17,332	600	1,200	2,000	6,000	20,000	

QUARTER EAGLES, OR $2.50 GOLD PIECES

	Mintage	Fine-12	EF-40	AU-55	MS-60	MS-63	Proof-65
1845	91,051	300	400	500	900	5,000	
1845-D	19,460	600	900	2,000	8,000	22,500	
1845-O	4,000	1,000	3,000	5,000	14,000	42,000	
1846	21,598	375	785	2,250	6,150	22,500	
1846-C	4,808	1,000	1,600	4,000	15,000	42,500	
1846-D	19,303	750	1,100	2,800	7,250	22,500	
1846-O	62,000	300	450	1,400	4,600	16,000	
1847	29,814	200	400	900	4,000	9,000	
1847-C	23,226	500	900	2,000	7,000	20,000	
1847-D	15,784	500	1,000	2,000	7,000	21,500	
1847-O	124,000	250	400	1,000	3,000	8,000	
1848	7,497	300	800	3,000	7,500	20,000	
1848 with CAL. above eagle	1,389	6,850	14,000	15,000	30,000	62,500	
1848-C	16,788	500	1,200	4,000	8,250	30,000	
1848-D	13,771	500	1,200	4,000	8,250	30,000	
1849	23,294	300	600	1,500	3,600	7,000	
1849-C	10,220	500	1,300	4,250	16,000	42,500	
1849-D	10,945	750	1,200	2,750	14,000	35,000	
1850	252,923	100	200	300	800	4,000	
1850-C	9,148	500	1,500	3,000	14,000	38,500	
1850-D	12,148	600	1,000	3,000	15,000	34,000	
1850-O	84,000	200	575	1,500	4,000	14,250	
1851	1,372,748	200	300	400	500	1,200	
1851-C	14,923	500	1,450	3,850	12,750	32,500	
1851-D	11,264	625	1,200	3,600	12,500	30,000	
1851-O	148,000	200	300	900	4,000	8,000	
1852	1,159,681	200	275	375	410	1,000	
1852-C	9,772	550	1,400	4,600	15,500	38,500	
1852-D	4,078	850	2,600	5,000	18,000	40,000	
1852-O	140,000	200	300	700	5,000	11,000	
1853	1,404,668	200	400	450	600	1,050	
1853-D	3,178	1,500	2,500	5,000	17,500	35,000	
1854	596,258	100	200	250	450	1,000	
1854-C	7,295	600	2,000	4,000	15,000	32,500	
1854-D	1,760	2,500	4,500	8,500	20,000	42,500	
1854-O	153,000	100	300	600	1,500	5,850	
1854-S	246	13,500	32,500	60,000	—	—	
1855	235,480	200	225	250	425	1,600	
1855-C	3,677	1,200	2,600	4,000	18,000	42,500	
1855-D	1,123	4,000	6,500	10,500	24,000	46,000	
1856	384,240	100	200	300	400	1,275	$74,850
1856-C	7,913	800	1,600	4,600	14,000	30,000	

QUARTER EAGLES, OR $2.50 GOLD PIECES

	Mintage	Fine-12	EF-40	AU-55	MS-60	MS-63	Proof-65
1856-D	874	6,000	12,000	22,000	37,000	85,000	
1856-O	21,100	225	775	1,800	6,250	24,000	
1856-S	72,120	100	400	900	6,000	22,000	
1857	214,130	200	300	340	350	1,500	—
1857-D	2,364	800	1,700	3,400	12,000	30,000	
1857-O	34,000	150	325	1,500	6,000	14,000	
1857-S	69,200	200	400	1,500	6,000	15,000	
1858	47,377	150	300	400	1,400	4,250	18,500
1858-C	9,056	600	1,300	2,500	12,000	30,000	
1859 . . 80	39,364	200	300	900	1,500	4,000	18,500
1859-D	2,244	1,200	2,200	6,000	22,000	41,850	
1859-S	15,200	200	1,500	2,500	6,000	14,000	
1860 . . 112	22,563	200	300	500	1,200	3,300	18,500
1860-C	7,469	775	1,600	6,250	20,000	32,500	
1860-S	35,600	250	700	1,500	4,600	9,000	
1861 . . 90	1,283,788	200	300	375	410	1,050	18,500
1861-S	24,000	300	1,800	3,000	6,000	15,000	
1862 combined total	98,543						
1862 regular date . . 35		200	300	500	1,500	3,000	18,500
1862/1 overdate		675	2,000	5,600	13,750	32,000	
1862-S	8,000	800	3,000	6,000	15,000	34,000	
1863 (proof only)	30	—	—	—	—	—	—
1863-S	10,800	400	1,500	3,000	6,000	13,000	
1864 . . 50	2,824	5,000	10,000	25,000	40,000	—	18,500
1865 . . 25	1,520	3,000	9,000	15,000	32,500	—	28,000
1865-S	23,376	225	740	1,200	3,800	9,000	
1866 . . 30	3,080	1,200	2,200	6,900	16,000	40,000	24,000
1866-S	38,960	300	900	2,500	8,000	20,000	
1867 . . 50	3,200	300	900	1,400	5,000	11,000	18,500
1867-S	28,000	300	900	1,900	5,000	10,000	
1868 . . 25	3,600	300	600	900	3,000	7,000	18,500
1868-S	34,000	200	600	1,500	4,000	9,000	
1869 . . 25	4,320	225	450	900	5,000	9,500	18,500
1869-S	29,500	200	600	925	4,000	10,000	
1870 . . 35	4,520	250	500	900	4,000	9,000	18,500
1870-S	16,000	225	400	1,000	5,000	12,000	
1871 . . 30	5,320	250	475	925	2,600	6,000	18,500
1871-S	22,000	200	400	900	3,000	6,000	
1872 . . 30	3,000	350	750	1,800	4,000	12,000	18,500
1872-S	18,000	200	500	1,200	4,000	11,000	
1873 closed 3 . . 25	55,200	300	375	600	1,100	3,000	18,500
1873 open 3	122,800	200	300	325	375	1,050	

QUARTER EAGLES, OR $2.50 GOLD PIECES

	Mintage	Fine-12	EF-40	AU-55	MS-60	MS-63	Proof-65
1873-S	27,000	200	500	1,000	3,500	8,000	
1874 . . 20	3,920	300	500	1,000	3,500	8,000	18,500
1875 . . 20	400	3,000	6,000	9,000	15,000	—	42,500
1875-S	11,600	100	300	800	4,000	8,000	
1876 . . 45	4,176	150	700	1,500	5,000	11,000	18,500
1876-S	5,000	200	600	1,100	5,000	11,000	
1877 . . 20	1,632	400	800	1,400	4,000	7,000	—
1877-S	35,400	200	300	375	1,000	3,000	
1878 . . 20	286,240	200	300	375	425	1,075	18,500
1878-S	178,000	200	275	300	500	1,650	
1879 . . 30	88,960	200	300	375	425	1,075	18,500
1879-S	43,500	150	300	500	1,200	3,500	
1880 . . 36	2,960	200	325	750	1,400	3,000	22,000
1881 . . 51	640	1,400	3,000	6,000	14,000	30,000	22,000
1882 . . 67	4,000	200	300	400	1,100	3,100	13,750
1883 . . 82	1,920	150	400	700	2,000	4,000	17,500
1884 . . 73	1,950	150	400	700	1,600	3,000	18,500
1885 . . 87	800	600	1,500	2,600	6,000	15,000	—
1886 . . 88	4,000	200	300	400	1,200	3,000	17,000
1887 . . 122	6,160	200	300	400	1,200	3,000	—
1888 . . 97	16,001	200	300	400	500	1,400	—
1889 . . 48	17,600	205	240	260	280	1,275	—
1890 . . 93	8,720	140	190	240	410	1,410	17,750
1891 . . 80	10,960	200	250	260	410	1,475	14,850
1892 . . 105	2,440	130	200	300	800	2,575	14,700
1893 . . 106	30,000	200	225	240	260	1,100	13,000
1894 . . 122	4,000	225	250	275	800	2,400	12,000
1895 . . 119	6,000	140	160	190	400	1,300	12,000
1896 . . 132	19,070	120	150	180	250	1,000	11,750
1897 . . 136	29,768	120	150	180	250	1,000	11,750
1898 . . 165	24,000	120	150	180	250	1,000	11,750
1899 . . 150	27,200	120	150	180	250	1,000	11,750
1900 . . 205	67,000	120	150	180	250	1,000	11,750
1901 . . 223	91,100	120	150	180	250	1,000	11,750
1902 . . 193	133,540	120	150	180	250	1,000	11,750
1903 . . 197	201,060	120	150	180	250	1,000	11,750
1904 . . 170	160,790	120	150	180	250	1,000	11,750
1905 . . 144	217,800	120	150	180	250	1,000	11,750
1906 . . 160	176,330	120	150	180	250	1,000	11,750
1907 . . 154	336,294	120	150	180	250	1,000	11,750

Indian Head Portrait (1908–1929)

	Mintage	AU-55	MS-60	MS-63	MS-65	Proof-65
1908 . . *236*	564,821	$150	$250	$1,000	$6,000	$16,500
1909 . . *139*	441,760	150	250	1,100	4,000	17,250
1910 . . *682*	492,000	150	300	1,200	8,000	15,000
1911 . . *191*	704,000	150	275	1,100	9,000	15,500
1911-D	55,680	900	3,000	6,000	32,500	—
1912 . . *197*	616,000	200	300	1,100	12,000	15,500
1913 . . *165*	722,000	200	300	1,100	11,000	15,000
1914 . . *117*	240,000	200	300	3,000	16,000	15,500
1914-D	448,000	200	300	1,300	18,000	
1915 . . *100*	606,000	200	300	1,000	7,000	16,750
1925-D	578,000	200	300	1,000	4,000	
1926	446,000	200	300	1,000	4,000	
1927	388,000	200	300	1,000	4,000	
1928	416,000	200	300	1,000	4,000	
1929	532,000	200	300	1,000	9,000	

$3 GOLD PIECES (1854–1889)

	Mintage	Fine-12	EF-40	AU-55	MS-60	MS-63	Proof-65
1854	138,618	$400	$600	$1,000	$2,000	$4,800	$33,000
1854-D	1,120	5,000	11,000	25,000	40,000	—	

QUARTER EAGLES, OR $2.50 GOLD PIECES

	Mintage	Fine-12	EF-40	AU-55	MS-60	MS-63	Proof-65
1854-O	24,000	380	800	2,000	4,000	—	
1855	50,555	400	750	1,000	2,000	5,350	—
1855-S	6,600	850	2,000	5,000	12,000	—	
1856	26,010	550	750	1,000	2,000	—	—
1856-S	34,500	500	900	2,000	7,500	—	
1857	20,891	500	875	1,000	3,500	8,000	33,000
1857-S	14,250	750	1,200	4,000	9,600	—	
1858	2,133	750	1,000	2,500	4,500	—	33,000
1859 . . 80	15,558	500	775	1,000	2,500	5,000	33,000
1860 . . . 119	7,036	600	775	1,000	2,500	5,000	33,000
1860-S	4,408	700	1,600	4,000	10,000	20,000	
1861 . . . 113	5,959	650	850	1,200	3,500	5,600	33,000
1862 . . 35	5,750	650	900	1,200	3,500	6,000	33,000
1863 . . 39	5,000	650	900	1,200	3,500	5,900	33,000
1864 . . 50	2,630	650	925	1,200	3,200	6,100	33,000
1865 . . 25	1,140	900	2,000	3,500	6,800	10,500	33,000
1866 . . 30	4,000	650	925	1,200	3,500	6,000	33,000
1867 . . 50	2,600	650	925	1,200	3,500	5,500	33,000
1868 . . 25	4,850	600	875	1,200	3,300	5,500	33,000
1869 . . 25	2,500	675	900	1,500	3,700	6,900	33,000
1870 . . 35	3,500	600	925	1,500	4,000	10,000	33,000
1870-S	(1 known)	—	750,000	—	—	—	
1871 . . 30	1,300	500	800	1,500	3,600	6,250	33,000
1872 . . 30	2,000	500	775	1,300	3,300	6,500	33,000
1873 closed 3 (restrikes) . . . (unknown)		2,000	4,000	8,000	16,750	—	
1873 open 3 (proof only)	25	—	—	—	—	—	70,000
1874 . . 20	41,800	400	650	800	2,000	4,850	33,000
1875 (proof only)	20	—	—	—	—	—	185,000
1876 (proof only)	45	—	—	18,000	—	—	85,000
1877 . . 20	1,468	600	2,550	5,000	6,000	15,000	42,500
1878 . . 20	82,304	400	725	900	2,000	4,600	30,000
1879 . . 30	3,000	400	800	900	2,100	4,600	30,000
1880 . . 36	1,000	300	1,400	1,600	2,100	4,600	32,500
1881 . . 54	500	400	1,750	3,000	4,000	5,800	30,000
1882 . . 76	1,500	400	725	900	2,000	5,100	30,000
1883 . . 89	900	400	925	1,500	2,000	5,100	30,000
1884 . . 106	1,000	650	1,250	1,600	1,900	5,450	30,000
1885 . . 109	801	700	1,300	1,800	2,000	5,400	30,000
1886 . . 142	1,000	700	1,275	1,900	3,250	6,250	30,000
1887 . . 160	6,000	450	750	850	2,000	5,000	30,000
1888 . . 291	5,000	475	790	850	2,000	5,000	30,000
1889 . . 129	2,300	475	750	850	2,000	5,000	30,000

$4 GOLD PIECES, OR "STELLAS" (1879–1880)

	Mintage	Proof-60	Proof-63	Proof-65
1879 with flowing hair (proof only)	425	$28,000	$37,500	$52,500
1879 with coiled hair (proof only)	10	50,000	70,000	80,000
1880 with flowing hair (proof only)	15	38,000	48,500	65,000
1880 with coiled hair (proof only)	10	80,000	100,000	120,000

HALF EAGLES, OR $5 GOLD PIECES (1795–1929)
Capped Bust Portrait Facing Right
with Small Eagle on Reverse (1795–1798)

	Mintage	Fine-12	EF-40	MS-60
1795.	8,707	$5,000	$8,000	$20,000
1796/5 overdate.	6,196	6,000	13,000	50,000
1797 combined total	3,609			

	Mintage	Fine-12	EF-40	MS-60
1797 with 15 stars.		8,000	20,000	60,000
1797 with 16 stars.		7,000	20,000	60,000
1798.	(7 known)	25,000	60,000	105,000

Capped Bust Portrait Facing Right
with Heraldic Eagle on Reverse (1795–1807)

	Mintage	Fine-12	EF-40	MS-60
1795 (mintage included in 1798)		$6,000	$14,000	$50,000
1797/5 overdate (mintage included in 1798)		8,000	15,000	75,000
1797 with 16 stars (mintage included in 1798).	(1 known)	—	—	—
1798 combined total	24,867			
1798 with small 8		1,500	3,000	8,000
1798 with large 8 and 13 stars		1,500	3,000	8,000
1798 with large 8 and 14 stars		2,000	2,600	—
1799.	7,451	1,800	3,500	12,000
1800.	37,628	1,600	2,000	6,000
1802/1 overdate.	53,176	1,600	2,000	6,000
1803/2 overdate.	33,506	1,600	2,000	6,000
1804 combined total	30,475			
1804 with small 8		1,600	2,000	6,000
1804 with small 8 over large 8		1,600	2,000	6,000
1805.	33,183	1,600	2,000	6,000
1806 with pointed 6.	9,676	1,400	2,500	5,800
1806 with round-top 6	54,417	1,400	2,500	5,600
1807.	32,488	1,400	2,500	5,600

Capped Draped Bust Portrait Facing Left
(1807–1812)

	Mintage	Fine-12	EF-40	MS-60
1807	51,605	$1,300	$2,400	$5,500
1808 combined total	55,578			
1808 regular date		1,300	2,400	5,500
1808/7 overdate		1,500	3,000	10,000
1809/8 overdate		1,500	2,250	5,250
1810 combined total	100,287			
1810 small date with small 5		8,000	35,000	87,500
1810 small date with tall 5 . . .		1,600	2,700	5,800
1810 large date with small 5		7,600	33,000	78,000
1810 large date with large 5		1,600	2,450	5,800
1811	99,581	1,600	2,450	5,800
1812	58,087	1,600	2,450	5,800

Capped Head Portrait (1813–1829)

	Mintage	Fine-12	EF-40	AU-55	MS-60	MS-63
1813	95,428	$1,500	$2,200	$3,000	$5,000	$12,000
1814/3 overdate	15,454	1,800	2,700	4,200	8,500	22,750
1815	635	38,250	55,000	100,000	—	—
1818 combined total	48,588					
1818 regular strike		2,000	3,000	4,000	6,000	12,000
1818 with 5D over 50		—	—	—	—	68,500
1819 combined total	51,723					
1819 regular strike		—	—	—	—	—
1819 with 5D over 50		—	—	—	—	—
1820	263,806	2,000	3,000	4,000	8,000	15,000
1821	34,641	2,500	6,500	9,500	—	—
1822 (3 known)	17,796	—	—	—	—	—
1823	14,485	2,500	3,500	6,000	12,500	18,000
1824	17,340	5,000	16,000	18,000	28,000	40,000
1825 combined total	29,060					
1825/1		4,000	6,000	8,000		
1825/4 (2 known)		—	—	—		
1826	18,069	3,000	7,000	12,000	19,000	32,750
1827	24,913	7,200	8,500	14,850	24,000	47,000
1828 combined total	28,029					
1828 regular date		—	—	—	—	—
1828/7 overdate		—	—	—	—	—
1829 large date	57,442	—	—	—	—	—

Size Reduced (1829–1834)

	Mintage	Fine-12	EF-40	AU-55	MS-60	MS-63
1829 small date (mintage included with large date)		—	—	—	—	—
1830	126,351	$4,000	$5,000	$6,000	$12,000	$30,000
1831	140,594	4,000	5,000	6,000	12,000	30,000
1832 combined total	157,487					
1832 with 12 stars (6 known)		30,000	48,000	—	—	—
1832 with 13 stars		4,000	8,000	11,000	14,000	26,000
1833 with large date	193,630	3,000	5,000	6,000	10,000	22,500
1834 combined total	50,141					
1834 with plain 4		3,000	5,000	5,200	12,000	24,000
1834 with crosslet 4		3,000	5,000	5,200	12,000	24,000

Classic Head Portrait (1834–1838)

	Mintage	Fine-12	EF-40	AU-55	MS-60	MS-63
1834 combined total	657,460					
1834 with plain 4		$300	$400	$800	$3,000	$8,000
1834 with crosslet 4		900	3,000	5,000	15,000	
1835	371,534	300	500	800	3,000	9,000
1836	553,147	300	500	800	3,000	9,000
1837	207,121	300	500	800	3,000	10,000
1838	286,588	300	500	800	3,000	10,000
1838-C	17,179	875	4,500	8,000	22,000	—
1838-D	20,583	725	3,000	5,000	16,750	—

Coronet Portrait (1839–1907)

No Motto over Eagle (1839–1866)

	Mintage	Fine-12	EF-40	AU-55	MS-60	MS-63	Proof-65
1839	118,143	$200	$350	$800	$2,500	—	
1839-C	17,205	1,000	2,500	3,000	12,000	—	
1839-D	18,939	1,000	1,300	3,000	8,000	—	
1840	137,382	100	1,000	1,500	3,500	—	
1840-C	18,992	1,500	2,000	4,000	15,000	—	
1840-D	22,896	1,000	5,000	6,000	12,500	—	
1840-O	40,120	400	900	2,000	9,250	—	
1841	15,833	500	1,000	1,800	4,000	—	
1841-C	21,467	1,000	1,675	3,000	8,000	—	
1841-D	29,392	1,000	1,200	3,000	9,000	—	
1841-O	50	(unknown in any collection)					
1842 combined total	27,578						
1842 with small letters		250	975	4,000	12,500	—	
1842 with large letters		500	1,800	4,000	16,500	—	
1842-C combined total	27,432						
1842-C small date		2,500	9,800	32,500	87,500	—	
1842-C large date		725	1,150	2,450	12,500	—	
1842-D combined total	59,608						
1842-D small date		600	1,200	3,850	9,000	—	
1842-D large date		1,800	3,600	9,000	18,500	—	
1842-O	16,400	600	2,650	8,250	19,500	—	
1843	611,205	300	210	305	2,000	—	
1843-C	44,277	400	1,150	3,000	10,000	—	
1843-D	98,452	525	850	2,600	8,000	—	
1843-O with small letters	19,075	300	900	3,000	9,600	—	
1843-O with large letters	82,000	200	900	3,000	13,250	—	
1844	340,330	100	150	475	2,000	5,000	
1844-C	23,631	600	1,600	4,800	10,000	—	
1844-D	88,982	400	1,000	2,100	8,000	—	

HALF EAGLES, OR $5 GOLD PIECES (1795–1929)

	Mintage	Fine-12	EF-40	AU-55	MS-60	MS-63	Proof-65
1844-O	364,600	150	325	600	3,000	11,000	
1845	417,099	100	200	350	2,000	6,500	
1845-D	90,629	400	900	2,000	8,000	—	
1845-O	41,000	300	600	2,000	6,000	—	
1846	395,942	100	160	400	2,500	9,000	
1846-C	12,995	700	1,500	4,000	20,000	50,000	
1846-D	80,294	500	600	3,000	10,000	—	
1846-O	58,000	100	600	4,000	15,000	—	
1847	915,981	100	150	400	2,000	8,000	
1847-C	84,151	300	1,000	2,000	8,000	—	
1847-D	64,405	300	1,000	2,000	5,000	—	
1847-O	12,000	510	3,000	5,000	10,000	25,000	
1848	260,775	100	300	400	3,000	8,000	
1848-C	64,472	400	1,000	3,500	9,500	—	
1848-D	47,465	300	800	2,600	9,000	—	
1849	133,070	100	200	750	3,000	—	
1849-C	64,823	300	950	3,000	10,000	—	
1849-D	39,036	500	1,000	3,000	10,000	—	
1850	64,491	200	750	2,000	4,000	10,000	
1850-C	63,591	300	1,000	2,000	6,000	—	
1850-D	43,984	300	1,650	3,000	10,000	—	
1851	377,505	100	200	300	2,000	9,000	
1851-C	49,176	490	750	2,000	8,000	—	
1851-D	62,710	475	910	2,000	8,000	—	
1851-O	41,000	400	910	3,000	15,000	—	
1852	573,901	100	175	200	1,200	8,000	
1852-C	72,574	400	800	2,000	8,000	25,000	
1852-D	91,584	400	800	2,000	10,000	—	
1853	305,770	100	200	200	1,600	9,000	
1853-C	65,571	300	800	1,500	9,000	—	
1853-D	89,678	300	800	1,500	9,000	22,500	
1854	160,675	100	300	600	3,000	—	
1854-C	39,283	400	1,200	3,000	9,000	—	
1854-D	56,413	300	900	1,500	8,000	—	
1854-O	46,000	200	400	900	6,000	—	
1854-S	268	—	—	300,000	—	—	
1855	117,098	100	200	300	3,000	7,000	
1855-C	39,788	400	1,400	3,000	12,000	36,500	
1855-D	22,432	500	1,100	3,000	12,000	—	
1855-O	11,100	400	2,000	4,000	20,000	—	
1855-S	61,000	200	800	2,000	9,000	—	
1856	197,990	100	200	300	2,000	9,000	

HALF EAGLES, OR $5 GOLD PIECES (1795–1929)

	Mintage	Fine-12	EF-40	AU-55	MS-60	MS-63	Proof-65
1856-C	28,457	400	1,000	3,000	8,000	—	
1856-D	19,786	400	1,000	3,000	8,000	—	
1856-O	10,000	400	1,650	5,000	15,500	—	
1856-S	105,100	225	700	2,000	5,000	—	
1857	98,188	100	150	300	2,000	9,000	—
1857-C	31,360	400	1,000	2,600	9,000	—	
1857-D	17,046	400	850	2,500	8,000	—	
1857-O	13,000	400	1,500	4,600	12,000	—	
1857-S	87,000	300	710	2,000	6,000	—	
1858	15,136	300	575	1,600	3,000	15,000	—
1858-C	38,856	300	1,000	3,000	9,000	—	
1858-D	15,362	300	1,000	1,600	8,000	—	
1858-S	18,600	300	1,675	4,000	12,000	—	
1859 . . 80	16,734	200	500	1,000	4,000	—	—
1859-C	31,847	300	1,000	2,000	12,500	50,000	
1859-D	10,366	400	1,700	2,800	8,000	—	
1859-S	13,220	900	2,950	12,000	—	—	
1860 . . 62	19,763	150	300	900	6,000	—	
1860-C	14,813	500	1,000	2,500	12,500	—	
1860-D	14,635	500	1,000	2,000	14,000	32,500	
1860-S	21,200	600	1,100	5,000	25,000	—	
1861 . . 66	688,084	100	150	200	2,000	6,000	65,500
1861-C	6,879	900	2,000	5,000	26,500	—	
1861-D	1,597	2,000	3,000	9,000	32,500	—	
1861-S	18,000	800	2,000	8,000	32,500	—	
1862 . . 35	4,430	300	1,500	2,000	20,000	—	—
1862-S	9,500	900	8,000	10,500	60,000	—	
1863 . . 30	2,442	500	2,000	4,000	22,500	—	—
1863-S	17,000	400	3,000	9,000	30,000	—	
1864 . . 50	4,170	200	1,200	3,000	12,500	—	65,000
1864-S	3,888	2,000	6,000	16,500	60,000	—	
1865 . . 25	1,270	600	2,000	3,850	28,000	—	—
1865-S	27,612	500	2,000	8,000	25,000	—	
1866-S	9,000	900	2,800	12,500	25,000	—	

Motto over Eagle (1866–1908)

	Mintage	Fine-12	EF-40	AU-55	MS-60	MS-63	Proof-65
1866 . . 30	6,700	$400	$1,000	$4,600	$12,000	—	—
1866-S	34,920	600	2,000	9,000	20,000	—	
1867 . . 50	6,870	200	1,000	4,650	8,650	—	
1867-S	29,000	900	2,500	8,500	15,000	—	
1868 . . 25	5,700	400	1,000	3,600	7,000	—	—

HALF EAGLES, OR $5 GOLD PIECES (1795–1929)

	Mintage	Fine-12	EF-40	AU-55	MS-60	MS-63	Proof-65
1868-S	52,000	300	1,100	6,000	10,000	—	
1869 . . 25	1,760	500	2,000	5,000	12,000	—	—
1869-S	31,000	525	2,300	7,800	23,500	—	
1870 . . 35	4,000	650	1,950	4,300	16,000	—	
1870-CC	7,675	2,400	6,400	12,250	39,000	—	
1870-S	17,000	1,075	2,800	7,800	25,000	—	
1871 . . 30	3,200	775	2,050	6,000	21,000	—	—
1871-CC	20,770	825	3,500	6,800	22,500	—	
1871-S	25,000	500	1,250	5,250	18,500	—	
1872 . . 30	1,660	725	1,900	3,750	17,000	42,000	—
1872-CC	16,980	775	3,250	5,900	19,500	—	
1872-S	36,400	500	1,350	6,000	20,500	—	
1873 combined total	112,480						
1873 closed 3 . . 25		150	175	550	2,400	11,500	—
1873 open 3	122,800	150	175	500	2,300	11,000	
1873-CC	7,416	1,400	4,300	10,500	25,000	—	
1873-S	31,000	615	2,700	7,800	20,000	—	
1874 . . 20	3,488	580	2,050	4,600	16,000	—	—
1874-CC	21,198	625	1,350	3,750	11,000	—	
1874-S	16,000	700	2,500	6,600	19,500	—	
1875 . . 20	200	42,000	57,000	96,000	—	—	—
1875-CC	11,828	1,250	3,700	10,500	30,000	—	
1875-S	9,000	725	2,750	8,650	22,000	—	
1876 . . 45	1,432	925	2,500	4,750	18,000	42,000	—
1876-CC	6,887	1,000	3,500	6,900	19,250	45,000	
1876-S	4,000	1,450	3,100	10,750	27,000	—	
1877 . . 20	1,132	750	2,400	4,200	11,400	—	—
1877-CC	8,680	850	2,600	6,450	17,000	—	
1877-S	26,700	330	700	3,000	8,000	—	
1878 . . 20	131,720	125	150	190	850	3,100	—
1878-CC	9,054	1,900	5,700	13,000	32,500	—	
1878-S	144,700	135	185	350	1,300	4,350	
1879 . . 30	301,920	125	145	210	450	1,700	—
1879-CC	17,281	400	900	2,000	6,000	—	
1879-S	426,200	160	240	285	875	3,950	
1880 . . 36	3,166,400	115	125	155	195	1,400	—
1880-CC	51,017	315	650	1,300	7,500	—	
1880-S	1,348,900	150	200	250	400	1,600	
1881 combined total	5,708,760						
1881 regular date . . 42		105	150	175	250	1,400	35,000
1881/0 overdate		300	600	1,500	5,000	—	
1881-CC	13,886	400	1,200	3,000	9,000	22,000	

HALF EAGLES, OR $5 GOLD PIECES (1795–1929)

	Mintage	Fine-12	EF-40	AU-55	MS-60	MS-63	Proof-65
1881-S	969,000	150	200	225	275	1,600	
1882 . . . *48*	2,514,520	150	200	225	275	1,600	35,000
1882-CC	82,817	285	425	800	4,900	9,000	
1882-S	969,000	150	200	225	275	1,600	
1883 . . *61*	233,400	150	200	225	600	3,400	—
1883-CC	12,958	400	600	2,900	14,000	—	
1883-S	83,200	150	200	275	995	4,900	
1884 . . *48*	191,030	150	175	200	900	4,000	—
1884-CC	16,402	400	700	3,500	13,000	—	
1884-S	177,000	200	275	300	600	4,100	
1885 . . *66*	601,440	105	120	125	200	1,600	—
1885-S	1,211,500	110	115	135	175	1,375	
1886 . . *72*	388,360	150	175	195	450	2,350	—
1886-S	3,268,000	110	120	150	175	2,000	
1887 (proof only)	87	—	—	—	—	—	—
1887-S	1,912,000	105	120	140	175	1,600	
1888 . . *95*	18,201	130	200	275	995	4,000	—
1888-S	293,900	135	240	650	2,750	—	
1889 . . *45*	7,520	220	450	795	1,400	3,900	35,000
1890 . . *88*	4,240	375	600	1,200	4,000	—	29,000
1890-CC	53,800	250	300	450	1,600	4,200	
1891 . . *53*	61,360	120	160	210	700	2,900	27,000
1891-CC	208,000	175	250	350	700	2,900	
1892 . . *92*	753,480	110	120	130	195	1,775	—
1892-CC	82,968	250	350	500	1,900	5,900	
1892-O	10,000	400	900	1,900	5,900	—	
1892-S	298,400	150	200	275	1,200	4,300	
1893 . . *77*	1,528,120	100	115	140	195	1,600	27,000
1893-CC	60,000	200	500	600	1,900	9,900	
1893-O	110,000	195	225	350	1,200	5,300	
1893-S	224,000	150	175	225	550	3,200	
1894 . . *75*	957,880	110	120	140	200	1,650	29,500
1894-O	16,600	160	250	375	1,500	5,500	
1894-S	55,900	250	300	550	3,300	8,900	
1895 . . *81*	1,345,855	105	115	140	200	1,650	29,000
1895-S	112,000	175	275	900	3,800	8,500	
1896 . . *103*	58,960	130	150	175	255	4,000	24,000
1896-S	155,400	185	250	600	2,000	6,700	
1897 . . *83*	867,800	110	115	145	195	1,500	—
1897-S	354,000	135	195	395	1,300	4,500	
1898 . . *75*	633,420	110	115	135	225	1,775	25,000
1898-S	1,397,400	120	130	140	190	2,000	

HALF EAGLES, OR $5 GOLD PIECES (1795–1929)

	Mintage	Fine-12	EF-40	AU-55	MS-60	MS-63	Proof-65
1899 . . 99	1,710,630	110	120	130	175	1,600	25,000
1899-S	1,545,000	120	130	140	225	1,600	
1900 . . 230	1,405,500	115	120	130	200	1,600	26,000
1900-S	329,000	130	150	250	850	3,000	
1901 . . 140	615,900	115	120	130	175	1,600	26,000
1901-S combined total	3,648,000						
1901-S regular date		105	115	135	175	1,500	
1901/O-S overdate		140	195	350	900	4,500	
1902 . . 162	172,400	105	115	135	175	1,500	25,000
1902-S	939,000	105	115	135	175	1,500	
1903 . . 154	226,870	105	115	135	175	1,500	25,000
1903-S	1,855,000	105	115	135	175	1,500	
1904 . . 136	392,000	105	115	135	175	1,500	25,000
1904-S	97,000	130	175	295	750	4,500	
1905 . . 108	302,200	115	125	145	195	1,600	27,000
1905-S	880,700	130	175	295	750	4,500	
1906 . . 85	348,735	115	125	145	195	1,600	27,000
1906-D	320,000	115	125	145	195	1,600	
1906-S	598,000	115	125	145	195	1,600	
1907 . . 92	626,100	115	125	145	195	1,600	27,000
1907-D	888,000	115	125	145	195	1,600	
1908	421,874	115	125	145	195	1,600	

Indian Head Portrait (1908–1929)

	Mintage	Fine-12	EF-40	AU-55	MS-60	MS-63	Proof-65
1908 . . 167	577,845	$100	$200	$225	$300	$2,300	23,000
1908-D	148,000	100	200	225	300	2,300	
1908-S	82,000	195	200	295	3,000	4,950	
1909 . . 78	627,060	100	200	225	300	2,300	24,000
1909-D	3,423,560	100	200	225	300	2,300	
1909-O	34,200	700	900	1,450	7,000	39,000	

HALF EAGLES, OR $5 GOLD PIECES (1795–1929)

	Mintage	Fine-12	EF-40	AU-55	MS-60	MS-63	Proof-65
1909-S	297,200	195	200	300	995	6,000	
1910 . . 250	604,000	100	200	225	300	2,300	23,000
1910-D	193,600	125	200	300	450	6,000	
1910-S	770,200	200	300	350	475	7,950	
1911 . . 139	915,000	100	200	225	300	2,300	24,000
1911-D	72,500	100	200	275	6,000	19,000	
1911-S	1,416,000	100	200	225	800	5,650	
1912 . . 144	790,000	100	300	500	600	2,300	24,000
1912-S	392,000	100	300	500	995	9,950	
1913 . . 99	915,901	100	200	225	300	2,300	24,000
1913-S	408,000	200	300	500	3,000	15,000	
1914 . . 125	247,000	100	200	225	300	2,300	28,000
1914-D	247,000	200	300	500	700	3,000	
1914-S	263,000	200	900	995	1,200	9,500	
1915 . . 75	588,000	100	200	225	300	2,300	30,000
1915-S	164,000	300	375	400	4,000	9,000	
1916-S	240,000	200	300	375	600	4,000	
1929	662,000	2,900	3,750	6,000	7,500	11,950	

EAGLES, OR $10 GOLD PIECES (1795–1933)

Capped Bust Portrait Facing Right
with Small Eagle on Reverse (1795–1797)

	Mintage	VF-20	EF-40	MS-60
1795 combined total	5,583			
1795 with 9 leaves below eagle		$37,000	$50,000	$150,000
1795 with 13 leaves below eagle		9,000	11,000	35,000
1796.	4,146	10,000	13,000	50,000
1797.	3,615	12,000	19,000	80,000

Capped Bust Portrait Facing Right
with Heraldic Eagle on Reverse (1797–1804)

	Mintage	VF-20	EF-40	MS-60
1797.	10,940	$2,500	$3,900	$12,950
1798/7 overdate with 9 stars				
left, 4 right	900	6,000	15,000	55,000
1798/7 overdate with 7 stars				
left, 6 right	842	12,000	50,000	—
1799.	37,449	2,300	4,000	8,500
1800.	5,999	2,800	4,700	10,000
1801.	44,344	2,300	4,700	9,000
1803.	15,017	2,300	4,700	9,000
1804.	3,757	3,000	6,000	19,000

Coronet Portrait (1838–1907)

No Motto over Eagle (1838–1866)

	Mintage	VF-20	EF-40	AU-50	MS-60	MS-63	Proof-65
1838	7,200	$785	$2,500	$4,500	$19,500	$75,000	
1839 with large letters	25,801	750	1,400	3,500	12,500	70,000	

Modified Portrait of Liberty, Smaller Letters (1839–1907)

	Mintage	VF-20	EF-40	AU-50	MS-60	MS-63	Proof-65
1839 with small letters	12,447	$1,500	$3,200	$6,700	$24,000	—	
1840	47,338	330	700	2,500	14,000	—	
1841	63,131	400	650	2,200	11,000	38,000	
1841-O	2,500	2,000	6,000	17,000	37,000	—	
1842 small date	18,623	350	500	2,000	8,000	29,000	
1842 large date	62,884	400	600	2,500	10,000	—	
1842-O	27,400	350	750	4,000	20,000	—	
1843	75,462	350	650	2,500	12,000	—	
1843-O	175,162	350	600	1,500	17,000	—	
1844	6,361	995	2,995	8,000	29,500	—	
1844-O	118,700	350	500	1,200	9,950	—	
1845	26,153	500	1,200	5,500	19,000	—	
1845-O	47,500	400	900	2,500	20,000	—	
1846	20,095	800	2,200	7,300	24,000	—	
1846-O	81,780	500	1,000	6,700	14,000	—	
1847	862,258	350	380	700	5,000	22,000	
1847-O	571,500	350	400	800	5,000	17,500	
1848	145,484	350	450	850	5,500	35,000	
1848-O	35,850	500	1,350	5,500	17,000	—	
1849	653,618	350	450	750	4,800	12,000	
1849-O	23,900	800	2,400	5,000	21,000	—	

EAGLES, OR $10 GOLD PIECES (1795–1933)

	Mintage	VF-20	EF-40	AU-50	MS-60	MS-63	Proof-65
1850 combined total	291,451						
1850 small date		600	900	2,000	18,000	—	
1850 large date		350	600	995	5,500	18,000	
1850-O	57,500	350	600	6,000	13,000	75,000	
1851	176,328	350	400	1,100	9,000	30,000	
1851-O	263,000	350	500	1,700	11,000	—	
1852	263,106	350	500	750	5,500	19,000	
1852-O	18,000	700	1,400	4,900	25,000	—	
1853 combined total	201,253						
1853 regular date		350	400	675	5,200	32,000	
1853/2 overdate		550	1,100	2,400	11,000	—	
1853-O	51,000	350	450	1,500	9,000	—	
1854	54,250	350	500	1,500	10,000	—	
1854-O combined total	52,500						
1854-O small date		350	1,000	2,700	11,000	—	
1854-O large date		450	1,600	3,600	13,000	—	
1854-S	123,826	350	500	1,500	13,000	—	
1855	121,701	350	400	800	5,500	—	
1855-O	18,000	600	1,900	5,000	15,000	—	
1855-S	9,000	1,400	3,500	7,500	29,000	—	
1856	60,490	350	400	800	5,000	14,000	—
1856-O	14,500	950	2,100	5,000	16,000	—	
1856-S	68,000	350	450	1,500	10,000	—	
1857	16,606	350	900	3,600	13,000	—	—
1857-O	5,500	1,100	2,400	5,500	25,000	—	
1857-S	26,000	400	950	2,500	11,000	—	
1858	2,521	5,500	12,000	25,000	65,000	—	
1858-O	20,000	350	700	1,800	14,000	—	
1858-S	11,800	2,000	4,500	12,000	32,000	—	
1859 . . 80	16,013	350	575	2,500	13,000	—	—
1859-O	2,300	3,500	9,500	25,000	47,500	—	
1859-S	7,000	3,000	7,000	17,500	45,000	—	
1860 . . 50	15,055	400	950	3,000	12,000	—	
1860-O	11,100	500	1,400	3,300	14,000	—	
1860-S	5,000	2,500	6,500	19,000	42,000	—	
1861 . . 69	113,164	350	400	800	5,400	17,000	—
1861-S	15,500	1,400	4,000	12,000	32,000	—	
1862 . . 35	10,960	400	1,200	3,900	12,000	—	—
1862-S	12,500	1,700	4,200	12,000	40,000	—	
1863 . . 30	1,218	4,000	10,000	24,000	57,500	—	—
1863-S	10,000	1,500	4,000	10,000	52,000	—	
1864 . . 50	3,530	1,800	3,950	9,000	27,000	—	—

EAGLES, OR $10 GOLD PIECES (1795–1933)

	Mintage	VF-20	EF-40	AU-50	MS-60	MS-63	Proof-65
1864-S	2,500	4,200	11,000	21,000	50,000	—	
1865 . . 25	3,980	1,500	5,000	11,000	35,000	—	—
1865-S combined total	16,700						
1865-S regular date		5,000	10,000	21,000	45,000	—	
1865-S with 865 over inverted							
186		3,600	8,000	15,000	50,000	—	
1866-S	8,500	3,600	6,000	20,000	45,000	—	

Motto over Eagle (1866–1907)

	Mintage	VF-20	EF-40	AU-50	MS-60	MS-63	Proof-65
1866 . . 30	3,750	$800	$2,000	$6,000	$17,000	—	$53,500
1866-S	11,500	1,700	4,000	9,500	25,000	—	
1867 . . 50	3,090	2,000	4,500	8,000	28,000	—	53,500
1867-S	9,000	2,300	8,000	16,000	42,500	—	
1868 . . 25	10,630	600	1,500	4,500	14,000	—	53,500
1868-S	13,500	1,700	3,900	8,500	33,000	—	
1869 . . 25	1,830	1,500	4,000	10,000	29,500	—	53,500
1869-S	6,430	1,500	3,900	9,000	35,000	—	
1870 . . 35	3,990	800	1,500	4,700	18,000	—	53,500
1870-CC	5,908	5,700	14,000	29,500	60,000	—	
1870-S	8,000	2,000	6,000	15,000	37,500	—	
1871 . . 30	1,790	1,500	3,500	7,000	25,000	—	53,500
1871-CC	8,085	1,700	5,000	16,000	45,000	—	
1871-S	16,500	1,500	3,900	9,500	30,000	—	
1872 . . 30	1,620	3,000	5,500	15,000	39,500	—	53,500
1872-CC	4,680	1,600	8,000	19,000	50,000	—	
1872-S	17,300	900	2,000	6,500	25,000	—	
1873 . . 25	800	4,000	10,000	29,000	55,000	—	53,500
1873-CC	4,543	2,600	9,000	20,000	45,000	—	
1873-S	12,000	1,150	3,000	7,000	29,000	—	

EAGLES, OR $10 GOLD PIECES (1795–1933)

	Mintage	VF-20	EF-40	AU-50	MS-60	MS-63	Proof-65
1874 . . 20	53,140	250	300	370	2,300	8,000	53,500
1874-CC	16,767	700	3,900	9,000	25,000	—	
1874-S	10,000	1,100	3,600	13,000	45,000		
1875 . . 20	100	40,000	—	—	—	—	170,000
1875-CC	7,715	3,800	10,000	21,000	50,000		
1876 . . 45	687	3,500	9,000	29,000	49,000	—	44,000
1876-CC	4,696	3,500	9,000	26,000	50,000	—	
1876-S	5,000	1,700	3,600	9,000	40,000	—	
1877 . . 20	797	2,500	6,000	14,000	45,000	60,000	60,000
1877-CC	3,332	2,000	5,000	9,000	31,000	—	
1877-S	17,000	500	1,500	5,000	25,000	—	
1878 . . 20	73,780	240	250	290	1,700	7,000	50,000
1878-CC	3,244	3,900	7,900	17,000	40,000	—	
1878-S	26,100	700	1,500	5,000	21,000	—	
1879 . . 30	384,740	240	280	290	500	3,000	44,000
1879-CC	1,762	4,500	8,000	20,000	49,000	—	
1879-O	1,500	1,800	7,000	15,000	40,000	—	
1879-S	224,000	240	280	290	1,800	8,000	
1880 . . 36	1,644,840	240	290	290	330	4,500	44,000
1880-CC	11,190	400	800	2,900	7,500	—	
1880-O	9,200	300	600	1,750	7,500	—	
1880-S	506,250	240	280	290	500	5,000	
1881 . . 40	3,877,220	240	250	280	300	1,300	42,500
1881-CC	24,015	400	600	1,100	5,600	14,000	
1881-O	8,350	330	700	2,000	7,300	—	
1881-S	970,000	240	280	290	300	6,000	
1882 . . 40	2,324,440	240	250	290	300	1,400	42,500
1882-CC	6,764	500	1,200	3,500	8,500	30,000	
1882-O	10,820	300	700	1,600	6,500	19,500	
1882-S	132,000	240	280	350	500	5,000	
1883 . . 40	208,700	240	280	290	370	5,000	40,000
1883-CC	12,000	400	700	2,200	7,000	27,000	
1883-O	800	3,000	8,000	17,000	34,500	—	
1883-S	38,000	300	350	375	1,100	7,000	
1884 . . 45	76,860	300	350	375	1,200	5,500	—
1884-CC	9,925	500	900	3,200	8,000	25,000	
1884-S	124,250	240	280	300	700	6,700	
1885 . . 65	253,462	240	280	300	500	4,950	38,000
1885-S	228,000	240	260	300	325	6,500	
1886 . . 60	236,100	240	260	300	500	3,500	38,000
1886-S	826,000	240	280	300	400	1,700	
1887 . . 80	53,600	240	280	400	1,000	7,000	38,000

EAGLES, OR $10 GOLD PIECES (1795–1933)

	Mintage	VF-20	EF-40	AU-50	MS-60	MS-63	Proof-65
1887-S	817,000	240	280	285	300	4,200	
1888 . . 75	132,921	240	265	325	1,000	7,000	37,000
1888-O	21,335	240	280	285	650	4,500	
1888-S	648,700	240	280	300	350	3,600	
1889 . . 45	4,440	250	375	900	2,600	8,500	37,000
1889-S	425,400	240	280	285	375	2,400	
1890 . . 63	57,980	240	280	300	1,300	6,500	36,000
1890-CC	17,500	360	400	550	1,600	7,000	
1891 . . 48	91,820	240	280	285	325	3,500	37,000
1891-CC	103,732	240	275	425	650	4,300	
1892 . . 72	797,480	240	280	300	310	1,300	36,000
1892-CC	40,000	300	400	550	2,100	8,000	
1892-O	28,688	300	370	400	600	5,500	
1892-S	115,500	240	280	300	425	3,750	
1893 . . 55	1,840,840	240	280	285	325	1,600	37,000
1893-CC	14,000	425	700	1,900	5,500	15,000	
1893-O	17,000	240	280	325	750	6,000	
1893-S	141,350	240	280	325	700	5,500	
1894 . . 43	2,470,735	240	280	285	325	1,300	37,000
1894-O	107,500	240	280	350	1,400	7,500	
1894-S	25,000	240	295	850	4,500	9,500	
1895 . . 56	567,770	240	280	285	300	1,300	37,000
1895-O	98,000	240	280	245	700	4,000	
1895-S	49,000	240	275	900	4,800	10,000	
1896 . . 78	76,270	240	280	285	325	1,900	36,000
1896-S	123,750	240	300	900	5,000	11,000	
1897 . . 69	1,000,090	240	280	285	325	1,300	36,000
1897-O	42,500	240	280	285	700	4,000	
1897-S	234,750	240	280	285	1,500	5,500	
1898 . . 67	812,130	240	280	285	350	1,350	36,000
1898-S	473,600	240	280	285	400	2,500	
1899 . . 86	1,262,219	240	280	285	325	1,300	34,000
1899-O	37,047	240	280	285	750	4,000	
1899-S	841,000	240	280	285	450	1,800	
1900 . . 120	293,840	240	280	285	350	1,300	30,000
1900-S	81,000	240	280	285	1,000	4,500	
1901 . . 85	1,718,740	240	280	285	325	1,300	30,000
1901-O	72,041	240	280	285	450	2,000	
1901-S	2,812,750	240	280	285	325	1,300	
1902 . . 113	82,400	240	280	285	350	2,100	30,000
1902-S	469,500	240	280	285	325	1,300	
1903 . . 96	125,830	240	280	285	325	1,300	30,000

EAGLES, OR $10 GOLD PIECES (1795–1933)

	Mintage	VF-20	EF-40	AU-50	MS-60	MS-63	Proof-65
1903-O	112,771	240	270	310	425	3,000	
1903-S	538,000	240	280	285	325	1,300	
1904 . . *108*	161,930	240	280	325	1,200	2,300	30,000
1904-O	108,950	240	300	350	450	2,800	
1905 . . *86*	200,992	240	280	285	325	1,300	30,000
1905-S	369,250	240	280	375	2,700	6,500	
1906 . . *77*	165,420	240	280	285	325	1,300	30,000
1906-D	981,000	240	280	285	325	1,300	
1906-O	86,895	240	280	300	700	3,000	
1906-S	457,000	240	280	300	700	3,200	
1907 . . *74*	1,203,899	240	280	285	325	1,300	30,000
1907-D	1,030,000	240	280	285	325	1,300	
1907-S	210,500	240	280	495	995	3,200	

Indian Head Portrait (1907–1933)

	Mintage	VF-20	EF-40	AU-50	MS-60	MS-63	Proof-65
1907 with wire rim and periods before and after E PLURIBUS UNUM	500	—	—	$6,000	$9,000	$14,000	56,000
1907 with rounded rim and periods	42	—	—	22,000	26,000	40,000	—
1907 with no periods	239,406	380	450	500	700	2,100	
1908 without IN GOD WE TRUST	33,500	450	550	600	995	3,200	
1908-D without motto . .	210,000	450	550	800	995	8,000	

Motto Added to Reverse (1908–1933)

	Mintage	Fine-12	EF-40	AU-55	MS-60	MS-63	Proof-65
1908 . . *116*	341,370	$400	$425	$460	$500	$1,300	$33,000
1908-D	836,500	425	490	600	900	3,200	
1908-S	59,850	500	600	700	2,700	7,000	
1909 . . *74*	184,789	400	490	350	700	1,750	35,000
1909-D	121,540	400	465	500	900	9,000	
1909-S	292,350	400	465	490	1,000	2,700	
1910 . . *204*	318,500	400	425	475	600	1,400	34,000
1910-D	2,356,640	400	455	475	600	1,400	
1910-S	811,000	400	455	500	1,100	4,600	
1911 . . *95*	505,500	400	450	475	500	1,300	33,000
1911-D	30,100	400	500	900	6,000	13,000	
1911-S	51,000	500	600	750	1,400	4,000	
1912 . . *83*	405,000	400	450	500	600	1,300	33,000
1912-S	300,000	500	600	700	1,100	3,000	
1913 . . *71*	442,000	400	460	475	600	1,300	34,000
1913-S	66,000	500	600	700	5,800	29,000	
1914 . . *50*	151,000	400	450	500	600	1,300	34,000
1914-D	343,500	400	450	500	600	1,300	
1914-S	208,000	400	450	500	700	4,200	
1915 . . *75*	351,000	400	450	500	600	1,300	34,000
1915-S	59,000	400	450	700	3,300	9,000	
1916-S	138,500	400	450	600	900	3,500	
1920-S	126,500	3,950	6,000	8,000	20,000	35,000	
1926	1,014,000	400	450	460	600	1,300	
1930-S	96,000	5,000	7,500	8,000	10,000	13,000	
1932	4,463,000	460	450	460	400	1,100	
1933	312,500	—	—	—	54,000	85,000	

DOUBLE EAGLES, OR $20 GOLD PIECES (1849–1933)

Coronet Portrait (1849–1907)

No Motto over Eagle (1849–1866)

	Mintage	VF-20	EF-40	AU-50	MS-60	MS-63	Proof-63
1849	1	(part of the U.S. Mint Collection)					
1850	1,170,261	$525	$600	$1,100	$3,000	$30,000	
1850-O	141,000	650	1,100	3,500	16,000	40,000	
1851	2,087,155	525	600	750	3,000	18,000	
1851-O	315,000	600	700	1,400	15,000	40,000	
1852	2,053,026	525	600	800	3,200	12,000	
1852-O	190,000	550	700	1,700	14,000	35,000	
1853 combined total	1,261,326						
1853 regular date		525	600	800	5,500	18,000	
1853/2 overdate		650	1,100	2,750	25,000	—	
1853-O	71,000	650	1,000	3,500	20,000	45,000	
1854	757,899	525	600	800	5,400	20,000	
1854-O	3,250	13,000	30,000	57,000	110,000	—	
1854-S	141,468	575	625	900	3,300	8,000	
1855	364,666	575	675	925	7,000	25,000	
1855-O	8,000	2,500	5,000	14,500	50,000	—	
1855-S	879,675	575	625	950	8,000	30,000	
1856	329,878	575	625	900	6,500	37,000	
1856-O	2,250	15,000	28,000	57,000	120,000	250,000	
1856-S	1,189,750	575	625	750	4,200	17,000	
1857	439,375	600	675	800	4,000	22,000	

DOUBLE EAGLES (1849–1933)

	Mintage	VF-20	EF-40	AU-50	MS-60	MS-63	Proof-63
1857-O	30,000	950	1,800	4,200	15,000	40,000	
1857-S	970,500	575	650	800	4,200	11,000	
1858	211,714	550	800	1,500	5,200	25,000	
1858-O	35,250	1,000	2,000	5,000	16,000	16,000	
1858-S	846,710	525	650	1000	9,000	21,000	
1859 . . 80	43,517	900	2,400	5,400	25,000	60,000	—
1859-O	9,100	3,000	6,200	12,000	35,000	65,000	
1859-S	636,445	525	650	900	4,000	11,000	
1860 . . 59	577,611	525	650	750	4,500	16,000	—
1860-O	6,600	3,000	5,500	13,000	35,000	65,000	
1860-S	544,950	525	650	1,000	6,000	20,000	
1861 combined total	2,976,387						
1861 with regular reverse . . 66		525	650	720	1,900	7,500	—
1861 with Paquet reverse (tall letters)		—	—	—	—	700,000	
1861-O	17,741	1,300	3,500	6,500	18,000	40,000	
1861-S combined total	768,000						
1861-S with regular reverse		525	650	1,100	7,300	27,000	
1861-S with Paquet reverse (tall letters)		5,000	9,000	20,000	57,000	—	
1862 . . 35	92,098	700	1,300	2,500	12,000	30,000	—
1862-S	854,173	525	650	1,800	10,000	25,000	
1863 . . 30	142,760	525	650	1,800	10,000	30,000	—
1863-S	966,570	525	650	1,400	5,500	20,000	
1864 . . 50	204,235	525	650	1,400	10,000	30,000	37,000
1864-S	793,660	525	650	1,250	2,700	8,000	
1865 . . 25	351,175	525	700	1,100	6,500	21,000	—
1865-S	1,042,500	525	650	1,100	7,000	22,000	
1866-S	120,000	1,600	3,200	10,000	18,000	—	

Motto over Eagle (1866–1907)

	Mintage	VF-20	EF-40	AU-50	MS-60	MS-63	Proof-65
1866 . . 30	698,745	$425	$500	$1,075	$6,500	$30,000	$110,000
1866-S	842,250	425	525	1,800	13,000	30,000	
1867 . . 50	251,015	425	500	700	1,300	18,000	110,000
1867-S	920,750	425	500	1,600	13,000	30,000	
1868 . . 25	98,575	425	525	2,000	7,000	30,000	115,000
1868-S	837,500	425	500	1,350	11,500	8,000	
1869 . . 25	175,130	425	500	1,300	5,000	16,000	115,000
1869-S	686,750	425	500	1,100	4,400	16,000	
1870 . . 35	155,150	425	525	1,500	6,000	20,000	110,000
1870-CC	3,789	25,000	55,000	120,000	—	—	
1870-S	982,000	425	500	800	4,700	20,000	
1871 . . 30	80,120	450	600	1,500	4,800	17,000	110,000
1871-CC	17,387	2,400	5,000	9,000	25,000	—	
1871-S	928,000	425	500	700	4,200	18,000	
1872 . . 30	251,850	425	500	675	3,200	18,000	110,000
1872-CC	26,900	1,100	1,800	4,700	19,000	40,000	
1872-S	780,000	425	500	650	2,300	9,000	
1873 combined total	1,709,800						
1873 closed 3 . . 25		500	700	1,150	4,000	15,000	110,000
1873 open 3		425	500	610	675	6,500	
1873-CC	22,410	925	1,600	4,500	20,000	—	
1873-S	1,040,600	425	500	650	1,400	15,000	
1874 . . 20	366,780	425	500	650	1,200	8,000	110,000
1874-CC	115,085	450	600	1,800	8,750	22,000	
1874-S	1,214,000	425	500	675	1,400	14,000	
1875 . . 20	295,720	425	500	650	800	7,000	200,000
1875-CC	111,151	425	550	850	2,100	16,000	

	Mintage	VF-20	EF-40	AU-50	MS-60	MS-63	Proof-65
1875-S	1,230,000	425	500	650	800	15,000	
1876 . . 45	583,860	425	500	650	800	8,000	90,000
1876-CC	138,441	450	600	750	4,500	16,000	
1876-S	1,597,000	425	500	650	800	10,000	

TWENTY DOLLARS Spelled Out (1877–1907)

	Mintage	VF-20	EF-40	AU-50	MS-60	MS-63	Proof-65
1877 . . 20	397,650	$500	$525	$625	$675	$2,750	$75,000
1877-CC	42,565	650	900	1,500	17,000	40,000	
1877-S	1,735,000	425	490	600	480	695	
1878 . . 20	543,625	425	490	600	480	695	70,000
1878-CC	13,180	800	1,500	4,500	15,000	—	
1878-S	1,739,000	425	490	600	950	8,000	
1879 . . 30	207,600	425	490	600	900	7,500	65,000
1879-CC	10,708	1,000	2,000	4,500	17,000	40,000	
1879-O	2,325	3,000	4,500	4,000	26,000	50,000	
1879-S	1,223,800	425	490	625	1,400	9,000	
1880 . . 36	51,420	425	490	700	3,000	12,000	65,000
1880-S	836,000	425	490	630	1,500	7,000	
1881 . . 61	2,199	3,500	7,000	14,000	40,000	75,000	65,000
1881-S	727,000	425	490	590	1,100	6,500	
1882 . . 59	571	7,000	15,000	28,000	60,000	100,000	70,000
1882-CC	39,140	600	700	1,200	7,000	20,000	
1882-S	1,125,000	425	490	600	700	8,000	
1883 (proof only)	92	—	—	—	—	—	70,000
1883-CC	59,962	575	700	1,100	5,000	18,000	
1883-S	1,189,000	425	490	600	650	3,300	
1884 (proof only)	71	—	—	—	—	—	70,000
1884-CC	81,139	575	650	850	3,000	15,000	
1884-S	916,000	425	490	600	700	3,000	
1885 . . 77	751	3,000	4,500	9,000	30,000	70,000	70,000
1885-CC	9,450	900	2,000	3,200	10,000	31,000	
1885-S	683,500	425	490	600	675	3,000	
1886 . . 106	1,000	5,000	10,000	20,000	35,000	70,000	70,000
1887 (proof only)	121	—	—	—	—	—	70,000
1887-S	283,000	425	490	600	675	2,800	
1888 . . 105	226,161	425	490	600	800	6,000	60,000
1888-S	859,600	425	490	600	700	2,000	
1889 . . 45	44,070	425	490	600	700	5,000	60,000
1889-CC	30,945	425	490	1,100	4,500	17,000	
1889-S	774,700	425	490	600	675	2,500	
1890 . . 55	75,940	425	490	600	690	2,500	60,000

DOUBLE EAGLES (1849–1933)

	Mintage	VF-20	EF-40	AU-50	MS-60	MS-63	Proof-65
1890-CC	91,209	425	800	1,050	3,000	15,000	
1890-S	802,750	425	500	600	650	2,400	
1891 . . 52	1,390	2,900	4,700	9,000	25,000	50,000	55,000
1891-CC	5,000	1,400	2,500	4,750	13,000	35,000	
1891-S	1,288,125	425	500	600	650	1,400	
1892 . . 93	4,430	1,000	1,400	2,500	7,000	18,000	55,000
1892-CC	27,265	700	800	1,200	3,500	18,500	
1892-S	930,150	425	500	600	650	1,400	
1893 . . 59	344,280	425	500	600	650	2,250	55,000
1893-CC	18,402	575	750	1,100	2,300	9,500	
1893-S	996,175	425	500	600	650	1,300	
1894 . . 50	1,368,940	425	500	600	650	1,300	55,000
1894-S	1,048,550	425	500	600	650	1,200	
1895 . . 51	1,114,605	425	500	600	650	900	52,000
1895 S	1,143,500	425	500	600	650	900	
1896 . . 128	792,535	425	500	600	650	900	52,000
1896-S	1,403,925	425	500	600	650	1,200	
1897 . . 86	1,383,175	425	500	600	650	900	52,000
1897-S	1,470,250	425	500	600	650	900	
1898 . . 75	170,395	425	500	600	900	5,000	52,000
1898-S	2,575,175	425	500	600	650	900	
1899 . . 84	1,669,300	425	500	600	650	900	52,000
1899-S	2,010,300	425	500	600	650	900	
1900 . . 124	1,874,460	425	500	600	650	900	50,000
1900-S	2,459,500	425	500	600	650	1,200	
1901 . . 96	111,430	425	500	600	650	900	50,000
1901-S	1,596,000	425	500	600	650	1,600	
1902 . . 114	31,140	425	475	600	900	4,000	50,000
1902-S	1,753,625	425	475	600	650	1,500	
1903 . . 158	287,270	425	475	600	650	900	50,000
1903-S	954,000	425	475	615	650	1,000	
1904 . . 98	6,256,699	425	475	575	625	850	50,000
1904-S	5,134,175	425	475	600	650	900	
1905 . . 92	58,919	425	475	600	1,300	19,000	50,000
1905-S	1,813,000	425	475	600	650	1,400	
1906 . . 94	69,596	425	475	600	900	3,000	50,000
1906-D	620,250	425	475	600	700	1,700	
1906-S	2,065,750	425	475	600	700	450	
1907 . . 78	1,451,786	425	475	600	650	900	50,000
1907-D	842,250	425	475	600	650	900	
1907-S	2,165,800	425	475	600	650	1,100	

Saint-Gaudens Portrait of Liberty (1907–1933)

	Mintage	AU-50	MS-60	MS-63	MS-64	MS-65	Proof-65
1907 extremely high relief, plain edge	*1 known*	—	—	—	—	—	$950,000
1907 extremely high relief, lettered edge (proof only)	*24*	—	—	—	—	—	400,000
1907 high relief with Roman-numerals date MCMVII, combined total	11,250						
1907 high relief with wire rim		4,500	7,500	10,000	15,000	30,000	
1907 high relief with flat rim		4,500	7,500	10,000	15,000	30,000	
1907 with Arabic numerals	361,667	600	650	850	1,600	4,500	
1908 without IN GOD WE TRUST	4,271,551	600	650	750	850	1,500	
1908-D without motto	663,750	600	650	800	1,800	14,000	

Motto Added to Reverse (1908–1933)

	Mintage	AU-50	MS-60	MS-63	MS-64	MS-65	Proof-65
1908 . . _101_	156,258	$550	$600	$1,100	$4,000	$14,000	$32,000
1908-D	349,500	550	600	800	1,200	3,700	
1908-S	22,000	1,300	3,000	11,000	18,000	35,000	
1909 combined total	161,282						
1909 regular date . . _74_		600	850	4,000	14,000	58,000	43,000
1909/8 overdate		625	1,700	7,750	18,000	50,000	
1909-D	52,500	650	1,250	3,500	5,500	40,000	
1909-S	2,774,925	550	600	800	1,300	5,200	
1910 . . _167_	482,000	550	600	800	1,800	7,000	41,000
1910-D	429,000	550	600	800	1,050	3,600	
1910-S	2,128,250	550	600	900	2,100	14,000	
1911 . . _100_	197,250	550	600	1,400	2,800	14,000	36,000
1911-D	846,500	550	600	800	900	1,700	
1911-S	775,750	550	600	800	1,200	4,400	
1912 . . _74_	149,750	550	600	1,700	3,300	15,000	41,000
1913 . . _58_	168,780	550	600	2,200	5,500	22,000	43,000
1913-D	393,500	550	600	900	1,900	5,000	
1913-S	34,000	750	1,100	4,750	11,000	43,000	
1914 . . _70_	95,250	550	625	1,500	3,000	14,000	41,000
1914-D	453,000	550	600	800	1,000	3,500	
1914-S	1,498,000	550	600	750	850	2,200	
1915 . . _50_	152,000	550	600	1,600	3,300	11,000	43,000
1915-S	567,500	550	600	750	850	2,100	
1916-S	796,000	550	600	750	850	2,100	
1920	228,250	550	600	1,500	5,000	20,000	
1920-S	558,000	9,000	20,000	45,000	70,000	95,000	
1921	528,500	13,000	42,000	65,000	95,000	140,000	

	Mintage	AU-50	MS-60	MS-63	MS-64	MS-65	Proof-65
1922	1,375,500	550	575	750	850	4,000	
1922-S	2,658,000	700	800	1,600	5,500	40,000	
1923	566,000	550	575	750	1,050	6,000	
1923-D	1,702,250	550	600	750	900	1,600	
1924	4,323,500	550	575	750	800	1,350	
1924-D	3,049,500	1,300	1,900	6,000	18,000	55,000	
1924-S	2,927,500	1,100	2,200	5,700	19,000	53,000	
1925	2,831,750	550	575	750	800	1,450	
1925-D	2,938,500	1,400	3,000	8,000	25,000	55,000	
1925-S	3,776,500	1,200	5,500	26,000	40,000	75,500	
1926	816,750	550	575	750	800	1,350	
1926-D	481,000	2,400	9,000	26,000	40,000	60,000	
1926-S	2,041,500	1,300	2,000	3,500	6,200	45,000	
1927	2,946,750	550	575	750	800	1,350	
1927-D	180,000	130,000	170,000	250,000	325,000	425,000	
1927-S	3,107,000	5,000	12,000	26,000	40,000	90,000	
1928	8,816,000	550	575	750	800	1,350	
1929	1,779,750	8,400	15,000	20,000	30,000	65,000	
1930-S	74,000	9,000	18,000	36,000	45,000	80,000	
1931	2,938,250	9,000	15,000	25,000	33,000	75,000	
1931-D	106,500	9,000	15,000	25,000	36,000	75,000	
1932	1,101,750	11,000	14,500	23,000	27,000	52,500	
1933	445,500					(minted but never officially issued)	

COMMEMORATIVE COINS (1892–PRESENT)

Traditional Commemoratives (1892–1954)

	Number Minted	Number Melted	EF-40	MS-63	MS-65	Proof-63
COLUMBIAN EXPOSITION HALF DOLLARS						
1892 . . 104	949,896	None	$10.00	$110	$590	$8,000
1893 . . 3 reported	4,052,104	2,501,700	10.00	100	700	15,000
ISABELLA QUARTER DOLLAR						
1893 . . 20	39,120	15,809	$190	$550	$1,700	$10,000

LAFAYETTE SILVER DOLLAR

	Number Minted	Number Melted	EF-40	MS-63	MS-65	Proof-63
1900 . . *1 known*	50,025	14,000	$190	$1,000	$6,250	100,000

LOUISIANA PURCHASE EXPOSITION GOLD DOLLARS

	Number Minted	Number Melted	EF-40	MS-63	MS-65	Proof-63
Combined total	250,058	215,250				
1903 Jefferson . . *100* . . .			$300	$800	$2,200	$8,000
1903 McKinley . . *100* . . .			285	765	2,200	8,000

LEWIS AND CLARK EXPOSITION GOLD DOLLARS

	Number Minted	Number Melted	EF-40	MS-63	MS-65	Proof-63
1904 . . *about 7.*	25,021	15,003	$400	$2,000	$5,800	$50,000
1905 . . *about 4.*	35,037	25,000	400	2,200	13,000	50,000

PANAMA-PACIFIC EXPOSITION HALF DOLLAR

	Number Minted	Number Melted	EF-40	MS-63	MS-65	Proof-63
1915-S . . *2 reported*	60,028	32,896	$145	$640	$2,050	$35,000

PANAMA-PACIFIC EXPOSITION GOLD DOLLAR

	Number Minted	Number Melted	EF-40	MS-63	MS-65	Proof-63
1915-S . . *1 reported*	25,033	10,034	275	675	2,200	75,000

PANAMA-PACIFIC EXPOSITION QUARTER EAGLE ($2.50 GOLD PIECE)

	Number Minted	Number Melted	EF-40	MS-63	MS-65	Proof-63
1915-S . . . *1 reported*	10,016	3,268	1,050	2,600	4,100	250,000

PANAMA-PACIFIC EXPOSITION $50 GOLD PIECES

1915-S round	1,510	1,027	18,500	30,000	95,000
1915-S octagonal	1,509	864	18,000	28,000	85,000

MCKINLEY MEMORIAL GOLD DOLLARS
1916 . . *at least 6*	20,020	10,049	$250	$650	$2,200	$30,000
1917 . . *at least 5*	10,009	14	275	1,200	3,400	30,000

ILLINOIS CENTENNIAL HALF DOLLAR
1918 . . *at least 2*	100,056	None	$60.00	$85.00	$550	$30,000

MAINE CENTENNIAL HALF DOLLAR
1920 . . *1 known*	50,027	None	$60.00	$120	$320	$25,000

PILGRIM TERCENTENARY HALF DOLLARS
1920 . . *2 reported*	200,110	48,000	$65.00	$70.00	$430	$25,000
1921 . . *1 reported*	100,052	80,000	85.00	125	850	25,000

	Number Minted	Number Melted	EF-40	MS-63	MS-65	Proof-63
ALABAMA CENTENNIAL HALF DOLLARS						
1921 with 2×2 . . . *1*	6,005	None	$130	$600	$2,900	$50,000
1921 without 2×2	64,038	5,000	65.00	450	2,800	
MISSOURI CENTENNIAL HALF DOLLARS						
1921 with 2×4 . . . *1*	4,999	None	$240	$700	$4,400	$85,000
1921 without 2×4	45,028	29,600	160	575	4,000	
GRANT MEMORIAL HALF DOLLARS						
1922 with star . . *4 reported*	5,002	750	$410	$1,675	$7,500	$50,000
1922 without star . . *4*						
reported	95,051	27,650	60.00	165	800	50,000
GRANT MEMORIAL GOLD DOLLARS						
1922 with star.	5,016	None	950	1,825	2,600	
1922 without star	5,000	None	1,200	1,650	2,600	
MONROE DOCTRINE CENTENNIAL HALF DOLLAR						
1923-S . . *2 reported*	274,075	None	$31.00	$105.00	$2,250	$25,000
HUGUENOT-WALLOON TERCENTENARY HALF DOLLAR						
1924 . . *1 reported*	142,079	None	$60.00	$90.00	$650	$25,000
CALIFORNIA DIAMOND JUBILEE HALF DOLLAR						
1925-S . . *1 reported*. . . .	150,199	63,606	$80.00	$220	$700	$50,000
FORT VANCOUVER CENTENNIAL HALF DOLLAR						
1925 . . *3 reported*	50,025	35,034	$180	$400	$900	$25,000
LEXINGTON-CONCORD SESQUICENTENNIAL HALF DOLLAR						
1925 . . *1 reported*	162,098	86	$60.00	$90.00	$575	$25,000
STONE MOUNTAIN HALF DOLLAR						
1925 . . *1 reported*	2,314,708	1,000,000	$35.00	$45.00	$185	$30,000
OREGON TRAIL MEMORIAL HALF DOLLARS						
1926 . . *2 known*	48,028	75	$75.00	$120	$230	$35,000
1926-S	100,055	17,000	75.00	120	235	
1928	50,028	44,000	135	160	350	
1933-D	5,250	242	225	280	425	
1934-D	7,006	None	115	185	350	
1936	10,006	None	105	135	240	
1936-S	5,006	None	120	175	335	
1937-D	12,008	None	90.00	220	230	
1938	6,006	None	190	220	300	
1938-D	6,005	None	190	220	300	

COMMEMORATIVE COINS (1892–PRESENT)

	Number Minted	Number Melted	EF-40	MS-63	MS-65	Proof-63
1938-S	6,006	None	190	200	300	
1939.	3,004	None	400	450	675	
1939-D	3,004	None	400	450	675	
1939-S	3,005	None	400	450	675	

SESQUICENTENNIAL OF AMERICAN INDEPENDENCE HALF DOLLAR

1926 . . 4 reported	1,000,524	859,408	$60.00	$165	$4,250	$50,000

SESQUICENTENNIAL OF AMERICAN INDEPENDENCE QUARTER EAGLE ($2.50 GOLD PIECE)

1926 . . 2 reported	200,224	154,207	250	585	4,750	250,000

VERMONT SESQUICENTENNIAL HALF DOLLAR

1927 . . 1 reported	40,033	11,892	$110	$180	$925	$30,000

HAWAIIAN SESQUICENTENNIAL HALF DOLLAR

1928 . . 50	9,958	None	$775	$1,600	$4,500	$18,000

DANIEL BOONE BICENTENNIAL HALF DOLLARS

1934. . . . . . , , . . .	10,007	None	$75.00	$85.00	$145	
1935 plain	10,010	None	75.00	80.00	140	
1935-D plain	5,005	None	75.00	80.00	140	
1935-S plain	5,005	None	75.00	100.00	140	
1935 with small 1934 on reverse.	10,008	None	75.00	90.00	140	
1935-D with small 1934 on reverse.	2,003	None	275	300	775	
1935-S with small 1934 on reverse.	2,004	None	275	300	775	
1936.	12,012	None	75.00	80.00	140	
1936-D	5,005	None	75.00	80.00	140	
1936-S	5,006	None	75.00	80.00	140	
1937 . . 1 known proof	15,009	9,810	75.00	80.00	140	25,000
1937-D . . 1 known proof	7,505	5,000	180	275	500	25,000
1937-S . . 1 known proof	5,005	2,500	180	275	500	25,000
1938.	5,005	2,905	225	300	475	
1938-D	5,005	2,905	225	300	475	
1938-S	5,006	2,906	225	300	475	

MARYLAND TERCENTENARY HALF DOLLAR

1934 . . 3 known	25,012	None	$105	$130	$330	$30,000

TEXAS INDEPENDENCE CENTENNIAL HALF DOLLARS

1934.	205,113	143,650	$70.00	$90.00	$125	
1935.	10,008	12	70.00	90.00	125	

	Number Minted	Number Melted	EF-40	MS-63	MS-65	Proof-63
1935-D	10,007	None	70.00	90.00	125	
1935-S	10,008	None	70.00	90.00	125	
1936	10,008	1,097	70.00	90.00	120	
1936-D	10,007	968	70.00	90.00	120	
1936-S	10,008	943	70.00	90.00	120	
1937	8,005	1,434	80.00	100	195	
1937-D	8,006	1,401	80.00	100	195	
1937-S	8,007	1,370	80.00	100	195	
1938	5,005	1,225	150	280	350	
1938-D	5,005	1,230	150	280	350	
1938-S	5,006	1,192	150	280	350	

ARKANSAS CENTENNIAL HALF DOLLARS

	Number Minted	Number Melted	EF-40	MS-63	MS-65	Proof-63
1935 . . *1 reported*	13,011	None	$65.00	$80.00	$260	$30,000
1935-D	5,505	None	65.00	85.00	260	
1935-S	5,506	None	65.00	85.00	260	
1936	10,010	350	65.00	80.00	260	
1936-D	10,010	350	65.00	80.00	260	
1936-S	10,012	350	65.00	80.00	260	
1937	5,505	None	70.00	90.00	450	
1937-D	5,505	None	70.00	95.00	450	
1937-S	5,506	None	70.00	95.00	450	
1938 . . *1 known proof*	6,006	2,850	100	140	750	40,000
1938-D . . *1 known proof*	6,005	2,850	100	140	750	40,000
1938-S . . *1 known proof*	6,006	2,850	100	140	750	40,000
1939	2,104	None	225	225	900	
1939-D	2,104	None	225	225	900	
1939-S	2,105	None	225	225	900	

	Number Minted	Number Melted	EF-40	MS-63	MS-65	Proof-63
CONNECTICUT TERCENTENARY HALF DOLLAR						
1935 . . *about 6*	25,012	None	$160	$190	$610	$45,000
HUDSON, N.Y., SESQUICENTENNIAL HALF DOLLAR						
1935 . . *2 reported*	10,006	None	$380	$450	$875	$45,000
OLD SPANISH TRAIL HALF DOLLAR						
1935 . . *2 reported*	10,006	None	$625	$725	$925	$45,000
SAN DIEGO/CALIFORNIA-PACIFIC EXPOSITION HALF DOLLARS						
1935-S . . *2 reported*	250,130	180,000	$45.00	$65.00	$85.00	$20,000
1936-D	180,092	150,000	60.00	75.00	105	
ALBANY, N.Y., CHARTER HALF DOLLAR						
1936	25,013	7,342	$190	$215	$335	
BRIDGEPORT, CONN., CENTENNIAL HALF DOLLAR						
1936	25,015	None	$90.00	$100	$300	
CINCINNATI MUSIC CENTER HALF DOLLARS						
1936	5,005	None	$195	$240	$350	
1936-D	5,005	None	195	240	325	
1936-S	5,006	None	195	280	475	
CLEVELAND CENTENNIAL/GREAT LAKES EXPOSITION HALF DOLLAR						
1936	50,030	None	$50.00	$60.00	$220	
COLUMBIA, S.C., SESQUICENTENNIAL HALF DOLLARS						
1936	9,007	None	$150	$180	$200	
1936-D	8,009	None	150	180	200	
1936-S	8,007	None	150	180	220	
DELAWARE TERCENTENARY HALF DOLLAR						
1936	25,015	4,022	$140	$180	$370	
ELGIN, ILL., CENTENNIAL HALF DOLLAR						
1936	25,014	5,000	$170	$195	$180	—
GETTYSBURG BATTLE HALF DOLLAR						
1936	50,028	23,100	$210	$240	$510	
LONG ISLAND TERCENTENARY HALF DOLLAR						
1936	100,053	18,227	$50.00	$60.00	$365	
LYNCHBURG, VA., SESQUICENTENNIAL HALF DOLLAR						
1936	20,013	None	$130	$160	$260	

	Number Minted	Number Melted	EF-40	MS-63	MS-65	Proof-63
NORFOLK, VA., TERCENTENARY HALF DOLLAR						
1936	25,013	8,077	$330	$360	$400	
PROVIDENCE, R.I., TERCENTENARY HALF DOLLARS						
1936	20,013	None	$60.00	$75.00	$310	
1936-D	15,010	None	60.00	80.00	310	
1936-S	15,011	None	60.00	80.00	350	
ROBINSON-ARKANSAS CENTENNIAL HALF DOLLAR						
1936	25,256	None	$65.00	$85.00	$280	
SAN FRANCISCO-OAKLAND BAY BRIDGE HALF DOLLAR						
1936-S	100,055	28,631	$70.00	$150	$275	
WISCONSIN TERRITORIAL CENTENNIAL HALF DOLLAR						
1936	25,015	None	$140	$160	$190	
YORK COUNTY, MAINE, TERCENTENARY HALF DOLLAR						
1936	25,015	None	$135	$140	$165	
ANTIETAM BATTLE HALF DOLLAR						
1937	50,028	32,000	$335	$385	$550	
ROANOKE ISLAND, N.C., HALF DOLLAR						
1937	49,080	21,000	$165	$185	$200	
NEW ROCHELLE, N.Y., HALF DOLLAR						
1938 . . *about 10*	25,003	9,749	$225	$285	$380	$30,000
IOWA STATEHOOD CENTENNIAL HALF DOLLAR						
1946	100,057	None	$55.00	$67.00	$95.00	

BOOKER T. WASHINGTON HALF DOLLARS

	Number Minted	Number Melted	EF-40	MS-63	MS-65	Proof-63
1946	1,000,546	Unknown	$8.00	$13.00	$40.00	
1946-D	200,113	Unknown	8.00	13.00	40.00	
1946-S	500,279	Unknown	8.00	13.00	40.00	
1947	100,017	Unknown	8.00	20.00	125	
1947-D	100,017	Unknown	8.00	20.00	90.00	
1947-S	100,017	Unknown	8.00	20.00	90.00	
1948	20,005	12,000	15.00	30.00	50.00	
1948-D	20,005	12,000	15.00	30.00	50.00	
1948-S	20,005	12,000	15.00	30.00	50.00	
1949	12,004	6,000	20.00	60.00	70.00	
1949-D	12,004	6,000	20.00	60.00	70.00	
1949-S	12,004	6,000	20.00	60.00	70.00	
1950	12,004	6,000	18.00	30.00	50.00	
1950-D	12,004	6,000	18.00	30.00	50.00	
1950-S	512,091	Unknown	18.00	30.00	50.00	
1951	510,082	Unknown	15.00	35.00	50.00	
1951-D	12,004	5,000	15.00	35.00	50.00	
1951-S	12,004	5,000	15.00	35.00	50.00	

GEORGE WASHINGTON CARVER/BOOKER T. WASHINGTON HALF DOLLARS

	Number Minted	Number Melted	EF-40	MS-63	MS-65	Proof-63
1951	110,018*	Unknown	$8.00	$20.00	$350	
1951-D	10,004*	Unknown	8.00	25.00	150	
1951-S	10,004*	Unknown	8.00	25.00	80.00	
1952	2,006,292*	Unknown	8.00	15.00	50.00	
1952-D	8,006*	Unknown	10.00	25.00	350	
1952-S	8,006*	Unknown	10.00	25.00	80.00	

	Number Minted	Number Melted	EF-40	MS-63	MS-65	Proof-63
1953	8,003*	Unknown	10.00	20.00	175	
1953-D	8,003*	Unknown	10.00	20.00	300	
1953-S	108,020*	Unknown	8.00	20.00	80.00	
1954	12,006*	Unknown	8.00	20.00	100	
1954-D	12,006*	Unknown	10.00	20.00	350	
1954-S	122,024*	Unknown	8.00	20.00	80.00	

* These are net mintages, after melting. The quantities actually minted and melted are unknown.

Modern Commemoratives (1982–Present)

(NOTE: For commemorative coins issued since 1982, the U.S. Mint has not disclosed the number actually minted and the number melted. The figures shown here are net mintages furnished by the Mint. The George Washington half dollar is of traditional 90-percent-silver composition. All other half dollars in the modern commemorative series are of copper-nickel clad composition, with no precious-metal content.)

	Net Mintage	MS-65	Proof-67
GEORGE WASHINGTON HALF DOLLAR			
1982-D uncirculated	2,210,458	$3.50	
1982-S proof	4,894,044	—	$3.50
LOS ANGELES OLYMPIC SILVER DOLLARS			
1983-P uncirculated	294,543	$9.00	
1983-D uncirculated	174,014	10.00	
1983-S uncirculated	174,014	10.00	
1983-S proof	1,577,025	—	$7.50
1984-P uncirculated	217,954	13.00	
1984-D uncirculated	116,675	23.00	
1984-S uncirculated	116,675	23.00	
1984-S proof	1,801,210	—	9.50
LOS ANGELES OLYMPIC EAGLES ($10 GOLD PIECES)			
1984-P proof	33,309	—	275
1984-D proof	34,533	—	250
1984-S proof	48,551	—	220
1984-W uncirculated	75,886	220	

	Net Mintage	MS-65	Proof-67
1984-W proof.	*381,085*	—	220

STATUE OF LIBERTY HALF DOLLARS
1986-D uncirculated.	928,008	$3.50	
1986-S proof	*6,925,627*	—	$3.25

STATUE OF LIBERTY SILVER DOLLARS
1986-P uncirculated	723,635	8.00	
1986-S proof	*6,414,638*	—	7.75

STATUE OF LIBERTY HALF EAGLES ($5 GOLD PIECES)
1986-W uncirculated	95,248	125	
1986-W proof.	*404,013*	—	125

CONSTITUTION BICENTENNIAL SILVER DOLLARS
1987-P uncirculated	451,629	$7.50	
1987-S proof	*2,747,116*	—	$7.00

CONSTITUTION BICENTENNIAL HALF EAGLES ($5 GOLD PIECES)
1987-W uncirculated	214,225	125	
1987-W proof.	*651,659*	—	125

1988 OLYMPIC SILVER DOLLARS
1988-D uncirculated.	191,368	$10.00	
1988-S proof	*1,359,366*	—	$7.00

1988 OLYMPIC HALF EAGLES ($5 GOLD PIECES)
1988-W uncirculated	62,913	$120	
1988-W proof.	*281,465*	—	$120

CONGRESS BICENTENNIAL HALF DOLLARS
1989-D uncirculated.	163,753	$12.00	
1989-S proof	*767,897*	—	$7.00

CONGRESS BICENTENNIAL SILVER DOLLARS
1989-D uncirculated.	135,203	18.00	
1989-S proof	*762,198*	—	13.00

CONGRESS BICENTENNIAL HALF EAGLES ($5 GOLD PIECES)
1989-W uncirculated	46,899	125	
1989-W proof.	*164,690*	—	125

EISENHOWER CENTENNIAL SILVER DOLLARS
1990-W uncirculated	239,777	$18.00	
1990-P proof	*1,137,805*	—	$10.00

	Net Mintage	MS-65	Proof-67
KOREAN WAR MEMORIAL SILVER DOLLARS			
1991-D uncirculated.	213,049	$15.00	
1991-S proof	618,488		$14.00
MOUNT RUSHMORE 50TH ANNIVERSARY HALF DOLLARS			
1991-D uncirculated.	172,754	$10.00	
1991-S proof	753,257	—	$10.00
MOUNT RUSHMORE 50TH ANNIVERSARY SILVER DOLLARS			
1991-P uncirculated	133,139	25.00	
1991-S proof	738,419	—	21.00
MOUNT RUSHMORE 50TH ANNIVERSARY HALF EAGLES ($5 GOLD PIECES)			
1991-W uncirculated	31,959	125	
1991-W proof.	111,991	—	125
UNITED SERVICE ORGANIZATIONS (USO) SILVER DOLLARS			
1991-D uncirculated.	124,958	$25.00	
1991-S proof	321,275	—	$16.00
1992 OLYMPIC HALF DOLLARS			
1992-D uncirculated.	161,607	$5.00	
1992-S proof	519,645	—	$7.00
1992 OLYMPIC SILVER DOLLARS			
1992-D uncirculated.	187,552	$22	
1992-S proof	504,505	—	$25
1992 OLYMPIC HALF EAGLES ($5 GOLD PIECES)			
1992-D uncirculated.	27,732	$130	
1992-S proof	77,313	—	$130
1992 WHITE HOUSE SILVER DOLLARS			
1992-D uncirculated.	123,803	$40.00	
1992-W proof.	375,851	—	$41.00
1992 COLUMBUS QUINCENTENARY HALF DOLLARS			
1992-D uncirculated.	135,702	$9.00	
1992-S proof	390,154	—	$9.00
1992 COLUMBUS QUINCENTENARY SILVER DOLLARS			
1992-D uncirculated.	106,949	$24.00	
1992-P proof	385,241	—	$23.00
1992 COLUMBUS QUINCENTENARY HALF EAGLES ($5 GOLD PIECES)			
1992-W uncirculated	24,329	$170	
1992-W proof.	79,730	—	$180

COMMEMORATIVE COINS (1892–PRESENT)

	Net Mintage	MS-65	Proof-67
1993 BILL OF RIGHTS HALF DOLLARS (SILVER)			
1993-W uncirculated	193,346*	$12.00	
1993-S proof	586,315*	—	$7.50
1993 BILL OF RIGHTS SILVER DOLLARS			
1993-D uncirculated	98,383*	$18.00	
1993-S proof	534,001*	—	$15.00
1993 BILL OF RIGHTS HALF EAGLES ($5 GOLD PIECES)			
1993-W uncirculated	23,266*	$160	
1993-W proof	78,651*	—	$150
1993 WORLD WAR II HALF DOLLARS			
1993-P uncirculated	200,271	$7.00	—
1993-P proof	316,681*	—	$9.00
1993 WORLD WAR II SILVER DOLLARS			
1993-D uncirculated	107,266	$24.50	—
1993-W proof	341,626	—	$25.00
1993 WORLD WAR II HALF EAGLES ($5 GOLD PIECES)			
1993-W uncirculated	23,668	$160	—
1993-W proof	67,011	—	$130
1994 WORLD CUP SOCCER HALF DOLLARS			
1994-D uncirculated	169,366*	7.25	
1994-P proof	608,064*	—	8.75
1994 WORLD CUP SOCCER SILVER DOLLARS			
1994-D uncirculated	80, 602*	22.00	
1994-S proof	576,452*	—	25.00
1994 WORLD CUP HALF EAGLES ($5 GOLD PIECES)			
1994-W uncirculated	22,463*	160	
1994-W proof	89,615*	—	160
1994 THOMAS JEFFERSON 250TH ANNIVERSARY SILVER DOLLARS			
1994-P uncirculated	600,000	33.00	
1994-S proof	600,000	—	36.00
1994 PRISONER OF WAR SILVER DOLLARS			
1994-W uncirculated	—	33.00	
1994-S proof	—	—	36.00
1994 VIETNAM VETERANS MEMORIAL SILVER DOLLARS			
1994-W uncirculated	—	31.00	
1994-P proof	—	—	29.00

	Net Mintage	MS-65	Proof-67

1994 WOMEN IN MILITARY SERVICE FOR AMERICA SILVER DOLLARS

	Net Mintage	MS-65	Proof-67
1994-W uncirculated	—	33.00	
1994-P proof	—	—	28.00

1994 U.S. CAPITOL SILVER DOLLARS

1994-D uncirculated	—	32.00	
1994-S proof	—	—	37.00

1995 CIVIL WAR BATTLEFIELD HALF DOLLARS

1995-S uncirculated	—	10.25	
1995-S proof	—	—	11.75

1995 CIVIL WAR BATTLEFIELD SILVER DOLLARS

1995-P uncirculated	—	29.00	
1995-S proof	—	—	32.00

1995 CIVIL WAR BATTLEFIELD HALF EAGLES ($5 GOLD PIECES)

1995-W uncirculated	—	190	
1995-W proof	—	—	225

1995 OLYMPIC BASKETBALL HALF DOLLARS

1995-D uncirculated	—	11.50	
1995-S proof	—	—	12.50

1995 OLYMPIC GYMNAST SILVER DOLLARS

1995-D uncirculated	—	32.00	
1995-P proof	—	—	35.00

1995 OLYMPIC BLIND RUNNER SILVER DOLLARS

1995-D uncirculated	—	32.00	
1995-P proof	—	—	35.00

1995 OLYMPIC TORCH RUNNER GOLD HALF EAGLES ($5 GOLD PIECES)

1995-W uncirculated	—	250	
1995-W proof	—	—	260

1995 SPECIAL OLYMPIC WORLD GAMES SILVER DOLLARS (PORTRAIT OF EUNICE KENNEDY SHRIVER)

1995-W uncirculated	—	32.00	
1995-P proof	—	—	37.00

* Tentative.

AMERICAN EAGLE BULLION COINS (1986–PRESENT)

$5 Gold (¹/₁₀ Ounce)

	Mintage	MS-67	Proof-67
1986 (MCMLXXXVI) uncirculated	912,609	$50.00	
1987 (MCMLXXXVII) uncirculated	580,266	50.00	
1988 (MCMLXXXVIII) uncirculated	159,500	50.00	
1988-P (MCMLXXXVIII) proof	*143,881*	—	$65.00
1989 (MCMLXXXIX) uncirculated	264,790	50.00	
1989-P (MCMLXXXIX) proof	*84,647*	—	65.00
1990 (MCMXC) uncirculated	210,210	50.00	
1990-P (MCMXC) proof	*99,349*	—	72.50
1991 (MCMXCI) uncirculated	165,200	50.00	
1991-P (MCMXCI) proof	*70,334*	—	72.50
1992 uncirculated	209,300	50.00	
1992-P proof	*64,874*	—	72.50
1993 uncirculated	210,709	50.00	
1993-P proof	*58,649*	—	72.50
1994 uncirculated	206,380	50.00	
1994-P proof	*62,794*	—	72.50
1995 uncirculated	—	50.00	
1995-P proof	—	—	72.50

$10 Gold (¹/₄ Ounce)

	Mintage	MS-67	Proof-67
1986 (MCMLXXXVI) uncirculated	726,031	$125	
1987 (MCMLXXXVII) uncirculated	269,255	125	
1988 (MCMLXXXVIII) uncirculated	49,000	125	
1988-P (MCMLXXXVIII) proof	*98,028*	—	$140
1989 (MCMLXXXIX) uncirculated	81,789	125	
1989-P (MCMLXXXIX) proof	*54,170*	—	140
1990 (MCMXC) uncirculated	41,000	125	
1990-P (MCMXC) proof	*62,674*	—	145
1991 (MCMXCI) uncirculated	36,100	125	
1991-P (MCMXCI) proof	*50,839*	—	145
1992 uncirculated	59,546	125	
1992-P proof	*46,269*	—	145
1993 uncirculated	71,864	125	
1993-P proof	*46,464*	—	145
1994 uncirculated	72,650	125	

AMERICAN EAGLE BULLION COINS (1986–PRESENT)

	Mintage	MS-67	Proof-67
1994-P proof	48,128	—	145
1995 uncirculated	—	125	
1995 proof	—	—	145

$25 Gold (½ Ounce)

	Mintage	MS-67	Proof-67
1986 (MCMLXXXVI) uncirculated	599,566	$250	
1987 (MCMLXXXVII) uncirculated	131,255	250	
1987-P (MCMLXXXVII) proof	143,398	—	$265
1988 (MCMLXXXVIII) uncirculated	45,000	250	
1988-P (MCMLXXXVIII) proof	76,528	—	275
1989 (MCMLXXXIX) uncirculated	44,829	250	
1989-P (MCMLXXXIX) proof	44,798	—	285
1990 (MCMXC) uncirculated	31,000	300	
1990-P (MCMXCI) proof	51,636	—	290
1991 (MCMXCI) uncirculated	24,100	250	
1991-P (MCMXCI) proof	53,125	—	275
1992 uncirculated	54,404	250	
1992-P proof	40,976	—	275
1993 uncirculated	73,324	250	
1993-P proof	43,819	—	275
1994 uncirculated	62,400	250	
1994-P proof	44,595	—	275
1995 uncirculated	—	250	
1995 proof	—	—	275

$50 Gold (1 Ounce)

	Mintage	MS-67	Proof-67
1986 (MCMLXXXVI) uncirculated	1,362,650	$400	
1986-W (MCMLXXXVI) proof	446,290	—	$410
1987 (MCMLXXXVII) uncirculated	1,045,500	400	
1987-W (MCMLXXXVII) proof	147,498	—	420
1988 (MCMLXXXVIII) uncirculated	465,000	400	
1988-W (MCMLXXXVIII) proof	87,133	—	430
1989 (MCMLXXXIX) uncirculated	415,790	400	
1989-W (MCMLXXXIX) proof	54,570	—	430
1990 (MCMXC) uncirculated	373,210	400	
1990-W (MCMXC) proof	62,401	—	430
1991 (MCMXCI) uncirculated	243,100	400	

AMERICAN EAGLE BULLION COINS (1986–PRESENT)

	Mintage	MS-67	Proof-67
1991-W (MCMXCI) proof	*50,411*	—	520
1992 uncirculated	275,000	400	
1992-W proof	*44,826*	—	550
1993 uncirculated	480,192	400	
1993-W proof	*34,369*	—	550
1994 uncirculated	221,663	400	
1994-W proof	*46,741*	—	550
1995 uncirculated	—	400	
1995-W proof	—	—	550

Proof Gold Coin Sets

1987 ($50 and $25 coins only)	$700
1988 ($50 and $25 coins only)	750
1989 (all four coins)	1,000
1990 (all four coins)	1,050
1991 (all four coins)	1,050
1992 (all four coins)	1,050
1993 (all four coins)	1,050
1994 (all four coins)	1,050
1995 (all four coins)	1,050

$1 Silver (1 Ounce)

	Mintage	MS-67	Proof-67
1986 uncirculated	5,393,005	$12.50	
1986-S proof	*1,446,778*	—	$20.00
1987 uncirculated	11,442,335	6.00	
1987-S proof	*904,732*	—	20.00
1988 uncirculated	5,004,500	7.50	
1988-S proof	*557,370*	—	80.00
1989 uncirculated	5,203,327	7.50	
1989-S proof	*617,694*	—	20.00
1990 uncirculated	5,840,210	7.50	
1990-S proof	*695,510*	—	24.00
1991 uncirculated	7,191,066	6.00	
1991-S proof	*511,924*	—	27.50
1992 uncirculated	5,540,068	6.00	
1992-S proof	*498,543*	—	24.00
1993 uncirculated	6,763,762	6.00	

	Mintage	MS-67	Proof-67
1993-S proof	403,625	—	24.00
1994 uncirculated	4,227,319	6.00	
1994-S proof	355,531	—	24.00

MODERN PROOF SETS (1950–PRESENT)

(NOTE: Since 1955, the United States Mint has packaged its annual proof sets in sealed holders. Proof sets made up of coins that have been removed from those holders and then reassembled may be worth substantially less than the prices listed here.)

	Number Sold	Issue Price	Market Value
1950	51,386	$2.10	$335
1951	57,500	2.10	250
1952	81,980	2.10	135
1953	128,800	2.10	100
1954	233,300	2.10	61.00
1955	378,200	2.10	52.00
1956	669,384	2.10	22.00
1957	1,247,952	2.10	11.00
1958	875,652	2.10	16.00
1959	1,149,291	2.10	13.00
1960 combined total	1,691,602	2.10	
1960 with small-date cent			16.00
1960 with large-date cent			8.00
1961	3,028,244	2.10	6.00
1962	3,218,019	2.10	6.50
1963	3,075,645	2.10	6.40
1964	3,950,762	2.10	6.50
1968-S	3,041,506	5.00	4.00
1969-S	2,934,631	5.00	3.50
1970-S combined total	2,632,810	5.00	
1970-S with small-date cent			80.00
1970-S with large-date cent			6.40
1970-S with no-S dime			575
1971-S combined total	3,220,733	5.00	
1971-S with regular nickel			3.00
1971-S with no-S nickel			800
1972-S	3,260,996	5.00	3.50
1973-S	2,760,339	7.00	4.00

MODERN PROOF SETS (1950-PRESENT)

	Number Sold	Issue Price	Market Value
1974-S	2,612,568	7.00	4.25
1975-S	2,845,450	7.00	5.50
1976-S	4,149,730	7.00	7.00
1977-S	3,251,152	9.00	5.00
1978-S	3,127,781	9.00	5.00
1979 combined total	3,677,175	9.00	
1979-S with clear S			56.00
1979-S with clogged S			5.50
1980-S	3,554,806	10.00	6.00
1981-S	4,063,083	11.00	6.50
1982-S	3,857,479	11.00	3.80
1983-S combined total	3,138,765	11.00	
1983-S with regular dime.			5.00
1983-S with no-S dime			420
1983-S Prestige set.	140,361	59.00	90.00
1984-S	2,748,430	11.00	8.50
1984-S Prestige set.	316,680	59.00	22.00
1985-S	3,362,821	11.00	5.50
1986-S	2,411,180	11.00	15.00
1986-S Prestige set.	599,317	48.50	21.00
1987-S	3,356,738	11.00	5.00
1987-S Prestige set.	435,495	45.00	18.00
1988-S	3,031,287	11.00	8.00
1988-S Prestige set.	231,661	45.00	23.00
1989-S	3,005,776	11.00	8.00
1989-S Prestige set.	209,952	52.00	30.00
1990-S with regular cent	2,789,378	11.00	17.00
1990-S with no-S cent	3,555	11.00	2,900
1990-S Prestige set.	506,126	46.00	47.50
1991-S	2,610,833	11.00	12.50
1991-S Prestige set.	256,954	49.00	70.00
1992-S	2,675,618	12.50*	15.00
1992-S silver set	1,009,586	21.00*	25.00
1992-S Prestige set.	183,285	56.00	60.00
1992-S Premier silver set	308,055	37.00	40.00
1993-S	2,337,819	12.50	15.00
1993-S silver set	589,712	21.00	20.00
1993-S Prestige set.	232,063	57.00	60.00
1993-S Premier silver set	201,262	37.00	39.00
1994-S	2,260,631	12.50	15.00
1994-S silver set	628,439	21.00	20.00
1994-S Prestige set.	175,670	56.00	60.00

	Number Sold	Issue Price	Market Value
1994-S Premier silver set	148,052	37.00	39.00
1995-S	—	12.50	15.00
1995-S silver set	—	21.00	20.00
1995-S Prestige set.	—	—	—
1995-S Premier silver set	—	—	39.00

* Some 1992-S proof sets were sold at an issue price of $11, then the price was raised to $12.50. Some 1992-S silver proof sets were sold at an issue price of $18.50, then the price was raised to $21.

SPECIAL MINT SETS (1965–1967)

	Number Sold	Issue Price	Market Value
1965.	2,360,000	$4.00	$4.50
1966.	2,261,583	4.00	5.50
1967.	1,863,344	4.00	7.50

TYPE COINS

Many collectors acquire U.S. coins by "type." This means they purchase just one specimen of a certain kind of coin —one Lincoln cent, for example, to represent the entire series of Lincoln cents. Because they are buying just one coin, they usually acquire a piece that is exceptionally attractive, one in a very high grade or level of preservation. But, to avoid paying a prohibitive premium, they select a date for which the mintage is fairly high—a so-called "common-date" coin. Coins acquired in this fashion are known as "type coins," and many buyers and sellers track the value of U.S. coins as a whole by following the performance of these "type coins."

The following chart was prepared by Heritage Rare Coin Galleries. It provides a convenient look at U.S. type coins and their values. In using it, you will note such terms as "Liberty" and "Indian Head." These refer to elements of the coins' designs. For assistance in identifying these coins, refer to the illustrations accompanying the price listings in Chapter Four.

United States Coins by Type
Values compiled by Heritage Rare Coin Galleries
Dallas, Texas

	MS-60	MS-63	MS-65
HALF CENT	$150	$225	$1,400
LARGE CENT	$150	$225	$700
FLYING EAGLE CENT	$200	$325	$1,800
INDIAN CENT	$20	$35	$110
TWO-CENT PIECE	$60	$140	$300
THREE-CENT NICKEL	$75	$95	$650
THREE-CENT SILVER	$125	$275	$900
SHIELD NICKEL	$90	$150	$500
"V" OR LIBERTY NICKEL	$60	$75	$400
BUFFALO NICKEL	$8	$10	$30
CAPPED BUST HALF DIME	$275	$500	$2,300
LIBERTY SEATED HALF DIME	$115	$200	$1,200
CAPPED BUST DIME	$525	$900	$5,000
LIBERTY SEATED DIME	$115	$150	$1,000
BARBER DIME	$110	$125	$600
MERCURY DIME	$4	$9	$18
TWENTY-CENT PIECE	$350	$750	$4,000
CAPPED BUST QUARTER	$775	$1,500	$12,000

TYPE COINS

	MS-60	MS-63	MS-65
LIBERTY SEATED QUARTER	$210	$400	$1,300
BARBER QUARTER	$160	$375	$1,100
LIBERTY STANDING QUARTER	$85	$150	$325
CAPPED BUST HALF	$500	$1,400	$5,000
LIBERTY SEATED HALF	$300	$500	$2,300
BARBER HALF	$325	$600	$1,900
LIBERTY WALKING HALF	$20	$30	$85
LIBERTY SEATED DOLLAR	$1,000	$2,000	$22,000
MORGAN DOLLAR	$15	$30	$85
PEACE DOLLAR	$9	$20	$150
ONE DOLLAR GOLD PIECE	$275	$1,350	$2,500
$2.5 LIBERTY GOLD	$225	$725	$2,300
$2.5 INDIAN GOLD	$265	$730	$4,500
$3 GOLD	$1,750	$4,250	$11,000
$5 LIBERTY GOLD	$180	$1,000	$5,000
$5 INDIAN GOLD	$325	$2,500	$10,000
$10 LIBERTY GOLD	$250	$1,100	$5,100
$10 INDIAN GOLD	$390	$1,050	$5,000
$20 LIBERTY GOLD	$420	$700	$4,000
$20 ST. GAUDENS GOLD	$425	$525	$1,300

COIN PERIODICALS

COINage Magazine. Miller Magazines Inc., 4880 Market Street, Ventura, CA 93003. One-year subscription (12 monthly issues) $23, two-year subscription $36. Add $9 per year for all foreign countries, including Canada.

Coins Magazine. Krause Publications Inc., Iola, WI 54990. One-year subscription (12 monthly issues) $19.95, two-year subscription $37.25. Surface rate for other countries: $35.20, except for Canada and Mexico, where the rate is $38.95. Air-mail subscriptions available; write for rates.

Coin World. Amos Press Inc., P.O. Box 150, Sidney, OH 45365. One-year subscription (52 weekly issues) $26, two-year subscription $46. Outside the United States, add $40 per year. Air-mail subscriptions available; write for rates.

Numismatic News. Krause Publications Inc., Iola, WI 54990. Six-month subscription (26 weekly issues) $14.95 U.S., $40.95 foreign, including Canada and Mexico. One-year subscription $27.95 U.S., $79.95 foreign. Two-year subscription $52 U.S., $156 foreign. Special U.S. subscriptions available, including first- and second-class plain-wrapper delivery, regular delivery by United Parcel Service, and second-day and standard overnight delivery by Federal Express. Write for rates.

The Numismatist. American Numismatic Association, 818 North Cascade Avenue, Colorado Springs, CO 80903-3279. Published monthly and mailed to all members of the ANA without cost other than annual dues.

World Coin News. Krause Publications Inc., Iola, WI 54990. Six-month subscription (13 biweekly issues) $12.95 U.S., $24.25 foreign, including Canada and Mexico. One-year subscription $24.95 U.S., $47.25 foreign. Two-year subscription $46.50 U.S., $91.25 foreign. Special U.S. subscriptions available, including first- and second-class plain-wrapper delivery and regular delivery by United Parcel Service. Write for rates.

COIN SPECIFICATIONS

HALF CENTS

Diameter: 23.5 millimeters ($^{15}/_{16}$ of an inch)

Weight: 6.739 grams (0.21666 ounce) in 1793–94 and part of 1795, 5.443 grams (0.175 ounce) thereafter

Composition: all-copper

Edge: Lettered (TWO HUNDRED FOR A DOLLAR) in 1793 and part of 1797, gripped in part of 1797, plain in all other cases

Designers: Adam Eckfeldt (1793), Robert Scot (1794–1808), John Reich (1809–1836), Christian Gobrecht (1840–1857)

LARGE CENTS

Diameter: 25–28 millimeters (about $1^1/_{16}$ inches) in 1793, 27–30 millimeters (about $1^1/_8$ inches) in 1794, 28–29 millimeters (about $1^1/_8$ inches) thereafter

Weight: 13.478 grams (0.433 ounce) in 1793, 1794 and part of 1795, 10.886 grams (0.349 ounce) thereafter

Composition: All-copper

Edge: Vine and bars in part of 1793, lettered (ONE HUNDRED FOR A DOLLAR) in 1793–94 and part of 1795, gripped in part of 1797, plain in all other cases

Designers: Henry Voigt (1793 Chain cent), Adam Eckfeldt (1793 Wreath cent), Joseph Wright and John Smith Gardner (1793–1796 Liberty Cap), Robert Scot (1796–1807), John Reich (1808–1814), Robert Scot (1816–1835), Christian Gobrecht (1835–1857)

FLYING EAGLE CENTS

Diameter: 19 millimeters (³⁄₄ of an inch)
Weight: 4.666 grams (0.150 ounce)
Composition: 88 percent copper, 12 percent nickel
Edge: Plain
Designer: James B. Longacre

INDIAN HEAD CENTS

Diameter: 19 millimeters (³⁄₄ of an inch)
Weight: 4.666 grams (0.150 ounce) from 1859 to 1863 and part of 1864, 3.110 grams (0.099 ounce) in the rest of 1864 and thereafter
Composition: 88 percent copper, 12 percent nickel from 1859 to 1863 and part of 1864; 95 percent copper, 5 percent zinc and tin in the rest of 1864 and thereafter
Edge: Plain
Designer: James B. Longacre

LINCOLN CENTS

Diameter: 19 millimeter (³⁄₄ of an inch)
Weight: 3.110 grams (0.099 ounce) from 1909 to 1981 and part of 1982, except for 1943; 2.689 grams (0.086 ounce) in 1943; 2.5 grams (0.080 ounce) for part of 1982 and thereafter

Composition: 95 percent copper, 5 percent zinc and tin from 1909 to 1961 and part of 1962, except for 1943–46; zinc-plated steel in 1943; 95 percent copper, 5 percent zinc in 1944–46, 1963–1981 and parts of 1962 and 1982; 97.5 percent zinc, 2.5 percent copper (copper-plated zinc) for part of 1982 and thereafter

Edge: Plain

Designers: Victor D. Brenner (obverse from 1909 to date and reverse from 1909 to 1958), Frank Gasparro (reverse from 1959 to date)

TWO-CENT PIECES

Diameter: 23 millimeters (⁹/₁₀ of an inch)
Weight: 6.221 grams (0.200 ounce)
Composition: 95 percent copper, 5 percent zinc and tin
Edge: Plain
Designer: James B. Longacre

SILVER THREE-CENT PIECES

Diameter: 14 millimeters (⁹/₁₆ of an inch)
Weight: 0.802 grams (0.026 ounce) from 1851–53, 0.746 grams (0.024 ounce) thereafter
Composition: 75 percent silver, 25 percent copper from 1851–53; 90 percent silver, 10 percent copper thereafter
Edge: Plain
Designer: James B. Longacre

NICKEL THREE-CENT PIECES

Diameter: 17.9 millimeters (⁷/₁₀ of an inch)
Weight: 1.944 grams (0.063 ounce)

Composition: 75 percent copper, 25 percent nickel
Edge: Plain
Designer: James B. Longacre

HALF DIMES

Diameter: 16.5 millimeters (about ⅔ of an inch) from 1792 to 1805, 15.5 millimeters (⁶/₁₀ of an inch) thereafter
Weight: 1.348 grams (0.04334 ounce) from 1792 to 1836 and part of 1837, 1.336 grams (0.04295 ounce) from 1838 to 1852 and parts of 1837 and 1853, 1.244 grams (0.040 ounce) for part of 1853 and thereafter
Composition: 89.25 percent silver, 10.75 percent copper from 1792 to 1836 and part of 1837; 90 percent silver, 10 percent copper for part of 1837 and thereafter
Edge: Reeded
Designers: Robert Scot (1792–1805), William Kneass (1829–1837 Capped Bust), Christian Gobrecht (1837–1873)

SHIELD NICKELS

Diameter: 20.5 millimeters (¹³/₁₆ of an inch)
Weight: 5 grams (0.161 ounce)
Composition: 75 percent copper, 25 percent nickel
Edge: Plain
Designer: James B. Longacre

LIBERTY HEAD NICKELS

Diameter: 21.2 millimeters (⁵/₆ of an inch)
Weight: 5 grams (0.161 ounce)
Composition: 75 percent copper, 25 percent nickel

Edge: Plain
Designer: Charles E. Barber

BUFFALO NICKELS

Diameter: 21.2 millimeters (⁵/₆ of an inch)
Weight: 5 grams (0.161 ounce)
Composition: 75 percent copper, 25 percent nickel
Edge: Plain
Designer: James E. Fraser

JEFFERSON NICKELS

Diameter: 21.2 millimeters (⁵/₆ of an inch)
Weight: 5 grams (0.161 ounce)
Composition: 75 percent copper, 25 percent nickel except for 1943–45 and part of 1942; 56 percent copper, 35 percent silver and 9 percent manganese during those years
Edge: Plain
Designer: Felix Schlag

DRAPED BUST DIMES

Diameter: About 19 millimeters (²⁵/₃₂ of an inch)
Weight: 2.696 grams (0.087 ounce)
Composition: 89.25 percent silver, 10.75 percent copper
Edge: Reeded
Designer: Robert Scot

CAPPED BUST DIMES

Diameter: About 18.8 millimeters (³/₄ of an inch) from 1809 to 1827 and part of 1828; 18.5 millimeters (⁷/₁₀ of an inch) for part of 1828 and thereafter
Weight: 2.696 grams (0.087 ounce)
Composition: 89.25 percent silver, 10.75 percent copper
Edge: Reeded
Designer: John Reich

SEATED LIBERTY DIMES

Diameter: 17.9 millimeters (⁷/₁₀ of an inch)
Weight: 2.673 grams (0.086 ounce) from 1837 to 1852 and part of 1853; 2.488 grams (0.080 ounce) for parts of 1853 and 1873 and from 1854 to 1872; 2.50 grams (0.084 ounce) from 1874 to 1891.
Composition: 90 percent silver, 10 percent copper
Edge: Reeded
Designer: Christian Gobrecht

BARBER DIMES

Diameter: 17.9 millimeters (⁷/₁₀ of an inch)
Weight: 2.50 grams (0.804 ounce)
Composition: 90 percent silver, 10 percent copper
Edge: Reeded
Designer: Charles E. Barber

"MERCURY" DIMES

Diameter: 17.9 millimeters (⁷/₁₀ of an inch)
Weight: 2.50 grams (0.084 ounce)

Composition: 90 percent silver, 10 percent copper
Edge: Reeded
Designer: Adolph A. Weinman

ROOSEVELT DIMES

Diameter: 17.9 millimeters ($7/10$ of an inch)
Weight: 2.50 grams (0.084 ounce) from 1946 to 1964, 2.27 grams (0.073 ounce) from 1965 to date
Composition: 90 percent silver, 10 percent copper from 1946 to 1964; 75-percent-copper, 25-percent-nickel alloy bonded to pure copper core thereafter
Edge: Reeded
Designer: John R. Sinnock

TWENTY-CENT PIECES

Diameter: 22 millimeters ($7/8$ of an inch)
Weight: 5 grams (0.161 ounce)
Composition: 90 percent silver, 10 percent copper
Edge: Plain
Designer: William Barber

DRAPED BUST QUARTER DOLLARS

Diameter: About 27.5 millimeters ($1^1/12$ inches)
Weight: 6.739 grams (0.217 ounce)
Composition: 89.25 percent silver, 10.75 percent copper
Edge: Reeded
Designer: Robert Scot

COIN SPECIFICATIONS

CAPPED BUST QUARTER DOLLARS

Diameter: 27 millimeters (1^1/$_{14}$ inches) from 1815 to 1828, 24.3 millimeter (^{19}/$_{20}$ of an inch) from 1831 to 1838
Weight: 6.739 grams (0.217 ounce)
Composition: 89.25 percent silver, 10.75 percent silver
Edge: Reeded
Designer: John Reich

SEATED LIBERTY QUARTER DOLLARS

Diameter: 24.3 millimeters (^{19}/$_{20}$ of an inch)
Weight: 6.68 grams (0.215 ounce) from 1838 to 1852 and part of 1853; 6.221 grams (0.2 ounce) from 1854 to 1872 and part of 1873; 6.25 grams (0.201 ounce) in part of 1873 and from 1874 to 1891.
Composition: 90 percent silver, 10 percent copper
Edge: Reeded
Designer: Christian Gobrecht

BARBER QUARTER DOLLARS

Diameter: 24.3 millimeters (^{19}/$_{20}$ of an inch)
Weight: 6.25 grams (0.201 ounce)
Composition: 90 percent silver, 10 percent copper
Edge: Reeded
Designer: Charles E. Barber

STANDING LIBERTY QUARTER DOLLARS

Diameter: 24.3 millimeters (^{19}/$_{20}$ of an inch)
Weight: 6.25 grams (0.201 ounce)
Composition: 90 percent silver, 10 percent copper

Edge: Reeded
Designer: Hermon A. MacNeil

WASHINGTON QUARTER DOLLARS

Diameter: 24.3 millimeters ($^{19}/_{20}$ of an inch)
Weight: 6.25 grams (0.201 ounce) from 1932 to 1964; 5.670 grams (0.185 ounce) from 1965 to date
Composition: 90 percent silver, 10 percent copper from 1946 to 1964; 75-percent-copper, 25-percent-nickel alloy bonded to pure copper core thereafter
Edge: Reeded
Designer: John Flanagan

FLOWING HAIR HALF DOLLARS

Diameter: About 32.5 millimeters ($1^9/_{32}$ of an inch)
Weight: 13.48 grams (0.433 ounce)
Composition: 89.25 percent silver, 10.75 percent copper
Edge: Lettered (FIFTY CENTS OR HALF A DOLLAR)
Designer: Robert Scot

DRAPED BUST HALF DOLLARS

Diameter: 32.5 millimeters ($1^9/_{32}$ of an inch)
Weight: 13.48 grams (0.433 ounce)
Composition: 89.25 percent silver, 10.75 percent copper
Edge: Lettered (FIFTY CENTS OR HALF A DOLLAR)
Designer: Robert Scot

CAPPED BUST HALF DOLLARS

Diameter: 32.5 millimeters (1⁹/₃₂ of an inch)
Weight: 13.48 grams (0.433 ounce)
Composition: 89.25 percent silver, 10.75 percent copper
Edge: Lettered (FIFTY CENTS OR HALF A DOLLAR)
Designer: John Reich

SEATED LIBERTY HALF DOLLARS

Diameter: 30.6 millimeters (1²/₁₀ of an inch)
Weight: 13.36 grams (0.430 ounce) from 1839 to 1852 and part of 1853; 12.44 grams (0.4 ounce) in part of 1853 and 1873 and from 1854 to 1872; 12.5 grams (0.402 ounce) in part of 1873 and from 1874 to 1891.
Composition: 89.25 percent silver, 10.75 percent copper in part of 1839; 90 percent silver, 10 percent copper thereafter
Edge: Reeded
Designer: Christian Gobrecht

BARBER HALF DOLLARS

Diameter: 30.6 millimeters (1²/₁₀ of an inch)
Weight: 12.5 grams (0.402 ounce)
Composition: 90 percent silver, 10 percent copper
Edge: Reeded
Designer: Charles E. Barber

WALKING LIBERTY HALF DOLLARS

Diameter: 30.6 millimeters (1²/₁₀ of an inch)
Weight: 12.5 grams (0.402 ounce)

Composition: 90 percent silver, 10 percent copper
Edge: Reeded
Designer: Adolph A. Weinman

FRANKLIN HALF DOLLARS

Diameter: 30.6 millimeters (1²/₁₀ of an inch)
Weight: 12.5 grams (0.402 ounce)
Composition: 90 percent silver, 10 percent copper
Edge: Reeded
Designer: John R. Sinnock

KENNEDY HALF DOLLARS

Diameter: 30.6 millimeters (1²/₁₀ of an inch)
Weight: 12.5 grams (0.402 ounce) in 1964; 11.5 grams (0.370 ounce) from 1965 to 1970; 11.34 grams (0.365 ounce) from 1971 to date
Composition: 90 percent silver, 10 percent copper in 1964; 40 percent silver from 1965 to 1970 (80-percent-silver, 20-percent-copper alloy bonded to a 20.9-percent-silver, 79.1-percent-copper core); 75-percent-copper, 25-percent-nickel alloy bonded to pure copper core from 1971 to date
Edge: Reeded
Designers: Gilroy Roberts (obverse) and Frank Gasparro (reverse)

FLOWING HAIR SILVER DOLLARS

Diameter: About 39 to 40 millimeters (1⁹/₁₆ inches)
Weight: 26.96 grams (0.867 ounce)
Composition: 89.25 percent silver, 10.75 percent copper

Edge: Lettered (HUNDRED CENTS ONE DOLLAR OR UNIT)
Designer: Robert Scot

DRAPED BUST SILVER DOLLARS

Diameter: 39.5 millimeters (1$\frac{5}{9}$ inches)
Weight: 26.96 grams (0.867 ounce)
Composition: 89.25 percent silver, 10.75 percent copper
Edge: Lettered (HUNDRED CENTS ONE DOLLAR OR UNIT)
Designer: Robert Scot

GOBRECHT SILVER DOLLARS

Diameter: 39.5 millimeters (1$\frac{5}{9}$ inches)
Weight: 26.96 grams (0.867 ounce)
Composition: 90 percent silver, 10 percent copper
Edge: Plain in 1836, reeded in 1839
Designer: Christian Gobrecht

SEATED LIBERTY SILVER DOLLARS

Diameter: 38.1 millimeters (1$\frac{1}{2}$ inches)
Weight: 26.73 grams (0.859 ounce)
Composition: 90 percent silver, 10 percent copper
Edge: Reeded
Designer: Christian Gobrecht

MORGAN SILVER DOLLARS

Diameter: 38.1 millimeters (1$\frac{1}{2}$ inches)
Weight: 26.73 grams (0.859 ounce)
Composition: 90 percent silver, 10 percent copper

Edge: Reeded
Designer: George T. Morgan

PEACE SILVER DOLLARS

Diameter: 38.1 millimeters (1½ inches)
Weight: 26.73 grams (0.859 ounce)
Composition: 90 percent silver, 10 percent copper
Edge: Reeded
Designer: Anthony de Francisci

TRADE DOLLARS

Diameter: 38.1 millimeters (1½ inches)
Weight: 27.216 grams (0.875 ounce)
Composition: 90 percent silver, 10 percent copper
Edge: Reeded
Designer: William Barber

EISENHOWER DOLLARS

Diameter: 38.1 millimeters (1½ inches)
Weight: 22.68 grams (0.729 ounce)
Composition: 75-percent-copper, 25-percent-nickel alloy
  bonded to pure copper core
Edge: Reeded
Designer: Frank Gasparro

ANTHONY DOLLARS

Diameter: 26.5 millimeters (1¹/₂₀ inch)
Weight: 8.1 grams (0.260 ounce)

Composition: 75-percent-copper, 25-percent-nickel alloy
  bonded to pure copper core
Edge: Reeded
Designer: Frank Gasparro

GOLD DOLLARS

Diameter: 13 millimeters (½ inch) from 1849 to 1853 and
  part of 1854; 14.86 millimeters (⁶⁄₁₀ of an inch) for part
  of 1854 and thereafter
Weight: 1.672 grams (0.054 ounce)
Composition: 90 percent gold, 10 percent copper and silver
Edge: Reeded
Designer: James B. Longacre

CAPPED BUST FACING RIGHT QUARTER EAGLES
($2.50 GOLD PIECES)

Diameter: About 20 millimeters (⁸⁄₁₀ of an inch)
Weight: 4.374 grams (0.141 ounce)
Composition: 91.67 percent gold, 8.33 percent copper and
  silver
Edge: Reeded
Designer: Robert Scot

CAPPED BUST FACING LEFT QUARTER EAGLES

Diameter: About 20 millimeters (⁸⁄₁₀ of an inch)
Weight: 4.374 grams (0.141 ounce)
Composition: 91.67 percent gold, 8.33 percent copper and
  silver
Edge: Reeded
Designer: John Reich

CAPPED HEAD QUARTER EAGLES

Diameter: 18.5 millimeters (³/₄ inch) from 1821 to 1827, 18.2 millimeters (⁷/₁₀ inch) from 1829 to 1834
Weight: 4.374 grams (0.141 ounce)
Composition: 91.67 percent gold, 8.33 percent copper and silver
Edge: Reeded
Designer: Robert Scot and John Reich

CLASSIC HEAD QUARTER EAGLES

Diameter: 18.2 millimeters (⁷/₁₀ of an inch)
Weight: 4.18 grams (0.134 ounce)
Composition: 89.92 percent gold, 10.08 percent copper and silver from 1834 to 1836; 90 percent gold, 10 percent copper and silver from 1837 to 1839
Edge: Reeded
Designer: William Kneass

CORONET QUARTER EAGLES

Diameter: 18.2 millimeters (⁷/₁₀ of an inch)
Weight: 4.18 grams (0.134 ounce)
Composition: 90 percent gold, 10 percent copper
Edge: Reeded
Designer: Christian Gobrecht

INDIAN HEAD QUARTER EAGLES

Diameter: 18 millimeters (⁷/₁₀ of an inch)
Weight: 4.18 grams (0.134 ounce)
Composition: 90 percent gold, 10 percent copper

Edge: Reeded
Designer: Bela Lyon Pratt

$3 GOLD PIECES

Diameter: 20.5 millimeters (⁸⁄₁₀ of an inch)
Weight: 5.015 grams (0.161 ounce)
Composition: 90 percent gold, 10 percent copper
Edge: Reeded
Designer: James B. Longacre

STELLAS ($4 GOLD PIECES)

Diameter: 22 millimeters (⁷⁄₈ of an inch)
Weight: 7 grams (0.225 ounce)
Composition: 85.71 percent gold, 4.29 percent silver, 10 percent copper
Edge: Reeded
Designers: Charles E. Barber and George T. Morgan

CAPPED BUST HALF EAGLES ($5 GOLD PIECES)

Diameter: 25 millimeters (1 inch)
Weight: 8.748 grams (0.281 ounce)
Composition: 91.67 percent gold, 8.33 percent copper and silver
Edge: Reeded
Designer: Robert Scot

CAPPED DRAPED BUST FACING LEFT HALF EAGLES

Diameter: 25 millimeters (1 inch)
Weight: 8.748 grams (0.281 ounce)
Composition: 91.67 percent gold, 8.33 percent copper and silver
Edge: Reeded
Designer: John Reich

CAPPED HEAD HALF EAGLES

Diameter: 25 millimeters (1 inch) from 1813 to 1828 and part of 1829; 23.8 millimeters ($^{15}/_{16}$ of an inch) for part of 1829 and thereafter
Weight: 8.748 grams (0.281 ounce)
Composition: 91.67 percent gold, 8.33 percent copper and silver
Edge: Reeded
Designer: John Reich

CLASSIC HEAD HALF EAGLES

Diameter: 22.5 millimeters ($^{7}/_{8}$ of an inch)
Weight: 8.36 grams (0.269 ounce)
Composition: 89.92 percent gold, 10.08 percent copper from 1834 to 1836; 90 percent gold, 10 percent copper and silver in 1837 and 1838
Edge: Reeded
Designer: William Kneass

CORONET HALF EAGLES

Diameter: 22.5 millimeters ($^7/_8$ of an inch) in 1839 and part of 1840; 21.6 millimeters ($^{17}/_{20}$ of an inch) for part of 1840 and thereafter
Weight: 8.36 grams (0.269 ounce)
Composition: 90 percent gold, 10 percent copper
Edge: Reeded
Designer: Christian Gobrecht

INDIAN HEAD HALF EAGLES

Diameter: 21.6 millimeters ($^{17}/_{20}$ of an inch)
Weight: 8.36 grams (0.269 ounce)
Composition: 90 percent gold, 10 percent copper
Edge: Reeded
Designer: Bela Lyon Pratt

CAPPED BUST EAGLES ($10 GOLD PIECES)

Diameter: 33 millimeters ($1^3/_{10}$ inches)
Weight: 17.496 grams (0.563 ounce)
Composition: 91.67 percent gold, 8.33 percent copper and silver
Edge: Reeded
Designer: Robert Scot

CORONET EAGLES

Diameter: 27 millimeters ($1^1/_{16}$ inches)
Weight: 16.718 grams (0.538 ounce)

Composition: 90 percent gold, 10 percent copper and silver from 1838 to 1872 and part of 1873; 90 percent gold, 10 percent copper for part of 1873 and thereafter
Designer: Christian Gobrecht

INDIAN HEAD EAGLES

Diameter: 27 millimeters ($1^1/_{16}$ inches)
Weight: 16.718 grams (0.538 ounce)
Composition: 90 percent gold, 10 percent copper
Edge: Starred (46 raised stars from 1907 to 1911, 48 raised stars thereafter; each star represents one of the states in the Union, and two new states—New Mexico and Arizona—joined the Union in 1912)
Designer: Augustus Saint-Gaudens

LIBERTY HEAD DOUBLE EAGLES
($20 GOLD PIECES)

Diameter: 34.2 millimeters ($1^1/_3$ inches)
Weight: 33.436 grams (1.075 ounce)
Composition: 90 percent gold, 10 percent copper and silver from 1849 to 1872 and part of 1873; 90 percent gold, 10 percent copper for part of 1873 and thereafter
Edge: Reeded
Designer: James B. Longacre

SAINT-GAUDENS DOUBLE EAGLES
($20 GOLD PIECES)

Diameter: 34.2 millimeters ($1^1/_3$ inches)
Weight: 33.436 grams (1.075 ounce)

Composition: 90 percent gold, 10 percent copper
Edge: Lettered (E PLURIBUS UNUM, with stars dividing the words)
Designer: Augustus Saint-Gaudens

WHERE TO LOOK FOR MINT MARKS

Mint marks appear in a number of different locations on U.S. coins. Today, the standard location on regular-issue coins—the five coins made for use in commerce—is the obverse, or "heads" side. In earlier times, however, most coins carried these letters on the reverse.

Following is a list of where to look for mint marks on various U.S. coins:

• **Lincoln cents (1909–present)**—on the obverse, below the date.

• **Indian Head cents (1908 and 1909 only)**—on the reverse, below the wreath.

• **Jefferson nickels (1938–1964)**—on the reverse, to the right of Monticello, except on part-silver war nickels of 1942–45; there, a large mint mark appears above Monticello.

• **Jefferson nickels (1968–present)**—on the obverse, below the date.

• **Buffalo nickels (1913–1938)**—on the reverse, below the words FIVE CENTS.

• **Liberty Head nickels (1912 only)**—on the reverse, to the left of the word CENTS.

• **Roosevelt dimes (1946–1964)**—on the reverse, to the left of the torch's base.

• **Roosevelt dimes (1968–present)**—on the obverse, above the date.

• **"Mercury" dimes (1916–1945)**—on the reverse, to the left of the fasces.

• **Barber dimes (1892–1916)**—on the reverse, below the wreath.

• **Washington quarters (1932–1964)**—on the reverse, below the wreath.

• **Washington quarters (1968–present)**—on the obverse, to the right of George Washington's pigtail.

• **Standing Liberty quarters (1916–1930)**—on the obverse, to the left of the date.

• **Barber quarters (1892–1916)**—on the reverse, below the eagle.

• **Kennedy half dollars (1964)**—on the reverse, to the left of the eagle's tail feathers.

• **Kennedy half dollars (1968–present)**—on the obverse, below John F. Kennedy's neck.

• **Walking Liberty half dollars (1916–1917)**—on the obverse, below IN GOD WE TRUST.

• **Walking Liberty half dollars (1917–1947)**—on the reverse, above and to the left of HALF DOLLAR. (Half dollars dated 1917 come in both mint-mark varieties.)

• **Barber half dollars (1892–1915)**—on the reverse, below the wreath.

• **Anthony dollars (1979–1981)**—on the obverse, above Susan B. Anthony's right shoulder.

• **Eisenhower dollars (1971–1978)**—on the obverse, below Dwight D. Eisenhower's neck.

• **Peace silver dollars (1921–1935)**—on the reverse, below the word ONE.

• **Morgan silver dollars (1878–1921)**—on the reverse, below the wreath.

• **Saint-Gaudens double eagles (1907–1933)**—on the obverse, above the date.

• **Liberty Head $20 double eagles**—on the reverse, below the eagle.